Quick Gu

This guide is (...own together. Three se ...nilar habitats. The Speci

WATERFOWL (Geese, Swans, Ducks)

UPLAND GAME BIRDS (Quail, Pheasant, Turkey, Grouse) - LOONS - GREBES - CORMORANTS - PELICANS - WADING BIRDS (Bitterns, Herons, Egrets, Ibis)

VULTURES - DIURNAL RAPTORS (Osprey, Eagles, Hawks)

RAILS, GALLINULE AND COOT - CRANE - SHOREBIRDS (Stilt, Avocet, Oystercatcher, Plovers, Sandpipers, Dowitchers, Snipe, Phalaropes)

MURRE AND GUILLEMOT - GULLS, TERNS, AND SKIMMER

PIGEONS AND DOVES - CUCKOOS (Cuckoo, Roadrunner) - OWLS - NIGHTHAWKS AND POORWILL - SWIFTS - HUMMINGBIRDS

KINGFISHER - WOODPECKERS - FALCONS - FLYCATCHERS (Wood-Pewee, Flycatchers, Phoebes, Kingbirds) - SHRIKES - VIREOS

CORVIDS (Jays, Magpies, Crow, Raven) - LARK - SWALLOWS (Martin, Swallows) - CHICKADEES AND TITMICE - BUSHTIT - NUTHATCHES AND CREEPER

WRENS - GNATCATCHER - DIPPER - KINGLETS - WRENTIT - THRUSHES (Bluebirds, Thrushes, Robin) - MOCKINGBIRD AND THRASHERS - STARLING - PIPIT - WAXWING - PHAINOPEPLA

LONGSPUR - WARBLERS (Warblers, Yellowthroat, Chat)

NATIVE SPARROWS (Towhees, Sparrows, Junco) - TANAGERS, GROSBEAKS AND BUNTINGS

BLACKBIRDS (Blackbirds, Meadowlark, Grackle, Cowbird, Orioles) - FINCHES (Finches, Crossbill, Siskin) - HOUSE SPARROW – EXOTICS

MOUNTAIN SPECIALTIES

NORTHERN MOJAVE DESERT/GREAT BASIN SPECIALTIES

PELAGIC SPECIALTIES

BIRDS OF
NORTHERN CALIFORNIA

By

David E. Quady
Jon L. Dunn
Kimball L. Garrett
Brian E. Small

R.W. Morse Company
Olympia, Washington

DEQ dedicates this book to Nancy, with gratitude for so much.

JLD dedicates this book to Harry S. Swarth for his many published contributions to field ornithology, notably his seminal 1920 work on Fox Sparrows, and for setting the standard of what an amateur can contribute.

KLG dedicates this book to the long line of natural historians at the Museum of Vertebrate Zoology in Berkeley who have catalogued the bird life of northern California with such grand insight.

BES dedicates this book to the people who have had the greatest positive impact on his life: Dr. Arnold Small and Millicent Small (parents) and his beautiful wife, Ana.

Published by R.W. Morse Company,
PO Box 12302, Olympia, Washington 98508

Library of Congress Control Number: 2013936348

EAN 9780964081093   **$24.95 Softcover**

First Edition 2015   © 2015 R.W. Morse Company

Sixth Printing 2021

Authors: David E. Quady, Jon L. Dunn, Kimball L. Garrett, Brian E. Small

Executive Editor: Christina Duchesne Morse

Printed: China, Imago USA

Design: Christina Merwin

Maps: Rusty Scalf

Bird Drawings: Eric Kraig

Cover Photograph: Nuttall's Woodpecker, Brian E. Small

Contents

Map of Northern California .... inside front cover

Quick Guide to Local Birds .... inside front cover

Common Local Birds vi

Introduction 1

Identifying Birds 4

Observing Local Birds 8

Map of Habitats of Northern California 10

Bird Habitats of Northern California and Their Birds 11

Helpful Resources 21

Species Accounts 24

Acknowledgments, Photographer Credits 492

Index/Checklist of Northern California Birds 496

About the Authors 501

Short Index to Species 502

Common Local Birds

Here are some of the most common birds in Northern California. For more information about each bird, go to its Species Account. Images on the next five pages are not to scale.

Mallard
page 38
(male) (female)

Turkey Vulture
page 106

California Quail
page 68

Great Blue Heron
page 94

Red-tailed Hawk
page 122

Double-crested Cormorant
page 86

American Coot
page 134

Willet
page 156

Killdeer
page 146

Sanderling
page 168

Ring-billed Gull
page 192

California Gull
page 196

Rock Pigeon
page 214

Eurasian Collared-Dove
page 214

Mourning Dove
page 218

Great Horned Owl
page 226

Anna's Hummingbird
page 248

Black Phoebe
page 282

Northern Flicker
page 262

Common Raven
page 304

California Scrub-Jay
page 300

Bushtit
page 322

Barn Swallow
page 316

Bewick's Wren
page 336

**European
Starling**
page 360

American Robin
page 352

**California
Towhee**
page 396

**Yellow-rumped
Warbler**
page 380

Fox Sparrow
page 408

White-crowned Sparrow
page 414

Brewer's Blackbird
page 436

(male)

(female)

(male)

Red-winged Blackbird
page 428

(female)

Bullock's Oriole
page 440

House Finch
page 442

(male)

Lesser Goldfinch
page 450

(female)

House Sparrow
page 454

Introduction

Bird watching, or birding, has become one of America's most popular outdoor activities. The US Fish & Wildlife Service recently estimated that 47 million adult Americans either watch or feed birds. Birding can be great family entertainment. It is easy to get started, inexpensive, healthful, and it helps us understand and appreciate the natural world.

Birds of Northern California will help beginning bird watchers identify the birds of this beautiful, diverse part of the state. This book will also help experienced birders learn more about the behavior, habitats, and seasonal occurrence of our local birds.

Given the popularity of bird watching and the wide array of habitats and birds in Northern California, it is little wonder that the people of this region enjoy seeing and studying its birds. Our habitats range from offshore marine waters and coastal estuaries to open grasslands, oak woodlands, coastal and mountain forests, and desert scrub. Urban plantings, parks, and agricultural areas add more habitat diversity. Because different bird species live in each type of habitat, we enjoy a great variety of birds: more than 600 species have been found in the region. In this book we include accounts for more than 390 species. Most of these are commonly observed year-round residents or annual visitors, but we also include scarcer species that are especially sought-after in Northern California, to emphasize our region's tremendous diversity of bird life.

GEOGRAPHICAL COVERAGE

Birds of Northern California covers the 48 northernmost of California's 58 counties, from Monterey, Kings, Tulare, and Inyo (often considered part of southern California) counties all the way north to the Oregon border. It encompasses the major metropolitan areas of San Francisco and Sacramento, seven national parks, fifteen national forests and more than 90 state parks and beaches. It includes coastal mountains, the Sierra Nevada, most of the Central Valley, and

1

portions of the Great Basin.

The map inside the front cover shows the geographical area covered by this book: more than 60% of California's nearly 164,000 square miles of land area. The region (the term used to refer to the book's area of coverage) also includes offshore waters along the mainland coast, although we focus mainly on those ocean-dwelling ("pelagic") species that can often be seen from shore or observed on one-day boat outings. Northern California extends from the Pacific Ocean on the west through the Sierra Nevada on the east to the Nevada state line, reaching 14,505' at the summit of Mt. Whitney. The landform map on p. 10 shows the region's major topographical features, and many names commonly used in the text. Average annual precipitation ranges from about 2.5 inches in Death Valley National Park to more than 70 inches in Redwood National Park.

CONSERVATION

The 14.5 million people living in the region covered by this guide see a very different landscape than the one that greeted its first European explorers. Within historic times the Central Valley's vast expanse of grasslands and marshes, as well as the largest freshwater lake west of the Mississippi River, essentially vanished along with its teeming wildlife, replaced by intensive agriculture and the homes of several million people. The Sierran forests were heavily logged to provide timber for the mines of Nevada and California, and some 90% of old-growth redwood forests fell to the saw, in part to rebuild cities after the 1906 earthquake. Before it was halted by law, hydraulic mining on the Sierra Nevada's west slope sent staggering quantities of sediment seaward, altering the character of waterways reaching all the way to the sea. This, and later deliberate diking and filling, destroyed much of the marshes of Suisun, San Pablo, and San Francisco bays, and reduced the bays' surface area by a third.

Since settlement of Northern California began, the Sharp-tailed Grouse has been extirpated (about 1915; reasons largely unknown), and the California Condor has been extirpated as a self-sustaining

2

breeding species. Alterations to the land and other environmental changes have also resulted in the loss (or near loss) from the region of breeding species such as Fulvous Whistling-Duck, Yellow-billed Cuckoo, and Bell's Vireo, and severe population declines in others. On the other hand, some native species have adapted well to our highly modified habitats, their populations growing and ranges expanding, and several non-native species now thrive in the region. Extensive areas are now protected within national and state parks, national forests, and a variety of reserves on land and beneath the sea. And habitat restoration is underway in many areas, perhaps most visibly in the San Francisco Bay Area's marshes.

Protecting native birds and their habitats requires scientific knowledge, financing, education, and political and grassroots activism. Those who enjoy birds and wish to protect them can contribute in some or all of these areas. We urge you to join and become active in one or more of the many conservation organizations such as local Audubon chapters (there are about 30 chapters and bird clubs in the region), The Nature Conservancy - California, the Save The Redwoods League, the Center for Biological Diversity, and the many local and regional organizations focused on particular habitat preservation issues.

A NOTE ON TAXONOMY

We follow the English names and scientific names used by the American Ornithological Society (AOS) through its 61st check-list supplement, published in 2020. Do not be surprised if some of the bird names in this book differ from those in older field guides. It was impracticable, however, to incorporate in this printing the significant revisions to the sequence of bird species made by the AOS in recent years.

Identifying Birds

It can be confusing when you first start trying to identify birds. They move around, they hide, and many species are distressingly similar to others! A holistic approach to bird identification means paying attention not just to colors and patterns, but to size, structure, shape, behaviors and sounds. First, look at the general shape, size, and color of the bird. Check the Common Local Birds (pages vi - x) and see if it is there. If not, scan through the Species Account pages. Read the description—especially the **boldfaced** text—to see how it matches your bird. Compare range, time of year, similar species, voice, and habitat.

The different colors and patterns of a bird's feathering ("plumage") and bare parts (bill, legs, feet, eyes) provide some of the best ways to identify a bird. Beware, however, that plumages may vary within the same species between the sexes, between adults and younger birds, by season, and by geographical location. Learn the parts of a bird; consult the diagrams on pages 5 and 6. Often birds can be identified by head pattern alone.

In some species the male and the female have distinctly different plumages. Good examples are Mallard, Anna's Hummingbird, House Finch, and Red-winged Blackbird. Usually the males have more brilliant colors, as in these examples, while the females have muted colors. Other species such as Rock Pigeon, California Scrub-Jay, American Crow, and California Towhee show no plumage differences between the sexes.

Most birds seen in Northern California in spring and summer display what is known as their breeding ("summer" or "alternate") plumage. Birds seen here in winter are usually in their non-breeding ("winter" or "basic") plumage. Often the breeding plumage is more colorful or highly patterned and the non-breeding plumage is more muted; many species, however, look the same year round.

Molting is the process of replacing worn feathers with new, fresh

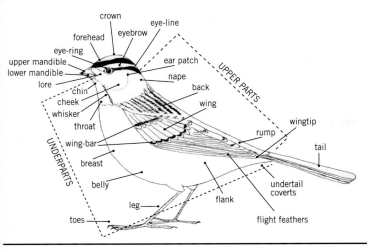

Parts of a Bird. It is helpful to know the names of the different parts of a bird. These sketches of a White-crowned Sparrow and an in-flight Mallard show the terms used to describe bird anatomy in this guide.

ones. Most local birds replace some or all of their feathers in a molt in summer or early fall when they change into their non-breeding plumage. Many birds undergo a partial molt again in late winter or spring to acquire breeding plumage. These molts occur over a period of several weeks or months. In some species, such as the European Starling, the bright "breeding plumage" results from the wearing of dull feather tips (revealing brighter colors underneath) rather than an actual molt. Many songbirds have only a very limited molt of head and body feathers before the breeding season. Molting is generally a longer and more complex process in larger birds than in small songbirds.

Most birds acquire different plumages as they mature. This is particularly true for gulls, which take up to four years and several plumage stages to gain their adult plumage. The term "juvenal

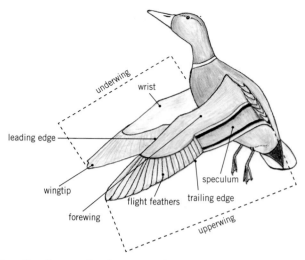

plumage" refers to the first true plumage worn by a young bird (a "juvenile") after it loses its initial downy feathers. Some species hold this plumage for only a few weeks after fledging while others may hold it into winter. "First-year plumage" refers to the plumage held during the first 12 months of a bird's life. "Immature" refers to all plumages before the bird gains its adult plumage. For many species in which the plumages of the sexes differ as adults, immature males may closely resemble females.

Colors, patterning, and size may vary considerably among birds of the same species and plumage stage that belong to different geographical populations. For instance, the Fox Sparrows that nest in the high mountains differ markedly in color, bill size, and vocalizations from the dark brown northwestern birds that winter over much of the region. Differences can be great even within the same local population; for example, the majority of our Red-tailed Hawks have light breasts and underwings, yet a certain percentage of birds have dark brown to blackish underparts and underwings with lighter-colored flight feathers. Such consistently different types are called "color morphs" (or just "morphs"); the word "phase" is often incorrectly used in this context.

Don't expect every bird you see to look exactly like the photographs in this guide. Birds, like people, are individuals. To appreciate how variable birds of the same species can be, study the ones that come regularly to your backyard feeder. Male House Finches, for example, can show a wide range of coloration from rich, deep red to golden yellow. You may find that, with practice, you can learn to recognize individual birds by the subtle differences in their markings.

In this book the birds are presented in family groupings, as shown in the Quick Guide to Local Birds at the beginning of this book. Learning the characteristics of the different bird families will make bird identification both easier and quicker. Birds in the same family tend to show similarities in appearance and behavior. Hummingbirds, for example, are all very small, with long, thin bills, extremely fast wing beats, and hovering flight. Once you see a bird with these characteristics, you are well on your way to identifying it as a hummingbird. A bird's structure, including head shape, general slimness or roundness of the body, and the shape and length of its wings, tail, legs, and bill, provides important clues to both the family to which it belongs and, often, its species.

Although we have focused above on colors, patterns and shapes, the field identification of birds is greatly simplified by behaviors and, especially, vocalizations that are unique to a species. Experienced birders can recognize virtually all of the area's species by their calls and songs alone. Be sure to use the sections on Voice to help arrive at your identifications, and pay close attention in the field to the sounds that birds make.

Observing and Learning the Birds

OBSERVING BIRDS

Adjusting your binoculars and becoming proficient with them are first steps that some beginners neglect. First, match the distance between the centers of your binoculars' two ocular lenses (the "eyepieces") with the distance between the centers of your eyes. Second, adjust the independent focusing mechanism (on one of your eyepieces) so that objects are equally crisp in each eye when you focus on them with the main focus wheel. If you normally wear glasses, adjust the eyecups on your binoculars to get your eyes as close to the eyepieces as possible – this provides a larger image than if your eyes are farther from the eyepieces. Ask an experienced birdwatcher, or a clerk in a nature store, if you need help with these steps Finally, learn how to quickly bring your binoculars up to your eyes once you've spotted a bird. Keep your eyes on the bird as you raise your binoculars; you will be less likely to lose track of it during that step.

When looking for birds in the field, move slowly and quietly, and stop often to listen and to scan your surroundings. Keep conversations to a minimum so that you can concentrate on the sounds around you. Some birdwatchers pick an interesting spot every 30 minutes or so, then sit and study the birds that appear. As the scene "quiets down," many species, unseen and unheard at the outset, may appear as time passes. You may be surprised at how long birds remain in view, and how closely they approach, if you simply sit still.

Experienced birdwatchers detect and identify many more bird species by sound than by sight. With practice and experience, you can learn to identify birds simply by their songs and calls. Be aware, however, that there can be important geographical variations (dialects) in the songs of a given species, and also that mimicking species such as Northern Mockingbirds, European Starlings, and Lesser and Lawrence's Goldfinches can sow confusion.

Each bird species has unique vocalizations, which you can study by using tapes, CDs, smart phone applications or web sites. Xeno-Canto (**http://www.xeno-canto.org**) and Cornell University's Macaulay Library (**http://macaulaylibrary.org**) are two excellent resources.

LEARNING THE BIRDS

Identifying birds (discussed in the preceding chapter) requires already having a certain store of knowledge, which this book aims to help beginning birdwatchers acquire. But what if you can't identify a bird that's in front of you – what should you do?

Oftentimes beginners pull out a field guide, an iPhone, or some other resource to refer to . . . and find that the bird has disappeared in the meantime. Usually a better way to learn the birds is to discuss field marks and vocalizations with other birders present, and take notes (and photographs if you can), while the bird is in front of you. Write down your notes as soon as possible. Once the bird is gone, you can pull out your resources to try to identify the bird. Later, back home, study and organize your notes, study the field marks of the birds you saw, and try to better prepare yourself to identify them when you see them next.

Many people keep a list of the birds they see in their yard or in their county, state, or lifetime. As lists grow, so does an incentive to learn more about birds, including their status and distribution. Experienced birdwatchers keep a detailed journal of what birds they see each day (and how many), when and where, and the birds' behaviors. Careful record keeping can contribute greatly to scientific understanding of birdlife. Sharing records via Cornell Laboratory of Ornithology's "**eBird**" initiative at **http://ebird.org** contributes to a vast, real-time, continent-wide database of bird abundance and distribution. Other "citizen science" projects with merit include annual Christmas Bird Counts, submitting notable sightings to North American Birds' regional editors, and various monitoring programs for sensitive bird species.

Habitats of Northern California

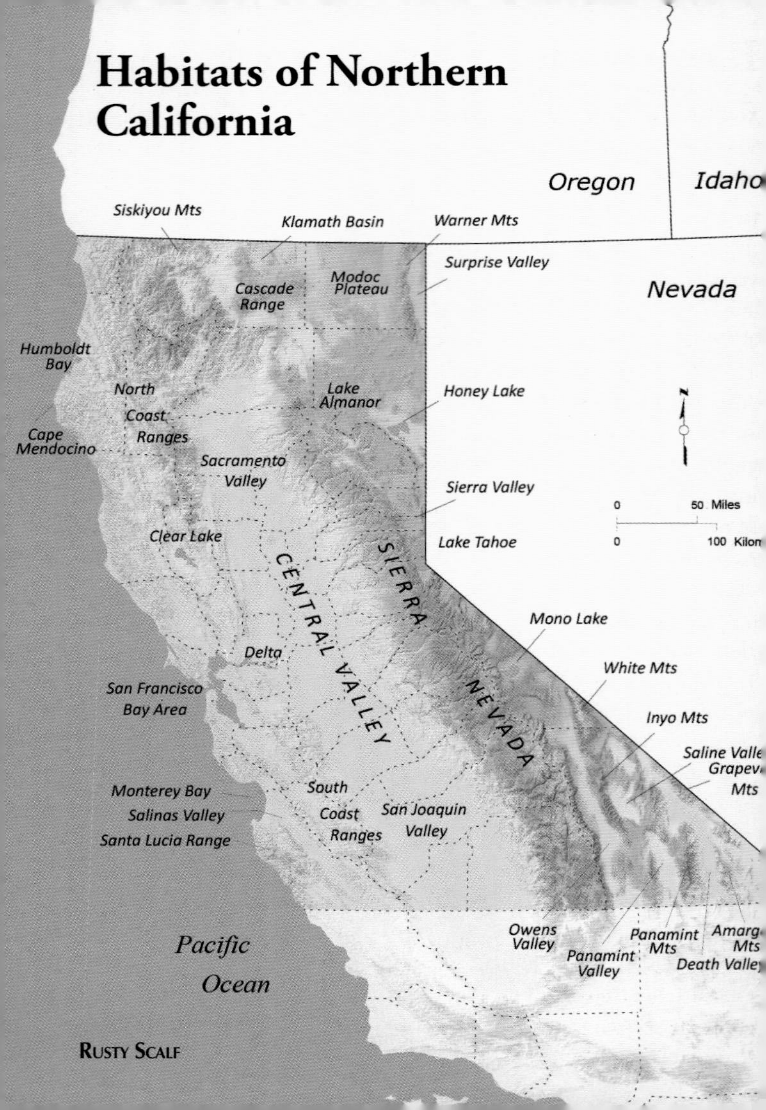

Oregon

Idaho

Siskiyou Mts

Klamath Basin

Warner Mts

Surprise Valley

Cascade Range

Modoc Plateau

Nevada

Humboldt Bay

North Coast Ranges

Lake Almanor

Honey Lake

Cape Mendocino

Sacramento Valley

Sierra Valley

Clear Lake

CENTRAL VALLEY

SIERRA

Lake Tahoe

Mono Lake

Delta

NEVADA

White Mts

San Francisco Bay Area

Inyo Mts

Saline Valley

Grapevine Mts

Monterey Bay

Salinas Valley

Santa Lucia Range

South Coast Ranges

San Joaquin Valley

Pacific Ocean

Owens Valley

Panamint Valley

Panamint Mts

Amargosa Mts

Death Valley

N

0   50 Miles

0   100 Kilom

RUSTY SCALF

Bird Habitats of Northern California and Their Birds

The environment that provides the resources for a bird or other living creature to live is termed its "habitat." Birds are quite diverse in the nature and specificity of their habitat requirements. You won't see a Wrentit on a lawn or a Nuttall's Woodpecker in a salt marsh, nor will you see Killdeer in trees or pelicans in redwoods. The key to finding and identifying birds is knowing their habitats and developing an understanding of which birds are likely to be seen where, and when. The more types of habitat you explore, the greater the variety of birds you will see.

We describe sixteen major habitat categories or unique geographical features in Northern California, only hinting at the incredible ecological complexity of the region. These habitats can merge into one another and overlap in complex ways, and each habitat type has many variations. Bird diversity is highest where various habitats adjoin. Some species, like the Mourning Dove or Red-tailed Hawk, are at home in a great variety of habitats, whereas others may seek habitats as specialized as rocky shorelines (Surfbird, Black Turnstone) or canyon walls (Canyon Wren).

OFFSHORE MARINE WATERS

These are open ocean waters off our coast, with California's waters extending – by common convention among birders – 200 nautical miles offshore from mainland and islands. Shearwaters, albatrosses, and storm-petrels forage here, as do auklets and murrelets. Red-necked and Red Phalaropes, Sabine's Gulls, and jaegers move through these waters on their annual migrations. Seabirds congregate in productive waters associated with undersea features, such as Noyo Canyon, offshore Mendocino County; Cordell Bank, offshore Marin County; the Farallon Islands, offshore San Francisco; and Monterey Canyon, offshore Monterey County.

Protected Marine Waters

Northern California's large sheltered bays – Humboldt Bay, Drake's Bay, San Francisco Bay, and Monterey Bay – host scoters, Red-breasted Mergansers, loons, grebes, Brown Pelicans, cormorants, gulls, and terns, as do other relatively protected inshore waters in the lee of coastal headlands. Impressive flights of migrating Brant, scoters, and loons may be seen passing coastal sea watching points, especially from March through May. Such sites include Point St. George, Patrick's Point, Point Arena, Bodega Head, Point Reyes, Pigeon Point, and Point Pinos.

Offshore Islands, Rocky Shore, Breakwaters and Jetties

The Farallon Islands and sea stacks off the Del Norte and Humboldt County coastlines such as Castle Rock provide nest sites for Fork-tailed and Leach's Storm-Petrels, three species of cormorants, Common Murres, Rhinoceros and Cassin's Auklets, and Tufted Puffins. Natural rocky shore habitat occurs in scattered locations along the coast, including at Bodega Head and Año Nuevo, and in seaside cities such as Fort Bragg and Santa Cruz; many stretches are protected in public parks. Rocky shores are mimicked by breakwaters and jetties as at Crescent City, Humboldt Bay, and Half Moon Bay. Wandering Tattlers, Black Turnstones, Surfbirds, cormorants, pelicans, and gulls occur on these rocky shores, and scoters feed on shellfish in adjacent waters.

Sandy Shore, Mud Flats, Estuaries and Salt Marsh

Important coastal estuaries with tidal flats and saltmarsh vegetation are found at Humboldt Bay, Bodega Bay, Elkhorn Slough, and the San Francisco Bay area, including San Pablo Bay, Suisun Bay, and Grizzly Bay. There are smaller estuaries at several river mouths along the coastline. Vast numbers of shorebirds, waterfowl, terns, and herons congregate at productive estuaries; our most important Black Skimmer breeding colonies are found in some of these sites. Sandy beaches in the area can be crowded with people in summer, but better protected beaches still attract many shorebirds, gulls, and terns, including nesting Snowy Plovers and Least Terns. Shorebirds, gulls, and others can be enjoyed along long, relatively uncrowded beaches at Drake's Bay in Pt. Reyes National Seashore and at Humboldt County's Big Lagoon and the sand spit that separates it from the ocean.

LAKES, RESERVOIRS, MARSHES, RIVERS AND STREAMS

Large natural lakes in the region include Lake Tahoe, highly saline Mono Lake, Clear Lake (Lake County), Eagle Lake, and Lower Klamath Lake. Large reservoirs that also provide good habitat include Trinity Lake, Lake Almanor, Black Butte Lake, Lake Berryessa, Camanche Reservoir, Salt Springs Reservoir, San Luis Reservoir, Crowley Lake, and Tinemaha Reservoir. Freshwater marshes in the great Central Valley – which comprises the valleys of the Sacramento and the San Joaquin Rivers and their tributaries – have been considerably diminished in extent by generations of agricultural and urban development. Remaining marshlands there are largely limited to state and federal wildlife refuges and wildlife areas and to private hunting clubs; other such marshes exist in the Great Basin region. In the Central Valley, flooded overflow areas along river courses and seasonally flooded rice fields provide additional habitat in winter. Many municipal wastewater treatment plants also provide open water or marshy habitat, and some permit public access. The Arcata Wastewater Treatment Plant and Wildlife Sanctuary is a model; Stockton's and Modesto's treatment plants offer limited access to their vast ponds.

Herons, cormorants, and Belted Kingfishers feed in these waters, along with a variety of waterfowl. Shorebirds can be abundant in migration on exposed mudflats, and rails, gallinules and bitterns skulk in marsh vegetation. Cattails or bulrushes support nesting Common Yellowthroats, Red-winged (and locally Tricolored) Blackbirds, and Marsh Wrens. Northern Harriers, and other raptors forage in the marshy areas, while Ospreys and (locally) Bald Eagles fish in the lakes. Common Mergansers and American Dippers feed in rivers and streams, near sea level and in the mountains

RIPARIAN WOODLANDS AND OASES

Portions of many rivers and streams have important riparian woodlands of willows, alders, cottonwoods and sycamores that attract many breeding and migrating birds. Widespread riparian breeders include Downy Woodpeckers, Common Yellowthroats, Yellow Warblers, Song Sparrows, and Bullock's Orioles. Remnant willow clumps in the Central Valley attract breeding Yellow-breasted Chat and Blue Grosbeaks. Shaded canyons host Pacific-slope Flycatchers, Warbling Vireos, and Purple Finches. Black-capped Chickadee nest in riparian woodlands of alder and willow near the coast and locally inland in the northwestern counties. Wet thickets in the higher mountains host breeding MacGillivray's and Wilson's Warblers. Several oases in the Great Basin region attract large numbers of passerines, including rarities, in migration. In Inyo County they include Deep Springs College (contact in advance for permission to bird), Scotty's Castle, and Furnace Creek Ranch; the latter also hosts Verdin year-round and Lucy's Warbler in the breeding season.

Among major rivers, the Sacramento and – to a lesser extent – the San Joaquin have some remaining stretches of good riparian woodland along their length. Nearly all of the rivers and streams flowing out of the mountains also have attractive stretches, as do the smaller rivers and creeks that flow into the San Francisco Bay Area's waters. Riparian woodlands of the lower Cosumnes River deserve special mention.

BRUSHLAND

Humid coastal scrub occurs from Monterey County northward as a climax plant community in scattered locations where soil or climatic conditions prevent forests from growing, and as a subclimax community where fires or logging have destroyed the forest. Inland foothill chaparral cloaks the lower flanks of dry interior hills and the foothills of the Sierra Nevada, and montane chaparral occurs at higher elevations in the Sierra Nevada and other mountain ranges. Structural characteristics are similar in these types of brushland: a tangle of shrubby plants of varying heights that may be too dense to permit passage by large mammals, punctuated here and there by short trees that rise above the dense vegetation. The climb along state route 120 up to Big Oak Flat passes through foothill chaparral, home to Wrentits, California Thrashers, and Spotted Towhees. There, a springtime pause at a turnout before dawn may be rewarded with a chorus of Common Poorwills. Further east and 3000' higher, as state route 120 approaches Crane Flat in Yosemite National Park, stretches of montane chaparral appear, especially on south-facing slopes. Its expanses offer breeding habitat for Mountain Quail, Dusky Flycatchers, MacGillivray's Warblers, Yellow Warblers, Green-tailed Towhees, and Fox Sparrows.

DESERT SCRUB AND WOODLANDS

The Great Basin is the name given to a vast area of the west from which no water drains to the sea. In Northern California the Great Basin region includes the area east of the crest of the Cascade/Sierra Nevada range, and it encompasses much of Modoc and Lassen counties in the northeast and much of Mono and Inyo counties in the southeast. Its lower elevations are a dry, cold, high (average elevation 4,000') desert in which killing frosts can occur in any month of the year. Sagebrush and associated plants cover much of the region. Characteristic breeding birds in more northerly areas include Sage Thrasher and Sagebrush Sparrow; Greater Sage-Grouse, formerly much more numerous and widespread, is now found only locally. LeConte's Thrasher is a very local resident in Mono and Inyo counties; Bell's Sparrow (subspecies *canescens*) is resident in Inyo County. Joshua tree woodlands in southern Inyo County host breeding Ladder-backed Woodpeckers, Cactus Wrens (very locally), and Scott's Orioles.

OAK SAVANNAS AND WOODLANDS

Savannas are grasslands with widely scattered trees as a sparse overstory; they are usually the driest and warmest environments of any tree-dominated vegetation type. Woodlands are open, sunlit, tree-dominated areas with more tree cover than savannas but less than forests; tree canopies provide more than 30% cover but seldom overlap. Woodlands generally occur in elevation bands higher than savannas but lower than forests, in which tree canopies overlap to produce deep constant shade. Oak savannas and woodlands are found in lowland and foothills over much of the region, the tree species varying by ecologic conditions. Evergreen coast live oak, interior live oak, and canyon oak woodlands are common and widespread, the former in coastal counties from Mendocino southward. Winter-deciduous oaks include the northerly Oregon oak, the higher elevation black oak, and the widespread and easily recognized blue oak and valley oak of lower elevations.

Characteristic birds of oak savannas and woodlands include Band-tailed Pigeon; Western Screech-Owl; Acorn, Lewis's (mainly in winter), and Nuttall's Woodpeckers; Ash-throated Flycatcher (summer); Hutton's Vireo; Oak Titmouse; White-breasted Nuthatch; Western Bluebird; and (locally around the fringe of the Central Valley) Yellow-billed Magpie.

COASTAL CONIFEROUS FOREST

The coastal coniferous forest extends semi-continuously from the Oregon state line to about San Francisco in a belt rarely more than 20 miles wide; patches are also present southward, to Monterey Co. Its towering coast redwoods, some more than 300' high, and other constituent trees thrive in the coastal fog belt's high-precipitation damp environment, and create a high, close canopy through which only filtered sunlight passes. The forest floor is carpeted with shade-resistant plants that live in shadow except when a treefall opens a window in the canopy. Soon, however, fast-growing smaller trees and shrubs shade the forest floor again, but they eventually give way to mature coniferous forest once again.

Among common breeding species in this habitat are Pacific-slope Flycatcher, Steller's Jay, Chestnut-backed Chickadee, Pacific Wren,

Golden-crowned Kinglet, Swainson's Thrush, Hermit Thrush, Varied Thrush, and Wilson's Warbler. Spotted Owl and Vaux's Swift are two other notable nesting species. Marbled Murrelets nest on large, high limbs in the coastal coniferous forest at scattered locations from Del Norte County south to Santa Cruz County.

PINYON-JUNIPER WOODLAND

East of the Sierra Nevada and on the Modoc Plateau, pinyon pines and junipers form mixed woodlands on flats and foothills in regions where precipitation averages only 10 to 20 inches per year. This "P-J" woodland, as it's often called, occurs in places as a broad belt between the high desert scrub and the open pine forests of higher elevations.

Bird density is low in comparison with oak woodlands or montane forests, but P-J woodlands boast two resident namesake species. Noisy flocks of Pinyon Jays roam these woodlands in search of pinyon pine nuts, and pairs of the much less conspicuous Juniper Titmice quietly forage for insects, berries, and seeds. Gray Flycatchers and Blue-gray Gnatcatchers are among the migrant species that breed here. In winter ripened juniper berries draw American Robins, Cedar Waxwings, Townsend's Solitaires and, very rarely, Bohemian Waxwings.

MONTANE FOREST

Above the oak woodlands, mixed and purely coniferous forests stretch upward, reaching – in our highest mountains – to the alpine meadows above timberline. In the central Sierra Nevada, montane forests extend from about 4,000' to 7,000' elevation. At low elevations, deciduous trees such as black oak and big leaf maple mix with ponderosa pine, incense cedar, and white fir. Climbing higher, deciduous trees become fewer, and other conifers, such as sugar pine, Jeffrey pine, and red fir, join the mix. Here and there, dry mountain slopes and forest openings are cloaked in a chaparral of *Ceanothus*, mountain mahogany and manzanita. Montane forest habitat occurs also in the middle levels of the Klamath Mountains and the Cascade Range, the inner portions of the north Coast Range south to about

Clear Lake (Lake County), the Warner Mountains, and, sparingly, the White Mountains. In these mountains, forests of similar composition to those of the Sierra Nevada occur at somewhat different elevations depending upon their latitude, annual precipitation, and other factors.

Where black oaks are present, with their acorns and their hordes of caterpillars and flying insects in summer, Flammulated Owls, Cassin's Vireos, and Nashville and Black-throated Gray Warblers breed. Typical mountain birds also include Hairy, White-headed, and Pileated Woodpeckers; Steller's Jay; Mountain Chickadee; nuthatches; Brown Creeper; and summering Red-breasted Sapsucker, Western Tanager, Black-headed Grosbeak, Fox Sparrow, and Green-tailed Towhee.

SUBALPINE FOREST

Overlapping with the upper elevations of montane forest, a subalpine coniferous forest extends upward to timberline in our highest mountains. Red firs, some in pure stands, dominate much of this zone, mixed with lodgepole pines in many areas. Climbing further upward, trees become sparser, smaller, and increasingly twisted by the winds; limber pines appear in the Sierra Nevada and bristlecone pines appear in the White Mountains, then give way to the treeless alpine zone. Besides in the Sierra Nevada and White Mountains, subalpine forest occurs in the Cascade Range, a few high parts of the Trinity and Siskiyou Mountains, and in the Warner and Inyo Mountains.

Bird life is sparser than at lower elevations. Resident species include Sooty Grouse, Northern Goshawk, Black-backed Woodpecker, Townsend's Solitaire, Pine Grosbeak (Sierra Nevada only), and Red Crossbill. Breeding summer visitors include Dusky Flycatcher, Mountain Bluebird, and "Mountain" White-crowned Sparrow (subspecies *oriantha*).

ALPINE ZONE

Beginning at about 10,500' elevation in the Central Sierra Nevada, wind-twisted conifers of the uppermost reaches of the subalpine forest give way to the treeless alpine zone, wherein lie alpine meadows ell-fields, lakes, talus slopes, perpetual snow fields and glaciers, and barren cliffs and peaks. Similar habitat also occurs in the highest portions of the Cascade Range, and the Warner and White Mountains, but in total the area of the alpine zone is relatively small. Food, in the form of insects, plant life, and seeds is present in vegetated areas for only a short period of the year, breeding bird species are few, and none is present year-round.

Alpine zone breeding species include White-tailed Ptarmigan (introduced into the Sierra Nevada), Rock Wren, Mountain Bluebird, American Pipit (Sierra Nevada only), and Gray-crowned Rosy-Finch. Rufous Hummingbirds pass through mid-summer on their southbound migration. Golden Eagles and Prairie Falcons occasionally soar over open areas in search of prey.

URBAN AND SUBURBAN PARKS AND RESIDENTIAL AREAS

The planting and irrigation of a diverse array of non-native vegetation has transformed urban and suburban habitats and made them attractive to many bird species. Our yards and local parks may host Cooper's Hawk, Anna's and Allen's Hummingbirds, Nuttall's and Downy Woodpeckers, Black Phoebe, California Scrub-Jay, American Crow, Bushtit, Northern Mockingbird, Yellow-rumped Warbler (winter), Cedar Waxwing (winter and spring), Brewer's Blackbird, Hooded Oriole (spring and summer), House Finch, and such non-natives as Rock Pigeon, European Starling, and House Sparrow. With an abundance of exotic fruiting and nectar-producing trees and shrubs, urban parks can be magnets for migrant and wintering species alike. Birders scour well-planted urban parks and residential neighborhoods in season, sometimes turning up impressive rarities.

FARMLAND, PASTURES, AND GRASSLANDS

Natural grasslands that covered much of the Central Valley's floor and its lower foothills are all but gone, converted to farming, (especially recently) to nut farms and vineyards, and to urbanization. Ground-nesting grassland birds such as Burrowing Owl, Horned

Lark, Grasshopper Sparrow, and Western Meadowlark still reside in rangeland and similar environments, but in much reduced numbers. Winter still draws species such as Ferruginous and Rough-legged Hawks, Sandhill Crane, Mountain Plover, Long-billed Curlew, Prairie Falcon, American Pipit, and Savannah Sparrow to suitable locations. Look for them in the Central Valley, Fall River Valley, Sierra Valley, Little Panoche Valley, and similar locations.

Intensive agriculture, of row crops, orchards, vineyards, alfalfa and rice, still provides habitat for some species, at least at some times of the year. In winter, orchards attract woodpeckers and sapsuckers, and flooded rice fields attract many species of waterfowl; flood-irrigated fields attract shorebirds during migration, sometimes in great numbers. At any time of year, pastures and farmyards with dairy cattle attract Cattle Egrets and blackbirds, sometimes including Tricolored and Yellow-headed Blackbirds.

BIRDING IN NORTHERN CALIFORNIA

One of the best ways to see new birds is to join your local Audubon chapter or other nature club on a field trip. Participants often visit new areas, learn how to identify new birds, and meet people who share a common interest. After studying the birds in your yard, visit local parks and open areas.

It is beyond the scope of this guide to describe specific birding locations in Northern California; there are simply too many excellent areas in every part of the region. We have mentioned some of them above; for more, we highly recommend the two different books titled "Birding Northern California," described in the Helpful Resources section. In addition to those two region-wide books, useful localized bird-finding guides have been published for the Klamath River region, Del Norte County, the Arcata area, Mendocino County, the Sacramento region, the San Francisco peninsula (available on-line), South San Francisco Bay, Napa and Solano counties, San Joaquin County, and Stanislaus and Merced counties. Many of these guides are currently still available.

Helpful Resources

Statewide Publications:

California Bird Records Committee (Robert A. Hamilton, Michael A. Patten and Richard A. Erickson, Eds.). 2007. *Rare Birds of California*. Western Field Ornithologists, Camarillo, CA.

Daniel S. Cooper. 2004. *Important Bird Areas in California*. Audubon California.

Grinnell, J. and A. H. Miller. 1944. *The Distribution of the Birds of California*. Pacific Coast Avifauna, No. 27 (reprinted in 1986 by Artemisia Press)

Regional Publications:

Edward C. Beedy and Edward R. Pandolfino. 2013. *Birds of the Sierra Nevada: Their Natural History, Status, and Distribution*. University of California Press.

William G. Bousman. 2007. *Breeding Bird Atlas of Santa Clara County, California*. Santa Clara Valley Audubon Society, Cupertino CA.

David Gaines. 1988. *Birds of Yosemite and the East Slope*. Artemisia Press, Lee Vining, CA.

Stanley W. Harris. 2005. *Northwestern California Birds*. 3rd Ed. Living Gold Press, Klamath River, CA.

John E. Hunter, David Fix, Gregory A. Schmidt, Jude Claire Power. 2005. *Atlas of the Breeding Birds of Humboldt County, California*. Redwood Region Audubon Society, Eureka, CA.

John Kemper. 1999. *Birding Northern California*. Falcon Publishing, Inc., Helena, MT.

Guy McCaskie, Paul De Benedictis, Richard Erickson, Joseph Morlan. 1988. *Birds of Northern California: An Annotated Field List*. 2nd Ed. Golden Gate Audubon Society, Berkeley, CA.

Jean Richmond. 1985. *Birding Northern California*. Mt. Diablo Audubon Society, Walnut Creek, CA. Download from http://

www.diabloaudubon.org/birds/books/BirdingNorCal.pdf

Don Roberson. 2002. *Monterey Birds. Status and Distribution of Birds in Monterey County, California*. 2nd Ed. Monterey Peninsula Audubon Society, Carmel, CA.

Don Roberson and Chris Tenney, Eds. 1993. *Atlas of the Breeding Birds of Monterey County California*. Monterey Peninsula Audubon Society, Carmel, CA.

W. David Shuford. 1993. *The Marin County Breeding Bird Atlas*. Point Reyes Bird Observatory. Bushtit Books, Bolinas, CA. Download from http://ia601703.us.archive.org/31/items/marincountybreed00shuf/marincountybreed00shuf.pdf

The four breeding bird atlases above span most of the length of the region. Each contains extensive distributional information, much of it also relevant to adjacent counties. Helpful breeding bird atlases, each with less extensive distributional information, have also been published for Alameda, Contra Costa, Napa, San Francisco (draft available online), San Mateo, Solano, and Sonoma counties.

IDENTIFICATION GUIDES:

Jon L. Dunn and Jonathan Alderfer. 2017. National Geographic Field Guide to the Birds of North America, 7th Ed. National Geographic Society, Washington, D.C.

Roger Tory Peterson. 2010. *A Field Guide to Birds of Western North America*, 4th Ed. Houghton Mifflin Harcourt, Boston.

David Allen Sibley. 2014. *The Sibley Field Guide to Birds*. 2nd Ed. Alfred A. Knopf, New York.

PHOTOGRAPHIC GUIDES:

Edward S. Brinkley. 2007. *National Wildlife Federation Field Guide to Birds of North America*. Sterling Publ. Co., New York.

Paul Sterry and Brian E. Small. 2009. *Birds of Western North America: A Photographic Guide*. Princeton University Press, Princeton.

Donald and Lillian Stokes. 2010. *The Stokes Field Guide to the Birds of North America*. Little, Brown and Co., New York.

JOURNALS:

North American Birds (indispensable quarterly reports of bird sightings, related Articles and summaries; published by the American Birding Association)

Western Birds (the quarterly journal of the Western Field Ornithologists)

ON-LINE BIRDING RESOURCES:

California Bird Records Committee: http://californiabirds.org

Cornell Laboratory of Ornithology's BirdSource, including eBird, Christmas Bird Counts, Great Backyard Bird Count, Feeder Watch, and other citizen science projects: http://www.birds.cornell.edu/Page.aspx?pid=1478

Joe Morlan's California Birding pages: http://fog.ccsf.cc.ca.us/~jmorlan/rare.htm

The American Birding Association's compilation of birding email lists: http://birding.aba.org/

Western Field Ornithologists: http://westernfieldornithologists.org

NATURE CENTERS, NATURE STORES AND INFORMATION CENTERS:

There are many good nature stores in Northern California, which you can locate with web search engines or telephone directory yellow pages. Their staffs will happily answer your bird and bird-feeding questions.

Species Accounts

The following pages present accounts and photographs of Northern California's most familiar bird species. Most species accounts are presented in a standardized format, shown on the sample page (opposite). Pages that treat three or more species employ a compressed version of this format. Species are grouped by families, color-coded and thumb-indexed. Separate sections at the back of the book treat 16 species commonest in the higher mountains, 20 species commonest in the northern Mojave Desert/Great Basin region, and 27 pelagic species (those usually best seen from boats at sea). The Quick Guide at the beginning of the book will help you locate the most common birds, while the Index on p. 494 will help you locate any species described in the book.

The following terms are used to describe the relative abundance of each species and the likelihood of finding it in a particular season. The American Birding Association developed the first four definitions.

- **Common:** Found in moderate to large numbers, and easily found in appropriate habitat at the right time of year.
- **Fairly Common:** Found in small to moderate numbers, and usually easy to find in appropriate habitat at the right time of year.
- **Uncommon:** Found in small numbers, and usually—but not always—found with some effort in appropriate habitat at the right time of year.
- **Rare:** Occurs annually in very small numbers. Not to be expected on any given day, but may be found with extended effort over the course of the appropriate season(s).
- **Casual:** Does not occur annually, but a pattern of occurrence is apparent over decades.
- **Accidental:** Seen only once or a few times in an area that is far out of the species' normal range.

NAME OF SPECIES
Its Latin name

Description: Length (and wingspan for larger species), followed by a description that includes differences in plumages between sexes and ages. Key field marks—unique markings or structural characters visible in the field that help distinguish one species from another—are shown in **boldfaced** type.

Voice: Describes the main song and calls of the species; these can be very important for species identification. Note that most species have a much greater vocal repertoire than described here.

Behavior: Highlights behaviors characteristic of this species, including feeding behavior, distinctive movements and displays, flight style, and breeding behavior.

Similar Species: Identifies similar-appearing species and describes how to tell them apart. Similar species whose names appear in **boldfaced** type are illustrated in this guide.

Where, When to Find: Describes the general locations and habitats where this species may be found in Northern California, sometimes suggesting some of the better locations to search for it. Identifies the times of year that the species is here and its relative abundance (see facing page for definitions of abundance terms).

Did you know? Provides other interesting facts about the species.

Date and Location Seen: A place for you to record the date and location of your first sighting of this species.

Note: Birds shown in the photographs in the Species Accounts are adults unless the captions indicate otherwise.

Immature

Adult

Greater White-fronted Goose
elgasi

escription: 28", wingspan 53". A **gray-brown** goose with **pinkish bill** and **orange** legs. The **rear underparts are contrastingly white;** there is a **white band across the base of the tail** and a narrow white tail tip. ADULT: **White feathering at base of bill,** irregular **black bars across the belly.** JUVENILE: Lacks white on face and black belly bars. Subspecies *elgasi* (the "Tule Goose"): **Larger** (by about 10%) and **much thicker necked; much darker chocolate-brown coloration, especially about head and neck.**

oice: Common flight call is a rather high yelping *kah-la-luck*.

ehavior: Thousands (*sponsa*) habituate the Central Valley's rice fields, and also graze on lawns and pastures. They roost in shallow water in marshes and other aquatic environs while *elgasi* remain in marshes, where they feed on tules.

imilar Species: Domestic geese, mostly derived from Old World Graylag and Swan Geese, can be common on city park lakes. They resemble White-fronteds, but lack black belly bars and distinct white face patch, are larger-billed, pot-bellied, and often tame or even aggressive.

here, When to Find: The widespread subspecies *sponsa* breeds in southwest Alaska; it is common to abundant throughout much of the Central Valley, mainly mid-September through March; many remain through April. Common migrant in northeastern California; some winter. Uncommon migrant (mainly late September and October) along the coast; a few winter. A few wild birds tame down and stay for extended periods at park lakes. The much scarcer *elgasi* (population estimate about 5,000, a state Species of Special Concern) winters entirely in the Sacramento Valley, mainly in Glenn and Colusa counties. Breeds in partly forested areas near the upper reaches of Cook Inlet, Alaska.

id you know? Given its distinct size and coloration differences, isolated breeding range, and different feeding behavior, *elgasi* may represent a distinct species.

ate & Location Seen: _____

Snow Goose
Adult

Immature

Ross's Goose
Adult

Immature

SNOW GOOSE/ROSS'S GOOSE
Anser caerulescens/Anser rossii

Description: 28"/23", wingspan 54"/44". Both are medium-large **white** geese with **black wingtips**. In SNOW, pink bill shows a black "grinning patch" along the sides where the mandibles meet; **much smaller ROSS'S has stubbier bill** with blue-gray base, much less black on bill sides. JUVENILE Snow in first fall and early winter is washed with gray on the neck, back, and wings; bill is dull pinkish-gray; juvenile Ross's is much whiter (gray limited to crown, back, wings). "Blue" plumage morph of Snow, rare over most of the West, is variably slate-gray on the back, breast, and neck.

Voice: Call is a raucous, fairly high yelping "*rowk*" or "*wow;*" call of Ross's is higher pitched.

Behavior: Grazes on grasses, grain, marsh vegetation, and rice fields, foraging in shallow water as well as on land.

Similar Species: Beware white domestic geese and outsized white Mallards (these all lack black wingtips), common around park lakes. Hybrid Snow x Ross's Geese are known.

Where, When to Find: Flocks of thousands of Snows and hundreds of Ross's winter (November to March) at refuges through much of the central and northern portions of the Central Valley. Common in northeastern California, but mainly as a migrant in late October-November and February-March. Ross's Geese, on average, linger later in the spring (into April). Both species are rather rare, but regular, from coastal areas during migration (especially in late fall) and winter. Rare migrants in the Sierra Nevada. Individual or very small numbers of both Snow and Ross's geese will sometimes take up residence in city parks and join domestic waterfowl in becoming very tame.

Did you know? Ross's Goose also has a very rare "blue" morph, darker than blue Snows, with white face contrasting with dark head and neck.

Date & Location Seen: _____

"Black Brant"
nigricans

Description: 25", wingspan 42". A small, stocky, dark coastal goose with **black head and neck**, irregular white ring on upper neck, **blackish brown breast and belly**, and **extensively white rear end** that nearly hides the black tail. The flanks are marked with white. Bill and legs black. JUVENILE lacks white neck ring. Our birds are "Black Brant" of the subspecies *nigricans*. The more easterly, paler bellied *hrota*, the "Atlantic Brant," is casual along the coast and has been recorded in the Great Basin. Beware worn, over-summering *nigricans* can also have pale bellies.

Voice: Flocks make a low, hoarse *cronk* call, but individuals are usually silent in our area.

Behavior: Feeds on eelgrass in coastal estuaries and large bays; in our region, mostly seen as a migrant offshore, where it flies in disorganized lines (sometimes mixing with scoters). Routinely sits on the ocean, unlike other regularly occurring geese.

Similar Species: Canada and Cackling geese always show a conspicuous white chinstrap and are browner overall.

Where, When to Find: Common migrant, especially in spring (March to mid-May) along the coast, most visible from coastal headlands. Fall migration (November-December) is farther offshore and largely bypasses our coastline. Locally common at large coastal estuaries in winter. Thousands winter at Humboldt Bay and hundreds are found at Bodega Bay. Much scarcer elsewhere. Some, even small groups, spend the summer along the coast. Casual spring migrant throughout the interior; a few have summered.

Did you know? This is a circumpolar goose with three, perhaps four, subspecies. Our "Black Brant" is a state Species of Special Concern; it's found also in northeast Asia.

Date & Location Seen: _____

_____

Canada Goose

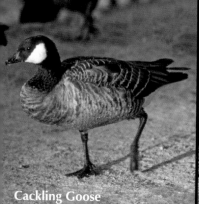

Cackling Goose
minima

Cackling Goose
"Aleutian" *leucopareia*

Description: 30-43"/23-33", wingspan 53-60"/43-48". A familiar small (CACKLING) to large (CANADA) brown goose with **black neck and white "chin strap."** Undertail and band across rump white. Bill and legs black. Subspecies size varies within each species. Cackling Geese have shorter, stubbier appearing bills than Canadas. One subspecies (*taverneri*) of Cackling is comparably sized to the smallest Canada Goose subspecies (*parvipes*); the two are virtually inseparable. Most Cackling Geese are either "Aleutian" (*leucopareia*) or smaller and darker breasted *minima*, the former having a prominent (usually) white neck ring that is indistinct or lacking in the latter subspecies.

Voice: Call of Canada is a low, familiar *"h-lonk."* Cackling's call is distinctly higher pitched.

Similar Species: Both species are unmistakable from other geese at rest, though not from each other. In flight separated from Greater White-fronted by darker coloration, especially the black neck (and white cheek) and the browner (much less gray) upper wing. Adult Greater White-fronteds with extensive black on belly are distinctive.

Where, When to Find: Migratory Canadas are uncommon to common winter visitors (October to March) and breed in northeastern California. Distinguishing them from now widely established resident (introduced) populations is problematic. "Aleutian" Cackling Geese commonly stage in spring migration along the coast of northwestern California after wintering there or in the Central Valley. Subspecies *minima* is uncommon to rare throughout the region (most in the Central Valley); it has declined here because large numbers now linger farther north to winter in Oregon's Willamette Valley. Cackling Geese are rare on the coast south of Humboldt County and east of the Sierra Nevada.

Did you know? The "Aleutian Goose" breeds almost exclusively in the Aleutians and nearly went extinct because of Arctic Fox predation. Populations have strongly rebounded due to predator control.

Date & Location Seen: _____

Immature

Adult

Description: 52", wingspan 66". Very large, white, and **long-necked**. ADULT: **Black bill,** black facial skin closes in front of eye (usually a yellow spot there), then cuts straight across forehead. JUVENILE: Overall clouded with gray, whiter by spring, and bill patchy pink.

Voice: Calls are loud and far carrying, a rather high-pitched whooping or yodeling.

Behavior: Forages on plant materials on land or in water. Gregarious, often in flocks; may roost on open water.

Similar Species: Swans are unmistakable, although sleeping American White Pelicans can be confused. The larger Mute Swan (*Cygnus olor*; 60", wingspan 75"), an introduced Old World species, is rapidly increasing, especially in the northern Bay Area and various foothill counties. Adults have a blackish knob at the base of an orange-pink bill; juveniles are dark gray. Trumpeter Swan (*Cygnus buccinator*; 60", wingspan 80") from northwestern North America is a very rare winter visitor, except small numbers now winter regularly in eastern Modoc County. Adults separated with difficulty from Tundra by longer bill, more Canvasback-like head profile; critical is that black facial skin extends back to include the eye, then cuts across the forehead in a V-shaped pattern. Juveniles in late winter and spring are darker than juvenile Tundras. Vocalizations strongly differ.

Where, When to Find: Common winter visitor (November to mid-March) in the Central Valley (rare south of Merced County) and in northeastern California. Generally uncommon coastally, and increasingly scarce from north to south; scarce on Sierra Nevada lakes. Found in a variety of wetland habitats, including flooded rice fields.

Did you know? Whistling Swan was Tundra's English name when it was treated as a separate species from the Old World "Bewick's Swan." A few subspecies *bewickii* (plus intergrades) appear annually in our region; adult *bewickii* shows extensive yellow at the base of the bill.

Date & Location Seen: _____

Male

Female

Description: 18 ½", wingspan 30". This distinctive duck sports a **drooping crest** and appears **long tailed** in flight. BREEDING MALE: Unmistakable with colorful green, black and white head pattern, **red bill base and eye ring,** deep reddish breast bordered behind by vertical black and white bars, glossy black upperparts, tan-yellow sides, and an iridescent blue wing patch. NON-BREEDING male (summer, fall) much duller but retains basic pattern. FEMALE: Broad **white ring** around eye, pointed in rear. Gray above, gray spotted with white below.

Voice: Calls include various high and rising whistles (males) and squeaks, almost exaggerated squeals in flight.

Behavior: Often perches low in trees or on fallen branches over the water. Feeds on invertebrates and plants in shallow water; does not dive. Nests in tree cavities or nest boxes.

Similar Species: Unmistakable, especially breeding males, but beware that there is a small established population of the Mandarin Duck (*A. galericulata*, 18"), native to east Asia, in Sonoma County, and individuals from that population (or escapees) are occasionally seen elsewhere in coastal regions. Male equally colorful but very different; female much like female Wood Duck, but paler (more grayish, less brownish) with long, thin white extension to eye ring, large white spots below, pale on bill tip.

Where, When to Find: Generally uncommon to rare throughout, scarcest in northeastern California and east of the Sierra Nevada, perhaps most numerous on small ponds and streams in the western Sierra Nevada foothills. Prefers wooded to partly wooded habitats throughout its range. Some migratory movements.

Did you know? Like Wood Duck in the genus *Aix*, ducks in the genera *Spatula, Mareca,* and *Anas* are also "dabblers," tipping their rear end up to feed just underwater rather than dive.

Date & Location Seen: _____

Mallard
Male

Mallard
Female

Gadwall
Male

Gadwall
Female

Description: 23″, wingspan 35″. **Our most familiar duck;** large and heavy-bodied with a **blue speculum bordered white in front and back**, white underwings, orange legs. MALE: **Green head, white neck ring**, reddish breast, pale gray body, curled black feathers at base of tail; bill yellow. FEMALE: Mottled brown, with dark line through eye, blotchy orange and dusky bill. **Voice:** Female's quacking is the quintessential duck noise; male utters short, rasping whistles. **Behavior:** Forages in shallow water; also grazes on land. **Similar Species:** Male unmistakable. Compare female with female Gadwall (below). **Where, When to Find:** Common resident throughout in wetlands, estuaries, lakes, and urban parks, where partly feral birds vary in color and especially shape (*i.e.*, heavier). There is an influx of wintering birds from late October to early March.

GADWALL *Mareca strepera*

Description: 20″, wingspan 33″. Both sexes rather plain with a **steep forehead and a square white patch on speculum.** MALE: Generally **grayish** (intricate pattern apparent at close range) with brownish head and **black rear end;** bill dark gray. FEMALE: Mottled brown and white, with white belly; **orange side to bill forms a straight line;** white wing patch often visible at rest. **Voice:** Female gives a nasal *quack*; male's call a reedy *rep, rep.* **Behavior:** Forages like *Anas* ducks. Usually in pairs or small groups. **Similar Species:** Gray color of male unique. Female most easily confused with female Mallard; note head shape, bill pattern, white belly and speculum. **Where, When to Find:** Uncommon to fairly common winter visitor (October to March) to estuaries, marshes, ponds and lakes throughout; less common and local during the summer.

Did you know? In our area, only male Mallards have curled-up tail feathers.

Date & Location Seen: _____

American Wigeon
Male

American Wigeon
Female

Eurasian Wigeon
Male

Eurasian Wigeon
Female

Description: 20"/20", wingspan 32"/32". AMERICAN a familiar wintering duck that grazes on lawns. Small **bill is blue-gray with black tip**. MALE: Pinkish brown with **white (or buffy) forehead, green patch around and behind eye,** white rear flank patch and black undertail. In flight shows white belly and **large white patch on forewing**. FEMALE: Gray-brown head, brown breast and flanks, white belly. In flight forewing is gray bordered behind by white. The much rarer EURASIAN WIGEON is similar but males have a **rufous head with a tawny-cream crown,** gray body; females told at close range by their warmer, more uniformly colored face, throat, and breast; in American the gray face and throat contrast with tawny-brown chest. Eurasian underwings are dusky in all plumages; American's are white.

Voice: The male American's call is an emphatic three-note whistle *whee whew whew* with a rise in the middle. The male Eurasian's call is distinctly different, a slurred, higher pitched one-note whistle. Females of both species give a low quack.

Behavior: Flocks of Americans graze on lawns that border park lakes and on mudflats; also feed by picking vegetation from the surface in shallow water (both fresh and salt). Eurasians are nearly always with Americans.

Where, When to Find: American is a common winter visitor (late September to early April) to freshwater lakes and estuaries throughout the region. They breed mainly in Alaska and Canada, uncommonly in the region, mostly in the eastern Sierra Nevada and Great Basin. Eurasian is a rare winter visitant, but where Americans occur in the many hundreds, up to a half dozen, sometimes more, Eurasians can be found; scarcer east of the Sierra Nevada.

Did you know? The name wigeon is derived from the French *vigeon*, a 'whistling duck.'

Date & Location Seen: _____

_____

Cinnamon Teal
Male

Cinnamon Teal
Female

Blue-winged Teal
Male

Blue-winged Teal
Female

Description: 16″, wingspan 23″. A small dabbling duck with a **light blue forewing patch**, mostly hidden at rest, yellowish legs. MALE: **Deep cinnamon-red** nearly throughout, with red eyes. Late summer males largely brownish. FEMALE: Mottled brown with a plain brown head; bluish forewing patch distinctive in flight. Fall immature males are similar; eyes gradually turn reddish. **Voice:** Male gives a low chatter, female quacks. **Behavior:** Forages by tipping up in shallow water and by dabbling with the bill in mud. **Similar Species:** See Blue-winged Teal (below). Female Green-winged Teal (p. 49) is smaller billed, has largely white undertail coverts. **Where, When to Find:** Common spring migrant (late January through April) throughout, a fairly common breeder, and a fairly common fall migrant (August-September). Uncommon to locally fairly common in winter; rare in the Sierra Nevada and Great Basin in winter.

BLUE-WINGED TEAL *Spatula discors*

Description: 15 ½″, wingspan 23″. Wing pattern like Cinnamon Teal. MALE: **Slate-gray** (tinged lilac) **head**, spotted brown body and **white face crescent and flank patch.** FEMALES and late summer/early fall males resemble female Cinnamon, but slightly grayer and more mottled overall with a stronger eye-line, broken white eye ring, and whitish area at base of smaller bill. **Voice:** Female quacks, male gives a gives a whistled *peeu*, unlike Cinnamon. **Behavior:** Like Cinnamon, with which it often associates. **Where, When to Find:** Uncommon throughout. Mostly noted in spring (March to early May) when males are easily identified, but actually more numerous in fall (mid-September through October), when all bear female-like plumage. A rare breeder, primarily in the Central Valley and Great Basin. Generally rare and local in winter, mostly from the Central Valley and Bay Area.

Did you know? These two closely related teal occasionally hybridize.

Date & Location Seen: _____

_____

Male

Female

Description: 19", wingspan 30". A medium-sized dabbler, rather chunky and with an **oversized, spatulate bill.** Shows bright orange legs. The large bill produces a front-heavy appearance in flight. MALE: **Green head** with yellow eye, white breast, **cinnamon sides.** In flight shows light blue-gray forewing with broad white rear border. As with other ducks the late summer and fall plumage is considerably muted. FEMALE: Mottled brown with broad buffy-white edges to side and flank feathers and whitish-gray edged tertials (a good field mark when at rest and bill is hidden); gray forewing with narrow white rear border. Female's large spoon-shaped bill with orange sides is distinctive.

Voice: Females quack; males give a soft *thup-tup*.

Behavior: Feeds like other dabblers by tipping up. Also sifts the water with its outsized bill in a circular motion, often in animated, spinning flocks.

Similar Species: Females of many other duck species resemble female Northern Shoveler in general plumage, but none shows the large, expanded bill of the shoveler.

Where, When to Find: Common winter visitor (mid-August to April) to wetlands throughout much of the region, although rather rare over most of the Sierra Nevada, and fewer in the Great Basin in winter. An uncommon breeder in the Central Valley and the Great Basin; rather rare in summer on the coast. Can be especially abundant on wastewater treatment ponds.

Did you know? Northern Shovelers have fringes along the sides of the bill that help them filter food items from water and mud. The Northern Shoveler's closest relatives are the Cinnamon and Blue-winged Teal. Although also called a "teal", Green-winged Teal is only distantly related to all three of these species.

Date & Location Seen: _____

Male

Female

escription: 21", wingspan 33". A slender, long-necked, dabbling duck with a **gray bill** and long pointed tail. In flight shows **white trailing edge to inner half of wing.** MALE: **Brown head**, white breast, **white stripe up side of neck.** Gray body with **elongated** black and white **tail feathers**. The speculum is green, bordered in front by buff, behind by white. FEMALE: Plain pale brown head and neck, mottled pale brownish body; central tail feathers rather **long and pointed** (but shorter than male).

ice: Female gives hoarse quacks; males give a thin, wheezy whistle, also a musical *droop* call (very similar to male Green-winged Teal's call), often doubled.

ehavior: Feeds like other dabblers by tipping up. Often seen flying in lines or "V"s.

milar Species: Other dabbling ducks have shorter, stocker necks and lack the pointed tail; most have some orange in the bill. Female Redhead (p. 51) is stockier, more solidly gray-brown on the body, and has pale gray flight feathers (visible in flight).

here, When to Find: Generally common to abundant winter visitor throughout (early August to mid-March), though fewer in the Sierra Nevada. Many migrate south along the coast in fall and flocks are frequently encountered well out to sea. Frequents a wide variety of wetland habitats; thousands are found in wet rice fields in the Central Valley. Generally an uncommon breeder throughout. This is an early spring and an early fall migrant.

id you know? This common Holarctic species is our most northerly breeding puddle duck, breeding across the Arctic.

ate & Location Seen: _____

Male

Female

Description: 14", wingspan 23". The smallest dabbling duck; all show a **bright green speculum** with a buffy-white border in front. Bill is small and dark. MALE: **Extensive bright green ear patch** borders **chestnut crown and face;** body gray with **white vertical stripe behind the breast;** undertail is **pale yellow and black.** FEMALE: Mottled brown; dark line through eye bordered indistinctly by buffy-brown lines, often with second blurry dark line through face; **whitish patch on sides of undertail.**

Voice: Male gives a high, peeping *dreep*, very similar to Northern Pintail. Female gives short, rough quacks.

Behavior: Like other dabblers, feeds at the surface of shallow water, but also routinely feeds shorebird-style on mudflats, including tidal channels, where their small size can make them relatively inconspicuous.

Similar Species: Compare female carefully to female Cinnamon and especially Blue-winged Teal (p. 43). Both are larger with larger bill (especially Cinnamon). Cinnamon is less mottled overall with a more subdued head pattern, but Blue-winged is more similarly patterned and colored; note pale sides to undertail, always mottled on both Cinnamon and Blue-winged. In flight (and sometimes at rest), easily separated by wing pattern.

Where, When to Find: Common winter visitor (September to early April) to wetlands throughout the region, though scarcer in the Sierra Nevada and adjacent foothills. An uncommon breeder in Great Basin wetlands; rarely breeds elsewhere in the region.

Did you know? Male "Eurasian" Green-winged Teal (subspecies *crecca*) shows a white horizontal stripe above the wing, lack the white vertical breast stripe of our subspecies *carolinensis*, and have a more conspicuous white border to the green facial patch; they occur nearly annually in coastal regions and in the Central Valley. Females of the two subspecies are virtually identical. Many Old World authorities treat *crecca* as a separate species.

Date & Location Seen: _____

Canvasback Male

Canvasback Female

Redhead Male

Redhead Female

CANVASBACK
Aythya valisineria

Description: 21", wingspan 29". A large diving duck with a **long sloping forehead** and a long black bill. MALE: **Nearly whitish body, deep chestnut head** (more blackish on forehead and forecrown), and red eyes. FEMALE: **Pale gray body contrasts sharply with light brown head and chest, pale gray wings. Voice:** Generally silent in our area. **Behavior:** Dives underwater for aquatic vegetation, some invertebrates; locally occurs in large rafts. **Similar Species:** Males can only be confused with Redhead (see below). Female's head-to-body color contrast is distinctive. **Where, When to Find:** A locally common winter visitor (late October-March) to coastal regions, the Central Valley, and the Great Basin; uncommon to rare on Sierra Nevada lakes and ponds. Has nested in the Central Valley; nests regularly in the Great Basin.

REDHEAD *Aythya americana*

Description: 19", wingspan 29". A large diving duck with a large round head. MALE: **Gray body** with **contrasting bright rufous-red head** and black breast. Blue-gray bill has black tip, preceded by white line. FEMALE: Uniformly buffy-brown with paler throat and faint eye ring; bill pattern similar to male. **Voice:** Males on the breeding grounds give a loud cat-like *ooaaoh*. **Behavior:** Forages like Canvasback. Usually found as singles, pairs, or very small groups, sometimes with Canvasback and scaup. **Similar Species:** Separated from Canvasback by head and bill shape, and by body color (grayer on males, browner on females). Female Ring-necked Duck (p. 53) is smaller, with a more angled head, less buffy coloration to body, grayer face, and bolder white eye ring. **Where, When to Find:** Rare to locally uncommon resident throughout the region, although from coastal areas known primarily during the winter.

Did you know? Redhead is a state Species of Special Concern; numbers have declined sharply and breeding range has contracted greatly since 1944.

Date & Location Seen: _____

Male

Female

escription: 17", wingspan 25". A small diving duck for which the term **"ring-billed duck"** is more descriptive – the gray bill has white rings at its base and near its black tip; **head is peaked at rear of crown.** In flight, gray flight feathers contrast with darker forewing. MALE: **Black back, distinct white crescent** separates **black breast** from **pale gray sides;** head is glossed purplish, chestnut ring at base of neck is hard to see. FEMALE: Dark slaty-brown above, **white eye ring** on **grayish face**, diffused whitish at base of bill.

ice: Generally silent in our area.

havior: Dives for aquatic plants, invertebrates. Usually found in small to moderate sized flocks; can be quite tame on park ponds.

nilar Species: Differs from scaup (p. 55) in having white rings on bill and a more peaked head, and lacking white wing stripe. Male scaup have gray (not black) back, whitish (not gray) sides; female scaup have distinct white patch at bill base and lack white eye ring. Female Redhead (p. 51) larger, paler brown, with more rounded head. The Tufted Duck (*A. fuligula*, 17"), a very rare, but annual winter visitor from Asia, has a bold, nearly complete white wing stripe; males have black backs and pure or nearly pure white sides; female has a dark chocolate brown head. Most birds show distinct tuft at back of head (shorter in females).

here, When to Find: Fairly common to locally common winter visitor (late September to early April) throughout, scarcest on the Central Valley floor. Prefers lakes and especially small wooded and park ponds, where scaup are scarce. Rare in summer; a few nest in the northern Sierra Nevada and Cascades.

d you know? As with most members of its genus, males have bright yellow eyes; females' eyes are duller, browner.

te & Location Seen: _____

**Lesser Scaup
Adult Male**

**Lesser Scaup
Female**

**Greater Scaup
Adult Male**

**Greater Scaup
Female**

LESSER SCAUP
Aythya affinis

Description: 16 ½", wingspan 25". In all plumages shows a **white stripe on inner half of wing** in flight, gray bill with small black "nail" on tip. MALE: **Iridescent purple (sometimes greenish) head** with **slight bump at rear of crown** (less evident on actively diving birds); chest, rump and undertail black; remaining **upperparts pale gray.** FEMALE: Brown throughout with white belly, **white patch at base of the bill. Voice:** Grating calls of females and rough whistles of males are rarely heard in our area. **Behavior:** Dives for aquatic invertebrates, some plant food. Often found in large flocks, sometimes mixed with other species of diving ducks. **Similar Species:** See Greater Scaup (below). **Where, When to Find:** Uncommon to common winter visitor (late October to mid-April) to ponds (including wastewater ponds), reservoirs, estuaries, and coastal lagoons. Small numbers nest in the northern Great Basin region. **Voice:** Grating calls of females and rough whistles of males are rarely heard in our area.

GREATER SCAUP *Aythya marila*

Description: 18", wingspan 28". **Larger than Lesser Scaup** with a larger and **very rounded head** and a **larger bill.** All plumages closely resemble Lesser; white wing stripe extends through the primaries. MALE: Averages paler than Lesser, dark nail extends to sides of bill tip. Head gloss averages greener, but very light dependent, and not diagnostic. FEMALE: Shows more of a whitish ear crescent than Lesser. **Voice:** Calls similar to Lesser, but lower pitched. **Behavior:** Like Lesser. **Where, When to Find:** Uncommon to abundant from coastal regions. Large rafts are found in the Bay Area and locally elsewhere in large estuaries. Elsewhere uncommon on larger lakes; prefers deeper, larger lakes than Lesser. Generally rare in the Central Valley.

Did you know? The name scaup perhaps comes from the Scottish 'scalp,' a bed of shellfish, upon which these ducks dine.

Date & Location Seen: _____

**Surf Scoter
Adult Male**

**Surf Scoter
Female**

**White-winged Scoter
Adult Male**

**White-winged Scoter
Immature**

Description: 20″, wingspan 30″. A heavy-set, dark diving duck of salt water. MALE: Entirely black except for **white patches on hindneck, forehead. Swollen bill has orange tip, white base with large black spot; eyes white.** FEMALE: Dark brown with blackish crown, **whitish patches on cheek** and at base of bill. IMMATURES of both sexes show pale belly. **Voice:** Generally silent in our region. **Behavior:** Dives for mollusks, especially around pier pilings, rocky shoreline, and bays with rocky bottoms. Often found in large flocks, including in flight past coastal points in migration. **Similar Species:** Compare with other scoters (below, p. 59). **Where, When to Find:** Common winter visitor and migrant (mid-October to April) along the coast and in San Francisco Bay. Rare migrant (mostly fall) inland. Small numbers (non-breeders) summer along coast.

WHITE-WINGED SCOTER *Melanitta deglandi*

Description: 21″, wingspan 34″. Slightly larger than Surf Scoter, with concave forehead shape; feathering extends farther out bill. Large white wing patch often hidden at rest. MALE: **Largely black with white on head limited to comma under eye;** flanks appear brownish in good light. Bill is intricately colored. FEMALE: Largely dark brown. **Voice:** Largely silent, even on the breeding grounds. **Behavior:** Unlike Surf Scoter slightly opens its wings as it dives. **Where, When to Find:** Generally rare to locally uncommon winter visitor (mid-October to April) along the coast and in bays. Numbers greatly reduced over recent decades; whether due to population decline or a change of wintering grounds is uncertain. Rare but annual migrant inland, especially in fall (November), mostly east of the Sierra Nevada crest.

Did you know? Prior to 2019 the Asian breeding Stejneger's Scoter *Melanitta stejnegeri* was considered conspecific with *M. deglandi;* adult males display black flanks and a more prominent nasal hook than *deglandi*. Accidental along the coast.

Date & Location Seen: _____

Black Scoter
Adult Male

Black Scoter
Immature Female

Harlequin Duck
Adult Male

Harlequin Duck
Female

BLACK SCOTER
Melanitta americana

Description: 19", wingspan 28". Rounded head distinct from other scoters. In flight, paler flight feathers contrast with rest of wing, most evident in adult males. MALE: **Entirely black** with **large swollen yellow-orange area at base of** black bill. FEMALE: Pale face contrasts with blackish crown; small concave bill. IMMATURES paler brown with pale belly; male's yellow at base of bill apparent by mid-winter. **Voice:** Unlike other scoter species, quite vocal, even in winter. Male gives an extended mellow whistle. Females give hoarse calls. **Behavior:** Usually associates with Surf Scoters, though can be found in small pure flocks. **Similar Species:** Adult male unmistakable. On female and immatures compare head shape and coloring with other scoters (p. 57). Pale flight feathers distinctive in flight. **Where, When to Find:** Our least abundant scoter. Rare to locally uncommon winter visitor (November-March) along coast; very rare on San Francisco Bay; casual inland, primarily in fall (November).

HARLEQUIN DUCK *Histrionicus histrionicus*

Description: 16 ½", wingspan 26". Small duck, with rounded head, stubby dark bill. MALE: **Colorful plumage (blue-gray and chestnut) with numerous white markings** diagnostic. FEMALE: Head shows three small white patches. JUVENILE: Resembles female. **Voice:** Largely silent in our area. **Behavior:** Found along rocky coasts, often stands on rocks; sometimes associates with other ducks, especially scoters. **Similar Species:** Female best told from female Surf Scoter (p. 57) by smaller size, rounder head, stubbier bill, and smaller circular white head patches. **Where, When to Find:** Rare but regular winter visitor (October-March) along rocky (primarily) sections of the coast; very rare in San Francisco Bay. Occasionally summers. Now casual inland.

Did you know? Harlequin Duck nested in the Sierra Nevada through the 1920s; there've been only a few breeding records in recent decades. A state Species of Special Concern.

Date & Location Seen: _____

**Long-tailed Duck
Adult Male**

**Long-tailed Duck
Female**

**Bufflehead
Adult Male**

**Bufflehead
Female**

LONG-TAILED DUCK
Clangula hyemalis

Description: 16" (male with tail 21"), wingspan 28". Formerly known as Oldsquaw. Extensively white plumage, including flanks, with short bill, rather short all-dark wings. MALE: Blackish-brown patch on rear of head, broad band across breast; **long, pointed tail, pinkish band across bill.** Becomes more extensively brown by late spring. IMMATURE male has pink band across bill, lacks long tail. FEMALE: Browner than male with short tail and all gray bill. Note mostly white face with dark patch. **Behavior**: Dives for mollusks and other invertebrates. In our area occurs as singles; sometimes associates with scoters, other diving ducks. **Voice**: Usually silent in our area; further north male gives well-known loud three-part yodeling calls in late spring and on breeding grounds. **Similar Species:** Unmistakable. **Where, When to Find:** Rare but annual to salt water along the coast and to the Bay Area in winter (late October to March). Casual inland in late fall and winter.

BUFFLEHEAD *Bucephala albeola*

Description: 13 ½", wingspan 21". Our **smallest duck**, with small gray bill. MALE: White below, mostly black above with **large white area on back of head,** large white wing patch. In good light, back of head shows purple and green gloss. FEMALE: Dark gray throughout with **oval white patch on sides of head,** small white speculum. IMMATURE male similar to female. **Voice:** Generally silent in our area. **Behavior:** Found in small, loose flocks; dives for aquatic invertebrates, small fish; flight is rapid. Nests in tree cavities. **Similar Species:** Much larger goldeneye females (p. 63) have dark brown heads. **Where, When to Find:** Common winter visitor (late October to April) throughout to bays, lakes, ponds and rivers. Uncommon breeder in the Cascade/Sierra Nevada range, non-breeders noted rarely elsewhere in summer.

Did you know? The Long-tailed Duck's plumages are complex, because it undergoes three complete molts during the year.

Date & Location Seen: _____

_____

**Common Goldeneye
Adult Male**

**Common Goldeneye
Female**

**Barrow's Goldeneye
Adult Male**

**Barrow's Goldeneye
Female**

COMMON GOLDENEYE
Bucephala clangula

escription: 18 ½", wingspan 26". MALE: **Green glossed head** with **large white lore spot;** all white underparts and mostly white scapulars. Extensive white on coverts and secondaries (visible in flight). FEMALE: **All brown head, gray below.** Dark bill with yellow tip; a few have all dull yellow bill. IMMATURE male like female; develops white lore spot by mid-December. **Voice:** Largely silent in our area; wings make whirring noise in flight. **Behavior:** Gregarious and rather shy, except on some park ponds. Dives for invertebrates and plants. Nests in tree cavities. **Similar Species:** See Barrow's Goldeneye (below). **Where, When to Find:** Fairly common to common winter visitor nearly throughout (November to March), fewer in southern Central Valley.

BARROW'S GOLDENEYE *Bucephala islandica*

escription: 18", wingspan 28". All plumages very similar to Common; the two hybridize occasionally. **Bill stubbier, forehead steeper, rear of head puffier.** MALE: **Purplish glossed head, white face crescent, black spur on sides of breast**, white spots on black scapulars. IMMATURE male like female, bill dark; usually develops trace of white crescent by late December. FEMALE: Similar to Common, but head darker and **bill nearly all orange-yellow.** Immature female has paler head; bill color variable. **Voice:** Largely silent in our area. **Behavior:** Nearly always with the more numerous Common; habits similar. **Similar Species:** Females and especially immature goldeneyes identifiable only with care at close range. Concentrate on head and bill shapes and bill color. Head shape less reliable when diving. **Where, When to Find:** Prefers bays, lakes, and rivers, often below dams. Rare to locally uncommon winter visitor (November to March) from coastal regions, Central Valley fringes, and the Cascade/Sierra Nevada range (formerly bred; no recent records).

id you know? *Bucephala* comes from Greek words: "ox-headed," describing the blunt foreheads of Bufflehead and goldeneyes.

ate & Location Seen: _____

**Common Merganser
Adult Male**
americanus

**Common Merganser
Adult Female**
americanus

**Red-breasted Merganser
Adult Male**

**Red-breasted Merganser
Female**

COMMON MERGANSER
Mergus merganser

Description: 25", wingspan 34". A low-slung diving duck with **slender, deep-based reddish bill.** MALE: **Green head** (looks blackish in poor light) with blackish along center of back, **white scapulars and underparts** except for blackish breast spur. Extensive white on coverts and secondaries; black bases to greater coverts sometimes visible at rest (forms dark bar) and especially in flight. FEMALE and young male with **deep rusty head, sharply separated from white chin and pale chest;** juvenile with pale lore stripe. **Voice**: Males give bell-like calls in display; both sexes give croaking calls. **Behavior**: Dives for fish; flocks often move together herding fish. Nests in tree cavities. **Similar Species**: See Red-breasted Merganser (below). **Where, When to Find:** Fairly common to common winter visitor (November to mid-April) nearly throughout. Uncommon nester throughout, except Central Valley, where nests only in northern Sacramento Valley. Strongly prefers fresh water.

RED-BREASTED MERGANSER *Mergus serrator*

Description: 23", wingspan 30". Shaped much like larger Common Merganser but with thinner bill, including base. MALE: **Dark green head with shaggy thin crest,** broad white neck ring, mottled reddish-brown breast; black and white wing patch. FEMALE: Tawny-brown head with thin shaggy crest; immature male similar. **Voice**: Largely silent in our area. **Behavior**: Dives for fish. Less gregarious than Common. **Similar Species**: Compare Common Merganser (above). Female and immature male told from Common by paler and more blended head, throat, and chest; lack contrasting white chin. **Where, When to Find**: Fairly common winter visitor (late October to April) along the coast, including bays and harbors. In our area strongly prefers salt water. Rare migrant and winter visitant inland, mostly on deep reservoirs.

Did you know? Merganser "teeth" – good for holding and grasping fish – are projections on the horny covering of the bill, not true teeth.

Date & Location Seen: _____

Hooded Merganser Adult Male

Hooded Merganser Female/Immature Male

Ruddy Duck Breeding Male

Ruddy Duck Female

HOODED MERGANSER
Lophodytes cucullatus

Description: 18″, wingspan 24″. A small, thin-billed, long-tailed diving duck with unique crest. MALE: **Puffy white crest outlined in black;** when folded back, white is reduced to a long thick stripe. Black above, tawny on sides, with two vertical black bars on sides of white breast. FEMALE: Dusky above, gray-brown on breast, sides; belly white; **puffy light tawny-brown crest**; bill has much yellow on sides; immature male similar. **Voice**: Mostly silent in our area. **Behavior**: Dives for small fish, aquatic invertebrates. In our area found singly, in pairs, or in small groups. Flight bullet-like, with rapid wing beats. Nests in tree cavities. **Similar Species:** Unmistakable. **Where, When to Find:** Uncommon to locally fairly common winter visitor (October to March) throughout, mostly on fresh water; scarcest on Central Valley floor. Prefers small ponds, rivers, and small lakes, especially with wooded margins. More numerous in recent decades. Small numbers nest in north coastal region and in Cascades.

RUDDY DUCK *Oxyura jamaicensis*

Description: 15″, wingspan 18 ½″. Small compact duck with **long stiff tail, often pointed upward**, short wings. MALE: **Large white cheek patch**, otherwise grayish-brown, except March to August, when body largely **deep chestnut, bill is sky blue.** FEMALE: Resembles non-breeding male but with **dark line across whitish cheek. Voice:** Mostly silent except for males in elaborate display when they give an accelerating series of popping notes, ending in a low croak. **Behavior**: Dives for aquatic plants, small fish, and invertebrates. **Similar Species:** Female and immature Bufflehead (p. 61) grayer with smaller bill than Ruddy, with white cheek spot. **Where, When to Find:** Common winter visitor throughout in a wide variety of wetland habitats. Fairly common breeder on marshy ponds throughout.

Did you know? Male Ruddy Ducks hold their colorful breeding plumage for fewer months than other ducks.

Date & Location Seen: _____

Mountain Quail
Male

Mountain Quail
Female

California Quail
Male

California Quail
Female

MOUNTAIN QUAIL
Oreortyx pictus

Description: 11″. A large, retiring quail with **long straight head plumes** that often seem like one, **chestnut throat outlined in white**, and **chestnut and white bars** on flanks. **Voice:** Breeding season call a loud, mellow *t'wook* (can be mistaken for Northern Pygmy-Owl); also a conversational *kew-kew-kew-kew…* series. **Behavior:** Often heard, but hard to see; much more wary than California Quail. Look for family groups along roads in late summer. **Similar Species:** Compare California Quail (below). **Where, When to Find:** Uncommon to fairly common in foothill and mountain chaparral and open coniferous forests with shrubby understory, to 10,000′. Descends on foot below the heavy snow line in fall and winter, when small coveys may be seen along snow-free roadsides.

CALIFORNIA QUAIL *Callipepla californica*

Description: 10″. A plump gray quail with short, rounded wings, medium-length tail, small black bill, and forward-curved topknot. **Belly is scaled with white,** brown flanks have white streaks. MALE'S **black throat outlined in white,** crown dark brown, **prominent forward-curved black topknot,** dark chestnut belly patch. FEMALE has gray-brown head and small, nearly straight topknot. **Voice:** Male's territorial call (during the breeding season) a cawing *waaaw;* location call a three-noted *chi-KA-go.* Flocks give sharp *pit, pit* calls. **Behavior:** Feeds in flocks on the ground, scratching with the feet for seeds and insects. One or more males stand watch as "sentinels." When flushed, quail explode into flight with whirring wing beats. **Similar Species:** Compare Mountain Quail (above). **Where, When to Find:** Common resident throughout the region in chaparral and oak and riparian woodland understory in lowlands and foothills, also in agricultural land. May form flocks of hundreds in some areas in winter. Absent from intensely farmed areas and higher mountain elevations.

Did you know? California Quail, sometimes called the "Valley Quail", is the State Bird of California.

Date & Location Seen: _____

_____

Ring-necked Pheasant

Male

Female

**Wild Turkey
Female**

**Wild Turkey
Male**

RING-NECKED PHEASANT
Phasianus colchicus

Description: 33" (male); 21" (female). Large chicken-like bird, introduced from Asia. **Long, pointed tail.** MALE largely **chestnut**, with intricate spotting, barring and scalloping patterns; glossy **dark green head, bare red face,** (usually) **white neck ring.** FEMALE brown above, paler gray-buff below, scaled throughout; long pointed tail (though shorter than male's). **Voice:** Male gives crowing *KOK'-kok*; all can give harsh notes when alarmed. **Behavior**: Feeds on ground among grain crops, farmlands, mixed grass and brush. Flushes explosively, rises steeply then flight levels off. A popular species for hunting. **Similar Species:** Sooty and Ruffed grouse (p. 73) are found in deep woodlands or mountains; both have shorter, fan-shaped tails. **Where, When to Find:** Fairly common, though declining, in the Central Valley and near wildlife areas. Populations managed for hunting, with new releases frequent.

WILD TURKEY *Meleagris gallopavo*

Description: 46" (male); 37" (female). Huge, familiar fowl with **bare reddish head and neck, bronzy plumage, fan-shaped tail** with pale band at tip. Much larger MALE has more wattled head, and a feathered chest "beard." **Voice**: male gives well-known "gobble." **Behavior**: Scratches on ground for acorns, other seeds, insects. Strong flyer (unlike overstuffed domestic versions); roosts in trees. **Similar Species:** Distinctive. Larger than all other regularly occurring chicken-like birds in the region. **Where, When to Find:** Multiple subspecies have been introduced for hunting; now fairly common in oak and riparian woodlands throughout the coast ranges, Sierra Nevada foothills, and wooded areas within the Central Valley.

Did you know? Pheasant declines are largely attributable to the reduction and industrialization of agriculture in the Central Valley. Turkeys, in contrast, are expanding in range and numbers.

Date & Location Seen: _____

Sooty Grouse
Female

Hooting Male

Ruffed Grouse

Description: 20". Large, longish-tailed **grayish bird; black tail has gray band at tip**. MALE has bare orange "comb" above eyes; exposes bare yellow neck sacs in display. **Voice**: Male gives series of very low-pitched hoots, difficult to locate. **Behavior**: Found in pairs or family groups. Forages from the ground to high in conifers, subsisting mainly on fresh conifer needles. Hooting male displays from a tall tree. **Similar Species**: Much larger than Mountain Quail (p. 69), which shares habitat. Much smaller, introduced White-tailed Ptarmigan (*Lagopus leucura*, 12 ½"), found locally in central Sierra Nevada's high meadows and alpine slopes, shows white underparts in summer. **Where, When to Find**: Resident in high mountain forests from the Sierra Nevada north to the Warner, Cascade, and Trinity ranges; locally in coastal county mountains south to Sonoma County. Females with young often found along meadow edges.

RUFFED GROUSE *Bonasa umbellus*

Description: 17". A secretive brown, **slightly crested** chicken-like bird of wet northwestern forests. **Rich brown** throughout, with paler barring and spotting; rufous **tail with black band near tip.** Black ruff on neck sides most visible during male's displays. **Voice**: Wing-beating of displaying male creates low, accelerating thumping sound. Alarmed birds give clucking sounds. **Behavior**: Forages, displays and nests on forest floor. Male display, often from atop a fallen log, involves fanned tail, erected "ruff," and wing-beating. Found in pairs and family groups. **Similar Species:** See Sooty Grouse (above). Much larger than quail within range. **Where, When to Find:** Uncommon resident in humid mixed coniferous/deciduous forest with a dense fern or shrub understory in Del Norte, Humboldt, Trinity, and western Siskiyou counties.

Did you know? Sooty Grouse were formerly considered conspecific with Dusky Grouse of the Rocky Mountains and Great Basin ranges east of California; known then as the "Blue Grouse."

Date & Location Seen: _____

Red-throated Loon
Breeding Adult

Red-throated Loon
Non-breeding Adult

Juvenile

Pacific Loon
Breeding Adult

Pacific Loon
Non-breeding Adult

Juvenile

Description: 25″, wingspan 36″. Loons are heavy-bodied, dagger-billed swimming and diving birds, not normally seen on land. This is the smallest loon, with **thin bill often tilted upwards. Upperparts rather plain** in all plumages. NON-BREEDING: Gray above, with small white spots; ADULT with gray cap, extensive white face and throat; JUVENILE'S neck washed with gray. BREEDING: Brick red **throat patch usually looks dark**. In flight, often dips neck below the horizontal. **Voice**: Usually silent in our area. **Behavior**: Forages closer to shore (even amongst breakers) than other loons as it pursues fish. **Similar Species**: See Pacific Loon (below). **Where, When to Find:** Common winter visitor (November to April) in inshore waters, harbors, and deeper portions of bays. Migrants pass by coastal points in small loose groups in November, also March-April. Uncommon (non-breeding) in summer. Very rare inland in late fall and winter; casual east of the Sierra Nevada.

PACIFIC LOON *Gavia pacifica*

Description: 26″, wingspan 36″. Small loon with straight bill. NON-BREEDING: Dark brown upperparts, crown (to eyes) and **neck sides, contrasting** sharply **with white throat** and a thin dark chin strap. JUVENILES paler brown above with paler barring; some lack chin strap. BREEDING: **Hindneck pale gray,** contrasting with black throat, **white patches on scapulars. Voice:** Largely silent in our area. **Behavior**: Migrants are often in flocks, many seen out to sea. **Similar Species:** See Common Loon (p. 77). Non-breeding adult Red-throated Loons have much more extensive white on the face, lack dark on the neck and are paler (grayer) above with white spots; juveniles show blended face and neck. **Where, When to Find:** Common migrant and winter visitor along coast (October to mid-May); some summer. Rare migrant inland.

Did you know? Loons' legs are set far back on their bodies, so they cannot walk efficiently on land.

Date & Location Seen: _____

Juvenile

Breeding Adult

Description: 32", wingspan 46". Our **largest regularly occurring loon**, with a heavy bill. In flight shows large feet, conspicuously held down; broad wings with relatively slow wing beats. NON-BREEDING: Brownish above (juvenile has pale gray cross-barring and duskier face), white below, **broad brownish partial collar intrudes on front of neck, white arcs around eye. Bill silver with entirely dusky ridge on top** (culmen). BREEDING: **Green-glossed black head, collar of white vertical bars on neck**, bordered below by black collar, extensive white markings above on scapulars. Bill black.

Voice: Far-carrying yodeling calls heard year-round (unlike other loons), though most vocal at nesting locations north of our region. Calls in flight as well as at rest.

Behavior: Dives for fish, often remaining submerged for long periods. Migrants (individuals or very small groups) move past, or just inland of, coastal points; often fly high; other loons tend to fly closer to the water.

Similar Species: Smaller non-breeding Pacific Loon (p. 75) shows an even line of sharp contrast between white foreneck and dark brown sides to neck, lacks white eye arcs and dark bar on sides of neck, and has a much smaller bill and feet. The slightly larger Yellow-billed Loon (*G. adamsii*, 35") is a very rare, but annual winter visitor to coastal areas, with a few inland records. Non-breeding Yellow-billeds are browner above and paler faced. Yellowish bill (in all plumages) is often tilted up as in Red-throated Loon.

Where, When to Find: Fairly common winter visitor (October to mid-May) along coast and deeper portions of bays, locally inland on large lakes. Otherwise generally rare in the interior. A few non-breeders summer; some older nesting records in northeastern California.

Did you know? The specific epithet *immer* evidently comes from the Icelandic name *himbrini* (the 'surf-roarer') for this species.

Date & Location Seen: _____

Non-breeding

Breeding Adult

PIED-BILLED GREBE
Podilymbus podiceps

Description: 13", wingspan 16". A small **brownish** diving bird with a **short, thick bill.** BREEDING ADULT has black throat patch on grayish-brown head and neck, **whitish bill with black ring near tip.** NON-BREEDING birds, including IMMATURES, have plain pale brownish bills; neck rufous-brown or tawny-brown. Young juveniles and downy young have black and white stripes on the face.

Voice: Quite vocal during the breeding season. Male's "song" is far carrying, a loud series of *kuh kuh kuh kow kow kow-ah*, etc. Interacting birds give an electric chatter, *huzza-huzza-huzza…*

Behavior: Dives for fish and crustaceans such as crayfish. When disturbed may slowly sink into water (only head and part of neck showing) rather than dive. Rarely seen in flight; shows almost no white in wing. Found in pairs or family groups, rarely flocks. Nest is a floating platform anchored to emergent vegetation.

Similar Species: Non-breeding Eared Grebe (p. 81) is slimmer-necked and slimmer-billed, grayer (less brown) overall with dusky foreneck; pale below.

Where, When to Find: Found in a wide variety of aquatic habitats, especially in winter when frequent even in salt water (coastal bays and estuaries). Breeds most frequently on marshy ponds and small to medium sized lakes. Basically resident, but withdraws from higher mountains and Great Basin if habitat freezes.

Did you know? Now that the Atitlán Grebe (*P. gigas*) from Guatemala is extinct, Pied-billed Grebe is the sole surviving representative of its genus. A great many other English names (some colloquial) have been ascribed to this species. These include American Dabchick, Hell-diver, and Water Witch.

Date & Location Seen: _____

_____

Eared Grebe
Non-breeding

Horned Grebe
Non-breeding

Eared Grebe
Breeding Adult

Horned Grebe
Breeding Adult

EARED GREBE
Podiceps nigricollis

Description: 13", wingspan 16". A small **slim-necked** grebe with a **thin, slightly upturned bill, peaked crown**, and red eyes. Shows **fluffy rear end** at rest. NON-BREEDING: Slaty-gray above, whitish with gray mottling below; dark down to cheek, neck variably washed with gray. BREEDING: Head and **neck black** with patch of golden plumes on side of head; flanks chestnut. **Voice**: Rising mellow whistles heard mainly at breeding colonies. **Behavior**: Dives for small fish, aquatic invertebrates. Often found in large flocks. **Similar Species:** Non-breeding birds, especially paler necked birds, closely resemble Horned Grebe (below). Note Eared's more peaked crown, all-dark lores, more upturned all-dark bill, and thinner, darker neck with a broader dark stripe down the hindneck. **Where, When to Find:** Found in a wider variety of wetlands than Horned Grebe, with peak numbers on saline ponds and lakes. Common winter visitor throughout, mid-September to April, except in higher Sierra Nevada and Great Basin. A few are found well offshore. Rather rare to uncommon and local nester, except in northeastern California where locally common.

HORNED GREBE *Podiceps auritus*

Description: 14", wingspan 18". A small **stocky-necked** grebe with a **short, straight pale-tipped bill, flat crown,** and red eyes. NON-BREEDING: White cheeks and foreneck; thin dark stripe down hindneck. BREEDING: Black head with **broad golden eyebrows** that extend back around back of head, **chestnut foreneck. Voice**: Silent in our area. **Behavior**: Dives for small fish. **Similar Species:** Compare with Eared Grebe (above) and Red-necked Grebe (p. 83). **Where, When to Find:** Common winter visitor in coastal areas, from mid-October to mid-April. Rare to locally fairly common inland, mainly on deep lakes and reservoirs. Very rare in summer; most summer records from Great Basin.

Did you know? Thousands of Eared Grebes gather every fall on Mono Lake.

Date & Location Seen: _____

_____

Non-breeding

Breeding Adult

escription: 20", wingspan 24". A **large, thick-necked grebe** with a large, wedge-shaped head and a **thickish, partly yellow bill** that is **almost as long as its head.** NON-BREEDING: Dark brownish, dark crown, pale gray cheeks (juveniles can show streaks until early winter), and dusky-gray neck. BREEDING: **Reddish front to neck**, dark crown down to its eye, **silver-gray throat and cheeks.**

ice: Silent in our area.

ehavior: Dives for small fish. Generally found as solitary individuals.

milar Species: Western and Clark's Grebes (p. 85) are slightly larger, but with thinner necks, thinner bills, and white (not dusky or red) fronts to their necks. Transitional (to breeding plumage) Horned Grebes (p. 81) can have reddish cast to neck and white cheeks, but are much smaller, and have a much shorter bill.

here, When to Find: Uncommon winter visitor (October to March) along the coast, including bays (e.g., Humboldt, Tomales, and San Francisco bays). Rare (non-breeders) in summer. Very rare but annual inland on large lakes and reservoirs in migration and winter.

id you know? The specific epithet *grisegena* is a combination of Latin words that together mean 'gray cheek.'

ate & Location Seen: _____

Clark's Grebe
Non-Breeding

Clark's Grebe
Breeding Adult

Western Grebe
Breeding Adult

scription: 25", wingspan 24". Our largest grebes, with **long slender necks** and bright red eyes. **Gray above, foreneck and underparts white**, with **black crown** and narrow black stripe down the hindneck. WESTERN: **Dull yellow to greenish-yellow bill**, black crown extends to eyes. CLARK'S: Best told in all seasons by **bright orange bill**. Eye largely surrounded by white in BREEDING (plumage more diffuse in winter), narrower dark stripe on hindneck, flanks paler gray, white in wings (visible in flight) more extensive.

ice: WESTERN: loud grating *kree-kreeek*. CLARK'S: single, drawn-out *kreeeek*.

havior: Dives for fish. Both species exhibit an elaborate breeding season display: birds rush along the surface of the water together, with gracefully curved necks. Gregarious, often in large flocks. The two species are often together and hybridization is frequent. Floating nests are anchored to vegetation. As in all grebes, the small downy chicks may ride on the backs of the parents.

ilar Species: This very distinctive species pair is unlikely to be confused with other species.

ere, When to Find: WESTERN: Common winter visitor October to April (some summer), along coast including adjacent bays; also locally common on larger inland lakes year-round. CLARK'S: Usually makes up small percentage (less than 10%) coastally; especially on in-shore ocean waters. More frequent inland. Both species are rare in winter on lakes in the Sierra Nevada and Great Basin. Both species breed in reed beds on large lakes when water levels are high enough, mostly in the Klamath Basin and Great Basin; also on Lake Almanor (Plumas County), Clear Lake (Lake County), and Lake San Antonio (Monterey County). WESTERN generally far outnumbers CLARK'S.

d you know? These two species were formerly treated as a single species.

te & Location Seen: _____

Breeding Adult
albociliatus

Immature

DOUBLE-CRESTED CORMORANT
Phalacrocorax auritus

scription: 33", wingspan 52". Large **blackish** seabird, with conspicuous **bare yellow or orange skin on the face and chin,** long thick neck and relatively long wings. ADULT: Black head, neck and underparts; scaled above with gray and black. Bright orange-yellow skin in front of eyes and on throat. BREEDING birds have white, black, or mixed double crest plumes. IMMATURE: Varies from brown to almost whitish on the neck and breast; belly darker; bare face skin yellow. Our only cormorant seen inland.

ce: Generally silent, but breeding and roosting birds make low guttural croaking sounds.

havior: Pursues fish underwater. On the surface it rides low in the water, with bill angled upwards. Often seen perched on shore, rocks or in trees with wings spread. More likely to fly high above the water (and over land) than other cormorants. Stick nests are built in tall trees near water, often among nesting herons; also nests on rocky slopes of offshore islands and islets.

nilar Species: See Brandt's Cormorant (p. 89). Very pale immatures on the water can be confused with loons.

ere, When to Find: Common year-round visitor to inshore marine waters and estuaries along the coast and in lakes and river channels throughout the lowlands. Breeding colonies are found at various coastal sites (especially San Francisco Bay, including on bridges there), on the Farallon Islands, and locally on offshore rocks. The Klamath Basin and Clear Lake (Lake County) usually host hundreds of nests; smaller colonies utilize inland lakes, marshes, and waterways at locations scattered throughout the region as water conditions permit.

you know? Populations of this cormorant have greatly increased; they now commonly feed on fish stocked into park lakes.

te & Location Seen: _____

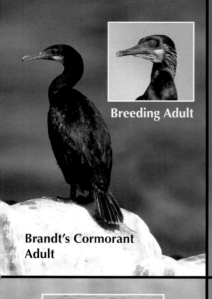

Breeding Adult

**Brandt's Cormorant
Adult**

**Brandt's Cormorant
Immature**

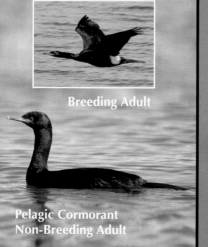

Breeding Adult

**Pelagic Cormorant
Non-Breeding Adult**

**Pelagic Cormorant
Immature**

Description: 34", wingspan 48". Restricted to marine waters and coastlines. Large, with relatively short wings, **short tail,** black bill. ADULT **entirely black**, with **buff chin patch**. BREEDING birds have blue-green gloss, thin white head plumes, bright blue gular pouch. IMMATURE duller, with light brown breast. **Voice:** Generally silent. **Behavior:** Pursues fish underwater, sometimes feeding in large flocks. Rests on rocky outcrops, jetties and breakwaters. Flies with neck held nearly straight. Places nests on rocky slopes. **Similar Species:** Double-crested Cormorant (p. 87) has yellow gular pouch and partly yellow bill; thicker neck is kinked in flight. See Pelagic Cormorant (below). **Where, When to Find:** Common year-round along the coast, especially rocky shorelines and breakwaters, rarely strays far into estuaries; can be very common far offshore. Breeds abundantly on the Farallon Islands, also on islets and coastal cliffs.

Description: 28", wingspan 39". **"Pencil-necked"** and **tiny-headed**, with a **very thin bill** that appears "pushed" into the facial feathering; **long tail**. Chin, throat feathering always dark. ADULT black throughout, glossier than other cormorants; BREEDING birds (February to May) show a **white patch on the flanks**, thin white neck plumes, small red facial patch. IMMATURE blackish-brown throughout. **Voice:** Generally silent. **Behavior:** Pursues fish underwater; rests on rocky outcrops, jetties and breakwaters, favors more vertical substrates. **Similar Species:** Brandt's Cormorant (above) has thicker neck, larger head, thicker bill, shorter tail; adult's plumage less glossy; never shows white flank patch. **Where, When to Find:** Uncommon to fairly common along the coast, especially rocky coastlines and jetties, rarely strays far into estuaries. Numbers greatest in winter, but non-breeders remain on the coast year-round.. Breeding grounds like Brandt's.

Did you know? Belying its name, Pelagic is our least "pelagic" cormorant.

Date & Location Seen: _____

**Brown Pelican
Breeding Adult**

Juvenile

**American White Pelican
Breeding Adult**

Non-breeding Adult

BROWN PELICAN
Pelecanus occidentalis

Description: 50", wingspan 79". An unmistakable **huge** seabird, generally gray-brown, with **long hooked bill and pouch.** ADULT: **Dark brown underparts,** frosted gray upperparts, whitish head and neck. BREEDING adults have brown hindnecks and bright red markings on bill and pouch. IMMATURE: Juveniles have **dark brown necks and upperparts, white bellies;** adult plumage develops over 3-4 years. **Voice:** Silent away from breeding colonies. **Behavior:** Plunges from 10-30' in the air to catch fish under the surface, using pouch as a scoop. Flies in lines or "Vs", with necks folded. Flocks rest on breakwaters, islets, pier pilings, sand flats. **Similar Species:** Unmistakable, but see American White Pelican (below); beware adult Browns can appear whitish above in some lighting. **Where, When to Find:** Fairly common to common post-breeding visitor, especially in summer and fall (fewer in winter), along entire coast and in much of San Francisco Bay. Casual inland. Nested sporadically until 1966 on Bird Island, Monterey County; no subsequent nesting in our region.

AMERICAN WHITE PELICAN *Pelecanus erythrorhynchos*

Description: 62", wingspan 108". **All white, with black flight feathers** (inner secondaries are white) and **huge orange bill**. **Voice:** Silent away from breeding colonies. **Behavior:** Feeds (usually in groups) by scooping fish while swimming on surface of shallow waters; does not plunge-dive like Brown. **Similar Species:** Sleeping swans can appear similar. **Where, When to Find:** Breeds mainly in Great Basin outside California; some in Klamath Basin. Migrates March-April and October; in winter, widely distributed and locally common in the region, mainly in the Central Valley. Foraging flocks can appear anytime. A state Species of Special Concern.

Did you know? The appearance of a likely escaped Pink-backed Pelican (*P. rufescens*, native to Africa) on the Farallon Islands and in coastal Santa Cruz County in 2002-3 was quite a shock!

Date & Location Seen: _____

Least Bittern
Breeding Adult

American Bittern

Least Bittern
Female

scription: 28″, wingspan 42″. A midsized, **long-billed heron streaked brownish on body and neck,** with a **long black stripe below its cheek**. In flight, **dark flight feathers contrast with paler upper wing coverts. Voice:** Distinctive deep, resonant *oonk-a-lunk* song delivered on wintering and breeding grounds, mainly dawn and dusk. Call like Black-crowned Night-Heron (p. 103), but higher-pitched. **Behavior**: Inconspicuous when motionless in tall brown marsh vegetation; often points bill skyward. **Similar Species:** Immature Black-crowned Night-Heron (p. 103) has much shorter neck and bill, more uniform wings. **Where, When to Find:** Uncommon and declining resident in brackish or freshwater marshes, and lake or pond edges with dense tules or rushes west of the Sierra Nevada divide; present on the Modoc Plateau only in summer.

LEAST BITTERN *Ixobrychus exilis*

scription: 13″, wingspan 17″. A tiny, secretive heron. **Large buff patch on shoulders** is **conspicuous in flight**. Bill and legs yellowish. ADULTS **cinnamon-buff throughout**, with buff patch on shoulders, dark back (blackish in MALES), and **buff stripes on white breast.** JUVENILES are more strongly striped below. **Voice**: Best detected by voice, a harsh *kek-kek-kek-kek* that slows at the end. Soft cooing song heard on breeding territory. **Similar Species**: Immature Green Heron (p. 101) is larger and darker. **Behavior**: Feeds within tules and cattails, clambering about low over the water's surface. Often suns early in the morning at edge of reeds, otherwise hard to see except when flying between patches of reeds. **Where, When to Find:** Rare summer resident and probable breeder in well-vegetated marshes or borders of ponds or reservoirs at scattered Central Valley locations; very rare elsewhere in non-breeding season. A state Species of Special Concern.

d you know? "Swamp-pumper" is a folk-name for the American Bittern; its gurgling song sounds like an old fashioned suction pump.

te & Location Seen: _____

Breeding Adult

Juvenile

Description: 46", wingspan 72". Our **largest and most widespread heron.** Largely **gray**, with darker flight feathers, **cinnamon or chestnut "thigh" feathering.** Strong, dagger-like bill shows much yellow; legs grayish. ADULT shows a **whitish face, pale crown, long black head plumes**, and plain pale lavender-gray neck. JUVENILE has a dark crown, and much gray streaking on foreneck and breast.

Voice: Calls are loud, deep and harsh, e.g., *grake* or *kronk*.

Behavior: Patiently hunts for fish, crayfish, frogs and other prey, standing on shore or in shallow water. Also hunts rodents in open fields. Often perches high in trees; stick nests are built in tall trees. Flies with ponderous wing beats, neck folded and retracted.

Similar Species: Often mistakenly called a "crane" by non-birders. Our true crane (Sandhill Crane, p. 137) flies with shallow wing beats and outstretched neck and has shorter legs and solid gray plumage, with a red cap.

Where, When to Find: Common year-round resident up to about 4,500' elevation, except withdraws from much of the Great Basin region and higher elevations in winter, when it is more numerous elsewhere. Found in all wetlands, including rivers, ponds, reservoirs, estuaries and even rocky coastlines. Small breeding colonies are found in tree groves near wetlands throughout the lowlands.

Did you know? This is the most widespread breeding heron in North America.

Date & Location Seen: _____

"High"
Breeding Adult

escription: 39", wingspan 51". A **large, all white heron** with a very long, slender neck, a **yellow bill**, and **black legs and feet**. All plumages are similar, but BREEDING ADULTS have lime green ("high breeding") facial skin and long white plumes on the breast, lower back and rump.

oice: Very low, harsh grating calls.

ehavior: Hunts very patiently, standing still for long periods or wading very slowly through shallow water. Feeds on a great variety of vertebrates, including fish, frogs, and rodents; also takes crayfish. Often feeds in open fields, and (like the Great Blue Heron, p. 95) it is sometimes seen foraging from rafts of kelp just offshore.

milar Species: Snowy Egret (p. 99) is much smaller, with a slender black bill and yellow feet. Cattle Egret (p. 99) also has dark legs and a yellow bill, but is much smaller, with a short neck and bill. These smaller egrets fly with faster wing beats.

here, When to Find: Common year-round resident and locally common breeder in coastal estuaries and freshwater wetlands throughout the lowlands. Fairly common summer visitor to foothill wetlands and the Great Basin region. Builds stick nests in trees, in colonies that may include Great Blue Herons, Snowy Egrets, and Double-crested Cormorants. Audubon Canyon Ranch on Bolinas Lagoon, Marin County, is a popular spot to observe a breeding colony.

id you know? Although white like Snowy and most other egrets, it is more closely related to the Great Blue Heron and recently has been placed in the same genus.

ate & Location Seen: _____

_____

Snowy Egret
Breeding Adult

Snowy Egret
Non-breeding

Cattle Egret
Breeding Adult

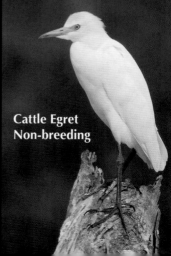

Cattle Egret
Non-breeding

Description: 24", wingspan 41". **Small, pure white egret** with a **slender black bill,** dark legs with **yellow feet**. ADULTS have yellow facial skin; develop a **white crest** and **long white plumes on the breast and rump** when breeding. JUVENILES lack plumes, legs greenish. **Voice**: Its rasping, grating notes are higher-pitched than Great Egrets' calls. **Behavior**: Forages almost exclusively in shallow water or at water's edge (not in dry fields). Foraging methods vary, from slow stalking to active running; often dabbles its bill or feet in water to lure or flush prey. **Similar Species:** Compare with Great Egret (p. 97), Cattle Egret (below). **Where, When to Find:** Fairly common and widespread resident in coastal and low elevation wetlands. Uncommon in the Great Basin region, where it is absent in winter.

CATTLE EGRET *Bubulcus ibis*

Description: 20", wingspan 36". Small, short-necked egret, white with **short yellow bill** (darker in JUVENILES) and **blackish legs**; BREEDING ADULTS have orange bill and legs, buffy patches on back, chest, crown. **Voice**: Generally silent; constant murmuring and *ruk-ruk* calls heard at breeding colonies. **Behavior**: Feeds mainly in fields, often around livestock or tractors, taking advantage of disturbance to insects; large flocks may gather as fields are flood-irrigated. **Similar Species**: Bare part colors suggest Great Egret (p. 97), but much smaller, stockier. Shorter-legged and shorter-billed than a Snowy, which has a darker bill. **Where, When to Find:** Locally common resident in agricultural areas of the Central Valley; much less numerous in coastal counties. Casual to the Great Basin region. Populations have declined somewhat in recent years.

Did you know? Cattle Egrets were unknown in the New World until the late 1800s and did not become well established until the 1950s, having colonized from Africa. They reached California in the early 1960s.

Date & Location Seen: _____

_____

Adult

Juvenile

Description: 18", wingspan 26". A small thick-necked, short-legged heron of wooded ponds, freshwater marshes, and riparian areas. ADULT is **slaty above** with only a hint of a green sheen; feathers of the wings have neat, narrow pale fringes. **Chestnut neck** with white stripe down the front, gray belly, **yellow to orange legs** and feet. JUVENILE is streaked with rufous on neck, breast; legs dull yellow; feathers of the wings boldly edged with buff.

Voice: Call is a loud *keeeow*, usually given when flushed; also a low *kuk, kuk*.

Behavior: Solitary or in pairs. Hunts patiently from shore or from branches low over water. Flicks tail when nervous. May perch well within willows or other riparian trees. Solitary nester, builds a stick nest in low to middle heights of trees, usually close to water.

Similar Species: Juvenile can suggest smaller Least Bittern (p. 93) but is darker (less buffy overall) and lacks buff wing patch.

Where, When to Find: Uncommon resident in the Central Valley and coastal areas, including foothills below about 3,000'. Less common elsewhere, and rare in the northeastern part of the region. Nests in pairs; other herons and egrets nest colonially. Withdraws from colder areas in winter. Favors tree-shaded areas, where it hunts small fish, frogs, and other prey by slowly stalking, often from low-hanging limbs.

Did you know? Green Herons engage in "baiting" – dropping an object onto water to attract curious prey within striking range, a behavior rare among other heron species. Crusts of bread, mayflies, and feathers are among the baits they've used.

Date & Location Seen: _____

Adult

Juvenile

Description: 25". A medium-sized, **stocky** heron with a **short, thick neck** and red eyes. ADULT has a **black crown and back**, white forehead, gray wings, **pale gray underparts**. Bill black, legs yellow. Adults usually show one or two long white head plumes. JUVENILES are streaked gray-brown below and have white spots on the wings and small white streaks on the back. Legs greenish to yellow, bill with much yellow at the base. Older IMMATURES are plainer gray-brown above and pale gray-buff below.

Voice: Call is an emphatic *kwok!* or *quark!*

Behavior: Sluggish, perching motionlessly at the water's edge for long periods before striking a fish, frog, or other prey. Most active at dusk and in the evening, but hunts through the day as well. During the day they are most often encountered as they roost in trees or reeds. Nests in small to large colonies in groves of trees (often planted eucalyptus groves) or in bulrush marshes, especially near coastal estuaries and harbors.

Similar Species: Juvenile differs from scarce American Bittern (p. 93) in grayer plumage tones, more uniformly colored wings, absence of black stripe below cheek.

Where, When to Find: Fairly common but somewhat local year-round resident in lowlands throughout the region, in coastal estuaries, harbors, lakes, and marshes where nearby trees are available for roosting. Less common at higher elevations; rare in the mountains. Most withdraw from colder locations in winter.

Did you know? This species and the Great and Cattle Egrets are the world's most widespread herons.

Date & Location Seen: _____

Breeding Adult

Non-breeding

Juvenile

escription: 23", wingspan 36". A dark wading bird with a **long decurved bill;** appears black in poor light or at a distance. ADULT has red eyes, pink facial skin, and **glossy green wings** with pink highlights. In BREEDING plumage **head, neck and underparts are deep chestnut**; pink facial skin is surrounded by narrow white line of feathering, legs extensively red. NON-BREEDING ADULT plumage is duller slaty overall, with small white streaks on the neck, limited pink in lores. IMMATURES resemble non-breeding adults, but less glossy on wings; facial skin and eye darker.

ice: When flushed gives a low, quacking *waarr, waarr.*

havior: Feeds mainly on insects and other invertebrates. Gregarious, flies in tight groups or lines where large numbers occur; in our area, often found singly or in small groups. Feeds in flooded fields, marshes, and along small channels. Nests in extensive freshwater marshes.

milar Species: See Glossy Ibis (below). At a distance in poor light might be mistaken for Long-billed Curlew (p. 159), often found in same habitat.

here, When to Find: Locally common year-round resident, nesting on and utilizing marshy ponds in the Central Valley; also utilizes flooded fields. Locally common migrant and uncommon summer resident east of the Cascade/Sierra Nevada range. Nesting locations include refuges in the Klamath Basin, the northern Great Basin region, and the Central Valley; also Sierra Valley. In spring and fall, migrants are fairly common in the Owens Valley, rare along the coast.

id you know? To date the closely related Glossy Ibis (*P. falcinnelus,* 23") of eastern North America has occurred sixteen times in our region, all since 2000. In all plumages it is dark-eyed with gray facial skin that is bordered above and below by narrow powder blue lines.

ate & Location Seen: _____

Turkey Vulture

**California Condor
Adult**

escription: 26″, wingspan 66″. A large, raptor-like bird. ADULT **blackish-brown**, with a **bare reddish head**. From below, shows **dark underwing linings, pale silvery flight feathers**. Appears small-headed in flight. JUVENILE'S head dull brownish. **Voice:** Silent. **Behavior:** Feeds on carrion, including road kills. Soars on slightly uptilted wings, rocking side to side. **Similar Species:** Distant flying adult Golden Eagle (p. 127) similar but does not rock in flight, and has a larger feathered head, pale brown hindneck and undertail. **Where, When to Find:** Fairly common throughout the lowlands in summer, less common at high elevations. Withdraws southward in fall (mainly September-November) from all areas to some extent, nearly totally from the northern mountains and Great Basin. Locally common in coastal regions in winter.

CALIFORNIA CONDOR *Gymnogyps californianus*

escription: 46″, wingspan 109″. A **huge** vulture that soars with wing tip feathers splayed. ADULT **blackish**, with a thin white line on upperwings, **bare orange head**. From below, shows **white underwing linings, black flight feathers**. JUVENILE'S head gray. All released birds have wing tags; most sport antennas for remote tracking. **Voice:** Generally silent. **Behavior:** Soars in very wide circles, flapping only occasionally. Perches on cliff faces, tall bare trees, man-made structures. **Similar Species:** Compare Turkey Vulture (above). Golden and Bald Eagles (p. 127) are smaller, have feathered heads. **Where, When to Find:** Now mainly seen near Pinnacles National Park and along the Big Sur coastline, Monterey County. Others are present in southern California, northern Arizona, and Baja California. Listed as Endangered (state and federal).

id you know? With the population down to 22 birds, the last two wild condors were captured on April 19, 1987. Captive breeding programs rebuilt numbers; first released in California in 1992, where now more than 100 fly wild and a few young have fledged.

ate & Location Seen: _____

escription: 23", wingspan 63". A large fish-eating hawk with a small, slightly crested head. Mostly **white on head and underparts, dark mask through eye**; blackish-brown above. Appears **gull-like in flight**, with wings angled and drooped slightly downward. JUVENILE is scaled with buffy on back and wings, has buffy wash below and on wing linings.

oice: Loud, shrill, downslurred whistles are heard primarily when birds interact.

ehavior: Often perches conspicuously on poles, bare trees, and mudflats. Courses or briefly hovers over water, plunging to surface to grab fish with their large feet; sometimes even submerges and swims for short distances. In flight, they carry the fish head first, to improve aerodynamics. Nest is a large stick structure on a conspicuous tall tree, pole, or structure.

imilar Species: Distant birds can suggest large gulls.

here, When to Find: Uncommon to fairly common breeding bird at scattered locations near the ocean shore, along major rivers, and at large lakes and reservoirs from Marin County northward, across the northern counties, and southward through the Cascade/Sierra Nevada range and the Great Basin. A few nest in the San Francisco Bay area; numbers are increasing there. Most birds leave the northern counties and the mountains in fall, moving southward, and toward the coast. Migrants and wintering birds occur widely in the Central Valley and coastal areas.

id you know? Like owls, an Osprey can turn its outer toe backward, splaying the toes on each foot into a broad X-shape, the better to grasp its fish prey as its talons strike.

ate & Location Seen: _____

_____

Adult

Immature

WHITE-TAILED KITE
Elanus leucurus

Description: 16", wingspan 42". An attractive small raptor with long, narrow wings and a long tail. **White head, underparts and tail;** pale gray upperparts with **black patch on shoulders**. In flight the underwing shows dark gray outer flight feathers and black patches at the "wrists." JUVENILE has a wash of cinnamon on the breast, crown and upperparts.

Voice: Short whistled notes; a longer rising whistle.

Behavior: Feeds mainly on small rodents. Flies buoyantly and habitually hovers ("kites") while searching for prey. Often feeds at dusk. Perches on thin twigs atop trees and shrubs. Large roost gatherings of two dozen or more birds are sometimes noted in fall and winter.

Similar Species: General coloration suggests a gull or large tern, but note black markings midway out the wings and distinctive hovering flight.

Where, When to Find: Uncommon year-round resident in open grasslands, oak savannas, marshes, agricultural areas, and lower foothills in the lower Sacramento Valley, San Francisco Bay area, coast ranges, and the northern coastal strip. Casual in the Great Basin and the Sierra Nevada, and on the Modoc Plateau. Populations move about seasonally in response to prey base supply, and vary from year to year in both numbers and locations.

Did you know? After sighting prey while hovering, kites often "parachute down," losing elevation slowly with wings held up in a steep "V". The technique is surprisingly effective.

Date & Location Seen: _____

Adult Female

Juvenile

Adult Male

scription: 16-20", wingspan 38-48". A long-winged, low-flying hawk with a banded tail; always shows a **conspicuous white rump** patch. The small head has an owl-like facial disk. ADULT MALE has **medium gray** head, dark gray upperparts; **whitish below** with some rusty spotting. **Black wing tips.** Larger adult FEMALE is brown, with **streaked underparts.** JUVENILE is **brown**; its unstreaked **pale rusty underparts** contrast with dark head.

ice: Generally silent away from breeding territories, where they give high whistles and lower, barking notes.

havior: Forages by coursing low over marshes, grasslands, and low open scrub, wheeling around to pounce on rodents and other prey. The wings are held slightly above horizontal in flight. Infrequently seen up high in soaring flight compared with other raptors. Nomadic in search of food. Nests on the ground in marshes and wet meadows.

nilar Species: Red-tailed Hawks (p. 123) and other buteos have broader wings, shorter tails, and lack a white rump patch. Cooper's Hawk (p. 117) flies with quick flaps and glides, has shorter wings, and lacks white rump.

here, When to Find: Uncommon to fairly common breeder (March-August) in marshes and wet meadows throughout the region. The majority breed in the Central Valley, San Francisco Bay area marshes, and northeastern wetlands and grasslands. Smaller numbers breed on the northwestern coastal strip, in the southern Great Basin and in the South Coast Range's interior valleys. In fall and winter an influx of visitors from more northerly breeding areas swells numbers considerably.

d you know? As its owl-like facial disk suggests – and unlike our other hawks –harriers frequently rely heavily on auditory cues, as well as visual ones, to detect and capture prey. A state Species of Special Concern. Prior to 2017 Northern Harrier was considered to be the same species as Hen Harrier *Circus cyaneus* of the Palearctic. The two species differ in morphology, plumage, and breeding habitat.

te & Location Seen:

Adult

Adult

Juvenile

scription: 10-14", wingspan 20-28". A small **short-winged,** somewhat **long-tailed** bird-eating hawk. The **tail is squared at the tip,** with gray and blackish bands. ADULT has **slate-gray upperparts, reddish barring below;** eyes red. JUVENILE is brown above, with some white spots; its underparts have rows of **teardrop-shaped reddish-brown spots.** Eyes yellow. FEMALES are larger than males.

ice: Silent except during breeding season, around the nest, where it gives a series of high pitched, short, squealed *kew* notes.

havior: Feeds on birds, which they ambush and chase – often around yards with feeders. Often seen flying between roost sites and feeding areas early in the morning and late in the afternoon. Usually perches within trees, only very rarely more openly and seemingly never on utility poles.

nilar Species: Closely resembles the larger Cooper's Hawk (p. 117). Cooper's appears to have relatively longer wings and tail, and its larger head projects farther in front of wings in flight. Tail-tip of Cooper's is rounded. Juvenile Cooper's has longer, sharper dark brown streaks below and more rufous tones to nape than juvenile Sharp-shinned.

here, When to Find: Rare summer resident and breeder (May-August) in open or somewhat broken northern forests; very rare in forested lowlands and mountains southward from the San Francisco Bay area and Lake Tahoe region. Fairly common and widespread fall migrant (mid-September through October) and winter visitor at lower elevations throughout the region in all sorts of vegetated habitats except open grasslands. Generally found in more heavily wooded areas than Cooper's Hawk favors.

d you know? Although difficult to distinguish from Cooper's in the field, the measurements of smallest male Cooper's and largest female Sharp-shinned do not overlap.

te & Location Seen: _____

Adult

Juvenile

Juvenile

Description: 14-20", wingspan 29-37". The larger of our two more common bird-eating hawks. **Tail** is somewhat **rounded in shape** and usually shows an obvious white band at the tip. ADULT has blackish cap, **dark gray upperparts, reddish barring below;** eyes red. JUVENILE is brown above with some lighter markings; its white underparts have **thin dark brown streaks.** Eyes yellow. FEMALES are larger than males.

Voice: An insistent, clucking *kek-kek-kek-kek-kek* is heard mainly on the breeding territory; juveniles give squealing whistle.

Behavior: Ambushes birds in brushy or wooded areas, often hunting around bird feeders. Perches more openly than Sharp-shinned, often on bare treetops, utility poles, fence posts. Normally flies with quick wing beats, glides and soars on flat wings. Displaying birds on territory fly high with deep, slow wing beats and white undertail coverts flared. Stick nest is usually high in a tree.

Similar Species: See very similar but smaller Sharp-shinned Hawk (p. 115). Red-shouldered Hawk (p. 119) has relatively longer wings and shorter tail and shows strongly checkered upperparts and upperwings. Compare Northern Goshawk (p. 459), a rare resident of northern mountains and the Sierra Nevada.

Where, When to Find: Fairly common year-round resident throughout the region. Nests (March-September) in riparian, oak and coniferous woodlands, suburban areas, and urban parks. Fall migration of some high elevation, northerly, and out of state breeders (peaking late September and October) swells lowland numbers in winter.

Did you know? Urban nesting has increased just in the past 20 years in the San Francisco Bay area. An 11-square mile area of Albany and Berkeley held 12 nests in each of two study years, one of the densest nest concentrations ever recorded.

Date & Location Seen: _____

_____

Adult *elegans*

Juvenile *elegans*

**Broad-winged Hawk
Juvenile**

scription: 17", wingspan 40". A strikingly attractive hawk of riparian and oak woodlands. Boldly **banded black and white tail, checkered pattern on wings,** and **pale crescents near the wingtips.** ADULT has **rich rufous-orange** on the breast, the barred belly, and the shoulder area. Wings boldly patterned in black and white. JUVENILE: reddish color below more limited to bars, spots; breast streaked with dusky, wing and tail pattern duller.

ice: Can be quite vocal, giving loud, repeated down-slurred *kee-oo, kee-oo…* calls.

havior: Hunts in woodlands and streamside forests, feeding on reptiles, frogs, crayfish, rodents and birds. Our birds fly with stiff, rapid wing beats (recalling a Cooper's Hawk). Their stick nest is built in a tall tree.

milar Species: Immature Red-tailed Hawk (p. 123) is larger, with broader wings and tail; it lacks reddish markings on underparts and shoulders and has finely barred brown tail. See Cooper's Hawk (p. 117). **Broad-winged Hawk** (*B. platypterus*; 16", wingspan 34") is usually pale below (dark morph rare), with more pointed wings that lack pale crescents. Rare but regular fall migrant (even rarer spring migrant) mainly along the coast; a few have over-wintered. An astounding 295 passed the Marin County headlands southbound on September 27, 2012.

here, When to Find: Locally common low elevation resident in riparian (especially sycamore) and oak woodlands and mature tree plantings (especially eucalyptus) in urban/suburban areas, valleys, foothills, and coastal lowlands. Historically limited to the southern part of the region west of the Sierra Nevada crest; now breeds throughout most of the region. Non-breeding visitor (especially in fall) in the far northeast.

d you know? Our California subspecies (*elegans*) differs from subspecies that occur in the eastern U. S. in appearance (more rufous below, broader white tail bands) and behavior (much quicker wing beats).

te & Location Seen:

Juvenile

Adult
Light Morph

Adult
Dark Morph

scription: 21", wingspan 52". A buteo with relatively slender, **pointed wings** and a fairly long tail. Plumage highly variable, but always shows **dark chest, light undertail**. Shows small whitish band on rump. All but darkest morph ADULTS have **white wing linings** contrasting with dark flight feathers from below, white chin, brown chest, and solidly brown upperparts. Some adults are extensively rufous or dark brown below and have rufous or even dark wing linings. JUVENILES usually show a pale eyebrow, dark whisker mark and some dark on chest; streaked below.

ice: On breeding territory gives a long, drawn-out *keeeeeah* scream.

havior: Flies with a slight dihedral, rocking side to side, sometimes catching large insects and consuming them on the wing; also feeds on rodents. Migrants may occur in flocks of a hundred or more birds. Nests are built in isolated tall trees in open areas.

milar Species: Red-tailed Hawk (p. 123) has broader, blunter wings, shorter and wider fan-shaped tail, and dark mark along the inner underwing's leading edge.

here, When to Find: Fairly common breeding summer resident (March through first week of August) in Central Valley, Great Basin, and Klamath Basin grasslands; rare but increasing and expanding westward in coast ranges. Formerly more common, now state listed as Threatened; numbers much reduced by habitat alteration and loss. Migrates by day, sometimes in large flocks, to and through central-interior California northbound (mid-February through at least April) and southbound (September-October); more rarely along the coast. Since 2000, increasing numbers have been found wintering in the Central Valley.

d you know? Most of the population migrates annually between North American breeding areas and wintering grounds on South America's pampas, a round-trip for Canadian and Alaskan breeders that can exceed 12,000 miles.

te & Location Seen: _____

Adult Dark Morph

Adult

Juvenile

scription: 22", wingspan 50". By far the most common and widespread large hawk in our region; found in all habitats. Bulky and broad winged, with **broad tail**. Nearly always shows **pale mottling on sides of back.** ADULT is variable, but our breeding birds always have **reddish-orange tails** (color best seen from above). Underparts vary from largely buffy to reddish brown or blackish, usually with some streaking. All but blackest birds show a **distinct dark patch along the leading edge of the inner portion of the underwing.** Most JUVENILES show some white on breast, dark mottling on belly. Tail finely barred blackish and gray-brown.

ice: Typical call is a harsh, drawn-out scream; also gives shorter, clipped notes.

havior: Hunts ground squirrels, gophers and other rodents, as well as snakes and birds. Courting birds fly in tandem with legs dangled; sometimes make long, acrobatic dives and rolls. Nest is a large stick structure in tall tree or man-made structure (e.g., electrical transmission tower), or on cliff ledge.

nilar Species: Red-shouldered (p. 119), Swainson's (p. 121), and Ferruginous (p. 125) Hawks differ in shape as well as plumage.

here, When to Find: Our "default" large hawk, common year-round in nearly all habitats including heavily urbanized areas. A winter influx (mainly October to March) to areas with minimal snow cover and a plentiful food supply brings birds of various color morphs; some dark morph birds also breed locally. "Harlan's Hawk" (subspecies *harlani*), dark with a dusky white tail, is a rare winter visitor from Alaska.

d you know? J. F. Gmelin described this species in 1788, based upon John Latham's 1781 account of a specimen from the island of Jamaica; hence the scientific name *jamaicensis*.

te & Location Seen: _____

_____

Ferruginous Hawk
Adult

Light Morph Juvenile

Dark Morph

Rough-legged Hawk
Light Morph Juvenile

Light Morph Female

Dark

Description: 23", wingspan 56". A large hawk with a **wide yellow "gape"** that extends beneath its eye. **Wings** are **long, broad**, and **pointed**. Light morph ADULTS are **mostly white below** with **mostly whitish tail** and **rusty feathering on the legs; upperparts gray and rusty** (ADULTS) or brown (JUVENILES). Scarce dark morph is dark chocolate brown, with whitish flight feathers. **Voice:** Harsh alarm calls *kree-a*, given in breeding season. **Behavior:** Hunts rodents from the ground or a perch, or in flight; sometimes hovers. Soars with wings in a dihedral. **Similar Species:** Compare smaller Rough-legged Hawk (below); Red-tailed Hawk (p. 123) usually has dark head, bellyband, and patagial. **Where, When to Find:** Uncommon winter visitor (mid-September to early April) in grasslands, agricultural fields inland and along the coast. Has nested in Lassen County grasslands.

ROUGH-LEGGED HAWK *Buteo lagopus*

Description: 21", wingspan 53". A **small-billed** hawk; predominantly **white tail** with **broad dark band** in many plumages; ADULT MALE'S white tail has several narrow black bands. From below, pale morph birds show **squarish black patch on "wrists."** ADULT FEMALES and JUVENILES have pale head with contrasting **dark belly**. Dark morph birds have dark wing linings and body. **Voice:** Usually silent in winter. **Behavior:** Hunts small rodents from the air; often hovers. **Similar Species:** Northern Harrier (p. 113) has white rump, not uppertail; Red-tailed Hawk (p. 123) usually has dark head; compare Ferruginous Hawk (above). **Where, When to Find:** Uncommon, irregular winter visitor (November - March) in grasslands, agricultural fields, marshes inland; rarer along the coast, more numerous in grassland fringes of the Central Valley and in northeastern California.

Did you know? Among our hawks and eagles, only these two northern-breeding hawks and Golden Eagle have legs (tarsi) that are completely feathered to the feet.

Date & Location Seen: _____

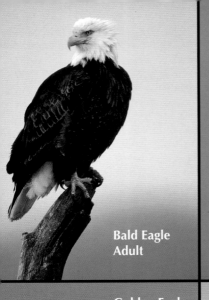

Bald Eagle
Adult

Bald Eagle
Immature

Golden Eagle
Adult

Golden Eagle
Juvenile

escription: 31-37", wingspan 70-90". ADULTS unmistakable with **white head and tail, large yellow bill**. JUVENILES mostly dark with **blotchy white on underwings and tail**; bill blackish gray. SUBADULTS variably intermediate; acquire adult plumage in 4-5 years. **Voice**: Calls include stuttered high-pitched twitterings or whistles. **Behavior**: Typically forages in aquatic habitats; prefers fish, also takes amphibians, crustaceans; takes sick or wounded waterfowl in winter, carrion at any time. **Similar Species**: Juvenile Golden Eagle (below) differs from juvenile Bald in smaller head and bill, longer tail, better-defined white wing patch and whitish tail base. **Where, When to Find**: Locally rare to uncommon breeding resident near large lakes, reservoirs, and rivers throughout, scarce in central and southern Sierra Nevada. Numbers increasing since DDT was banned; California still considers breeding populations Endangered. Migrants from the north swell numbers in winter, especially in the Klamath Basin.

escription: 30-40", wingspan 80-88". A very large **dark brown** raptor, with **very long wings**, sometimes angled slightly upward when soaring. Legs are feathered; toes are bright yellow. ADULT has pale golden-brown hindneck, light brown undertail, and grayish tail base. JUVENILE has **large white patches** at base of tail and at base of flight feathers on wing. **Voice**: Weak chippering calls heard on breeding territory. **Behavior**: Feeds on rabbits, ground squirrels, other medium-sized diurnal mammals. Also scavenges carrion. **Similar Species**: See Bald Eagle (above). **Where, When to Find:** Uncommon resident of remote mountains and open terrain. Best found in the Great Basin, upper elevations of the Sierra Nevada, and hills ringing the Central Valley. More numerous and widespread in migration and winter.

id you know? Older style wind turbines in Alameda County's Altamont Pass area kill many breeding and migrating Golden Eagles annually.

ate & Location Seen: _____

_____

Virgina Rail

Juvenile

Ridgway's Rail
obsoletus

Description: 9 ½". A small, dark, short-tailed marsh bird. **Long, thin, slightly decurved bill** is mostly red-orange. ADULT has gray face, **bright rusty underparts** with **black and white vertical bars on flanks**. Feathers of **upperparts edged rusty**. JUVENILE'S upperparts and breast blotched with sooty; little rusty coloration. **Voice:** Calls include a grunting, accelerating *wek, wek, wek, wek…*; a sharp *gi-dik, gi-dik*; and other high, sharp notes. **Behavior:** Feeds mainly on invertebrates, small fish and amphibians. Walks through marsh vegetation, flicking its short, raised tail. Sometimes feeds more openly on mudflats, pond shores, but usually shy and hidden. Flight appears weak and labored. **Similar Species:** Much larger Ridgway's Rail (below) is restricted to tidal salt and brackish marshes. **Where, When to Find:** Uncommon to fairly common breeder in freshwater marshes and more freshwater portions of coastal estuaries throughout. Can occupy even tiny marshes, assuming some open water, at least partly bordered by cattails and sedges. Some winter withdrawal from northerly and higher elevation areas, but can winter under harsh conditions.

RIDGWAY'S RAIL *Rallus obsoletus*

Description: 14 ½". **Much larger, and thicker-billed, than Virginia Rail** (above), with paler underparts. Feathers of **upperparts edged grayish**. **Voice:** Song a series of ten or more dry *kek kek kek* notes, accelerating and then slowing; call a few slower, sharper *kek* notes. **Behavior:** Similar to Virginia Rail. **Where, When to Find:** Uncommon year-round resident in salt marshes in the San Francisco Bay area. Numbers reduced due to loss of habitat and mammalian predation; state and federally Endangered. Most visible when foraging on exposed mud flats at very low tides.

Did you know? Ridgway's Rail was part of a three-way split in 2014 of the former Clapper Rail. The populations resident in saltwater marshes of the east coast, gulf coast, and West Indies retain the name Clapper Rail.

Date & Location Seen: _____

Sora
Adult

Sora
Juvenile

Black Rail

Yellow Rail

Description: 8 ¾". This small rail has a **short yellowish bill**. Flicks tail upward, showing creamy-white undertail. ADULT has a **black facemask** (including throat in breeding season), **gray neck and breast**, barred flanks, and scaly black, brown and white upperparts. JUVENILE is browner, with duller bill, buffy yellow breast; this plumage held into winter.

Voice: Song heard on breeding grounds an upslurred, whistled *koo-ree*. Commonest call is a hurried, descending whinny, *wee-ee-ee-ee-ee-ee….* Also various high, sharp *keek* and *kee-oo* notes.

Behavior: Easily our most visible rail. Feeds mostly on invertebrates. Skulks in marshes, but often feeds openly on mudflats close to vegetation. Flight appears weak and labored, with legs often dangling.

Similar Species: Virginia Rail (p. 129) has longer, thinner red-orange bill, rusty breast. The mainly nocturnal *kik-kee-do* song of the tiny, secretive, state Threatened **Black Rail** (*Laterallus jamaicensis*, 6") is heard far more often than the bird is seen; calls include harsh *grrr*. Rare to locally uncommon resident in San Francisco Bay area salt marshes, also small wet meadows in Butte, Yuba, Nevada, and Placer counties. Secretive **Yellow Rail** (*Coturnicops noveboracensis*, 7 ¼") utters metallic *tick-tick, tick-tick-tick* call mainly at night; summers (and presumably nests) in scattered high elevation wet meadows in the northeastern part of the region. Very rare winter visitor to San Francisco Bay area marshes; a state Species of Special Concern.

Where, When to Find: Fairly common, local breeder in foothills marshes and wet meadows; scarcer in the Central Valley and along the coast. Populations depart from higher elevation and colder regions in fall and winter. Fairly common migrant and winter resident in Central Valley and San Francisco Bay area marshes.

Did you know? Palo Alto Baylands, Oakland's Arrowhead Marsh, and Grizzly Island Wildlife Area have hosted all five rail species mentioned above.

Date & Location Seen: _____

_____

Adult

Juvenile

Description: 14". A dark, chicken-like marsh bird. ADULT'S **bill and forehead shield bright red** (brightest in breeding season). **Slaty head** and underparts with a **brown-tinged back**, white horizontal **"racing stripe" along flanks,** white patches on sides of undertail. Legs and long unlobed toes yellow. JUVENILE is duller and paler gray below; bill is mostly dusky.

Voice: Various high laughing, cackling notes, a loud *keeek*, and other miscellaneous "marsh sounds."

Behavior: Swims in well-vegetated ponds and marshes while bobbing head back and forth. Also walks nimbly along pond shores and even over floating vegetation. Feeds mainly on aquatic invertebrates and vegetable matter. More reclusive than American Coot.

Similar Species: American Coot (p. 135) is stockier with a white bill, lobed toes; lacks the white stripe along the flanks.

Where, When to Find: Fairly common year-round in freshwater marshes, ponds, and languid rivers in the Central Valley and western foothills of the Sierra Nevada; locally common in the San Francisco Bay area; much scarcer in coastal counties from Mendocino southward to Monterey. Casual elsewhere.

Did you know? This species was split in 2011 from the Old World species *Gallinula chloropus*, known as the Common Moorhen. This split returned our bird's English name to Common Gallinule, by which it was known for much of the 20th century.

Date & Location Seen: _____

Downy Chick

Description: 15″. An abundant and familiar **slaty** bird with a **black head**, suggesting a plump chicken on land and a **white-billed** duck on the water. Small white streaks on sides of undertail (can be flared out when birds are interacting); wing shows a white trailing edge in flight. Small dark red shield on forehead, thin dark band near bill tip. Legs are greenish-yellow, **toes have lobes**. DOWNY YOUNG show a seemingly bald bright red crown, orange-red bill, and stiff, bright orange hair-like down feathers on face and neck; these are lost within days of hatching. JUVENILE is pale gray below.

Voice: Coots make a variety of creaking, grating and trumpeting notes.

Behavior: Food consists of aquatic vegetation and invertebrates, obtained by diving and dabbling, and while walking on mudflats. Also grazes on land, especially on lawns and golf courses. Flies somewhat reluctantly, pattering along the water surface to get airborne; flight is rapid and a bit unsteady.

Similar Species: Duck-like, but note lobed (not webbed) toes and sharply pointed white bill. See Common Gallinule (p. 133).

Where, When to Find: Abundant year-round resident on lakes, ponds, and slow-moving streams bordered by thick growths of cattails, tules, or rushes; also estuaries and coastal lagoons in winter. Withdraws in fall and winter to some extent from colder and higher elevation areas where surface water freezes; winter visitors swell the lowland populations.

Did you know? Not closely related to ducks, but has come to resemble them via convergent evolution. Unlike other rail species, (but similar to web-footed ducks) they have lobed toes that aid in paddling, and diving for food.

Date & Location Seen: _____

escription: 34-48", wingspan 73-90". This stately, **tall pale gray bird** has a **distinctive "bustle" of long curved feathers on the hindquarters.** ADULTS show bare red crown. JUVENILE (called a "colt") lacks red crown patch; head and neck vary from pale to tawny; takes two and a half years to acquire full adult plumage.

ice: Far-carrying, bugling *gar-oo-oo* calls that Aldo Leopold likened to "a baying of some sweet-throated hound." Young birds give a wholly different, high-pitched cricket-like call.

havior: Nests in wet meadows and marshes on built-up mounds of vegetation. Pairs usually fledge only one young (generally two eggs laid), which travels with its parents for nearly a year. Omnivorous; forages in open grasslands, grain fields, edges of wetlands. Flies with shallow, "flicking" wing beats, neck extended, long legs projecting behind.

nilar Species: Compare with Great Blue Heron (p. 95), which lacks a bustle and flies with its neck folded and retracted, but is often mistakenly called a "crane."

here, When to Find: "Greater" Sandhill Crane (state Threatened), subspecies *tabida*, is an uncommon summer resident breeder in Siskiyou, Lassen, Modoc, Plumas, and Sierra counties. It and the much smaller "Lesser" Sandhill Crane (*canadensis*) from the Arctic (a state Species of Special Concern) are locally common winter (October to March) visitors to the Delta region and south to Tulare County. The Lodi Crane Festival, in early November, and the nearby Isenberg Crane Sanctuary offer good opportunities to enjoy large numbers of wintering Sandhill Cranes.

d you know? Fossils show that Sandhill Cranes have existed for 2.5 million years, which perhaps explains why some think of their haunting calls as a voice from the Pleistocene.

te & Location Seen: _____

Black-necked Stilt
Male

Black-necked Stilt
Female

American Avocet
Non-breeding Male

American Avocet
Breeding Female

BLACK-NECKED STILT
Himantopus mexicanus

Description: 14". A large, slender **black and white** shorebird with **extremely long pink legs; slender straight bill.** MALE: Back glossy black. FEMALE: Back brownish. JUVENILES have paler heads and buffy fringes above. **Voice**: Call is a high *keek* note, like a Long-billed Dowitcher. On breeding grounds gives an incessant series of yapping notes, *yike! yike! yike!* **Behavior**: Forages by walking on mudflats and in shallow water, picking for invertebrate prey. Found in a wide variety of wetland habitats; especially numerous at wastewater treatment plants. **Similar Species:** American Avocet (below) has upturned bill, white areas on wing, blue-gray legs. **Where, When to Find:** Increasing. Fairly common resident in coastal regions north to the San Francisco Bay area; rare north of there in migration. Common summer resident in the Central Valley (where small numbers winter) and the Great Basin. Rare migrant (late March-early May, July-early October) in the Sierra Nevada.

AMERICAN AVOCET *Recurvirostra americana*

Description: 18". A large shorebird with **long blue-gray legs** and **long, thin upturned bill; pied black and white wings.** BREEDING: Head and neck a rich tawny color. NON-BREEDING: Head and neck grayish. JUVENILES have buffy necks. The MALE'S bill is longer, less upturned than FEMALE'S. **Voice**: A high, loud, *kleep, kleep;* especially vocal on breeding grounds. **Behavior**: When feeding in shallow water, leans forward and sweeps bill from side to side to stir up invertebrate prey. Avocets can swim well for a shorebird. **Similar Species:** Unmistakable. **Where, When to Find:** Fairly common to common breeder in most regions, though absent on northern coast. Winters commonly in the coastal region north to Humboldt Bay, the Central Valley, and Owens Lake. Rare migrant in the Sierra Nevada (March-May, July-October).

Did you know? Hybrids ("Avostilts") have been noted on several occasions in the wild.

Date & Location Seen: _____

Adult

Juvenile

escription: 17". A large **blackish bird of rocky shores** with a **bright orange-red, knife-like bill.** Black head and underparts, blackish-brown back. Legs pinkish; eyes yellow, surrounded by a bare red orbital ring. The JUVENILE has a duller orange bill with a dark tip, and slightly duller, browner plumage with paler brown fringing above.

oice: Loud piping whistles are readily heard over the crashing surf. Calls often given in a long series, *wheeep, wheeep, wheep, whee-whee-whee-whee.*

ehavior: Forages on mollusks, barnacles and other intertidal invertebrates on rocky shorelines; the bill can be used to sever the adductor muscles of bivalves. Can be very vocal, with small groups often chasing and flying about. Eggs are laid on a rocky ledge above the high tide line.

imilar Species: Unmistakable.

here, When to Find: Fairly common along the entire rocky coastline and on the Farallon Islands. Uncommon and local around rocky portions of San Francisco Bay but recorded rarely to casually nearly throughout the Bay area. Accidental farther inland.

id you know? This species is resident south along the coast and the Channel Islands to northern Baja California and north to southern Alaska and out the entire chain of the Aleutian Islands to Attu Island. It was given its scientific name by J. J. Audubon for his friend, Rev. John Bachman (pronounced "back-min").

ate & Location Seen: _____

Black-bellied Plover
Breeding Adult Male

Black-bellied Plover
Juvenile

Pacific Golden-Plover
Non-breeding

American Golden-Plover
Juvenile

BLACK-BELLIED PLOVER
Pluvialis squatarola

Description: 11 ½". Large plover with **large**, stubby **black bill**. In flight shows **prominent white wing stripe, white rump, black "armpits" patch**. NON-BREEEDING plumage seen most frequently: gray overall, spotted whitish above. BREEDING plumage (April-September): face and most of underparts black, more solidly in MALE; undertail and sides of neck white. JUVENILE: Like non-breeding but buffier overall. **Voice:** Loud, plaintive whistle, dropping in pitch, then rising, *kleee-ooo-weee*. **Behavior:** Feeds mainly on beaches, mudflats, turf farms, with typical plover gait of running and abruptly stopping; picks prey from surface. Large flocks roost communally. **Similar Species:** See American and Pacific golden-plovers (below). **Where, When to Find:** Common winter visitant in coastal regions; uncommon (non-breeders) in summer. Locally fairly common to common in winter in the Central Valley. Uncommon to rare migrant (April-May, late July-October) in the Great Basin and Sierra Nevada. Juveniles arrive early September.

PACIFIC GOLDEN-PLOVER *Pluvialis fulva*

Description: 10". Primarily an Asian breeding species. This and **American Golden-Plover** (*P. dominica*, 10 ½") smaller than Black-bellied; in flight both lack black "armpits," rump uniform with back. NON-BREEDING Pacific with golden cast above; American more like Black-bellied, best separated from both by longer wing tip projection past tertials. In BREEDING (rarely seen in American here), underparts extensively black. **Voice:** A rich whistled upslurred *chu-wheet*. American gives a fainter, less rich, *ku-wheep*. **Behavior:** Both species are often with Black-bellied. **Where, When to Find:** Pacific a rare migrant and winter visitant (late July to May) in coastal regions and, even more rarely, in the Central Valley; recorded Owens Valley. American a rare fall (September-October) migrant, mostly along the coast; nearly all are juveniles.

d you know? These two golden-plovers were once treated as one species.

ate & Location Seen:

Snowy Plover
Breeding Male

Snowy Plover
Non-breeding

Semipalmated Plover
Breeding Male

Semipalmated Plover
Juvenile

Description: 6 ½". A **small, pale** plover of beaches and extensive alkali flats. **Slender, black bill, grayish legs, partial breast band.** BREEDING MALES have black band on forecrown, breast band black. **Voice**: Calls on breeding grounds include a short hard *krip* and rising *ch'loooy*. **Behavior**: Typical run and stop feeding action, characteristic fast running pursuit of prey. Resting birds sit in shallow depressions; often difficult to locate. Eggs laid on bare scrape on upper beach, estuary margin, interior alkali flat. **Similar Species:** See Semipalmated Plover (below). **Where, When to find:** Uncommon winter visitant to coastal beaches and San Francisco Bay area salt ponds (August-April); breeds locally in those areas. Fairly common breeder at Owens Lake (casual in winter), scarcer and more erratic elsewhere in the Great Basin. Uncommon and local migrant and breeder in the Central Valley.

SEMIPALMATED PLOVER *Charadrius semipalmatus*

Description: 7 ¼". A small plover, **dark brown back** and **complete breast band; stubby bill, yellow or orange legs.** BREEDING birds have face and breast band black (MALES) or mottled with brown (FEMALES). JUVENILES fringed with pale above. **Voice**: Call is a distinctive rising *chu-weep*. **Behavior**: More sedate than Snowy Plover when feeding; prefers wetter mud. **Similar Species:** Snowy Plover (above) paler with incomplete breast band, slimmer bill and darker legs. Much larger Killdeer (p. 147) with two breast bands, orange at base of tail in flight. **Where, When to Find:** Common migrant (mid-April to mid-May, July-September) and fairly common winter visitor coastally; a few summer. Uncommon to fairly common migrant (rare in winter in Central Valley) in all inland regions. Juveniles arrive in early August.

Did you know? Beach development led to listing of our coastal Snowy Plovers as federally Threatened; interior breeding population is a state Species of Special Concern.

Date & Location Seen: _____

escription: 10 ½". Perhaps our most familiar shorebird, this noisy plover of
upland as well as wetland habitats is dark brown above with **two black
breast bands,** red eye ring. In flight its **orange rump and tail base** are
distinctive; appears long tailed and long winged, with a prominent white
wing stripe. JUVENILE shows pale rusty fringes to the feathers of back
and wings. The tiny downy young appear "fluffy," and have only a single
breast band.

ice: Quite vocal day and night, especially on the breeding grounds, but
calls actively year-round. Call is a piercing *kill-deee,* frequently repeated.
When disturbed also gives a strident *teeeee-deer-deer* and a rapid trill.

havior: Forages on a variety of open substrates, from mudflats to gravel
washes to lawns, plowed fields, and short crops. Found in pairs or family
groups in breeding season in a wide variety of wetland habitats, including
around small ponds. The eggs are laid on a gravelly substrate such as a
river or creek bottom, vacant lot, or the edge of a gravel road or railroad
right-of-way. As in other shorebirds, breeders move slowly away with a
"broken wing act'" to lure intruders from their eggs. In fall and winter
flocks of dozens, even hundreds, of birds are sometimes found.

nilar Species: Our other plovers all have one breast band, or lack a band
altogether.

here, When to Find: Generally fairly common to common throughout
the region and present year-round, with migratory movements. Rare to
uncommon in the Great Basin and our higher mountains in mid-winter;
migration begins by the end of February in spring, and in fall continues
into November, or later.

d you know? Along with the Common Poorwill and a few other species,
the Killdeer is named for its call.

ate & Location Seen: _____

Non-breeding

scription: 9". **A plain sandy-brown plover** of dry fields. Whitish below except for broad diffuse brownish wash across breast, slender black bill. In flight prominent whitish wing-bar, white underwing coverts. BREEDING: Sometimes seen in our area in early spring; lores and forecrown black. JUVENILES: Fringed above with pale buff.

ice: Migrants and wintering birds give a harsh *krrr* note.

havior: Like other plovers, forages with typical run and stop behavior. Most often found in small flocks, although out-of-range birds usually found as individuals. Seldom associates with other plover species.

milar Species: Compare p. 143. The widespread Black-bellied Plover is larger with a thicker bill and, in non-breeding and juvenal plumage, more patterned upperparts. In flight it has a contrasting white rump and black "armpits." Non-breeding Pacific and American golden-plovers (both rare) are more patterned and darker above, with a thicker bill, especially in Pacific. In flight both species have grayish, not white, underwings.

here, When to Find: Rare to locally uncommon winter visitor (November-March) to the western portions of the Central Valley from Sutter and Yolo counties south; also the fringes of the lower foothills and valleys adjacent to the San Joaquin Valley. Favored locations include the Delta Region of eastern Solano County, Panoche Valley, and southwestern Kings County. Rare in fall in the Owens Valley and at Crowley Lake. Casual on beaches along the coast in fall and winter. Prefers non-lumpy bare earth fields, burned and very short grass fields. Migrants in fall sometimes found on alkali flats near water.

d you know? This state Species of Special Concern has severely declined in recent decades and deserves "Threatened" status. The total population numbers well under 10,000. Winter habitats in our region have disappeared with developments, including nut farms.

te & Location Seen:

Spotted Sandpiper
Adult

Spotted Sandpiper
Juvenile

Solitary Sandpiper
Juvenile

scription: 7 ½". Walks with **constant teetering; short legs.** NON-BREEDING: Brown above, white below, white eyebrow, brownish patches on sides of breast, short white wing stripe. Bill dark, legs dull greenish yellow or flesh. BREEDING: Thin dark bars above, **heavy black spotting below;** pink based bill. **Voice:** High staccato whistled notes, *peet-weet*, also a series of *whee-whee-whee-whee* notes. **Behavior:** Found singly or in pairs; small, loose groups in migration. Distinctive flight of intermittent bursts of rapid, shallow, wing beats. Found along streams, shores of lakes or small ponds; in winter, also rocky coastlines. Nests in creek bottoms or along lake and pond shorelines. **Similar Species:** Behavior suggestive of larger, plain winged Wandering Tattler (p. 153). **Where, When to Find:** Uncommon to fairly common year-round along the coastal slope and the fringe of the Central Valley. Fairly common breeder in the northern Sacramento Valley and Sierra Nevada; local breeder in the Great Basin. Fairly common migrant throughout; uncommon in winter.

SOLITARY SANDPIPER *Tringa solitaria*

scription: 8 ½. A rare visitor. A **rather small sandpiper** with fairly short legs, **distinct white eye ring.** BREEDING: Neck streaked with dark, spotted with pale above. JUVENILE: More brownish overall, neck washed with brown. In flight, dark center to barred tail, dark underwing. **Voice:** High, shrill *peet-weet*. **Behavior:** Like its name, usually solitary. Some tail bobbing as it feeds. **Similar Species:** Larger and darker than Spotted Sandpiper (above) with longer legs and pale spots above. Flight very different. See Lesser Yellowlegs (p. 155). **Where, When to Find:** Rare spring (mid-April to mid-May) and fall (late July-September) migrant nearly throughout region. Juveniles appear by early August. Prefers small ponds, streams.

d you know? Spotted Sandpiper is one of our later spring migrant shorebirds. Numbers are still passing through interior areas in late May.

te & Location Seen: _____

Breeding

Non-breeding

escription: 11″. A **long winged, short-legged shorebird** nearly always associated with rocky coastlines, including man-made jetties. Legs greenish-yellow. In flight, long wings are uniformly dark. NON-BREEDING: **Overall dark gray,** paler on belly; dark line through eye contrasts with a thin, broken eye ring. BREEDING: **Strongly barred with dark gray on underparts**, paler in vent region.

bice: A series of rapid, mellow whistles on one pitch.

ehavior: Walks methodically over rocks, bobbing its tail in a manner reminiscent of a Spotted Sandpiper. Usually solitary, but often loosely associates with other rocky shorebirds such as Black Turnstones and Surfbirds.

imilar Species: The smaller Spotted Sandpiper (p. 151) has similar behavior, but flies with shallow, rapid wing beats and has white wing stripe; paler underparts; browner, less gray upperparts. Much larger Willet (p. 157) has long gray wings and legs and a striking wing pattern in flight.

here, When to Find: Uncommon to fairly common migrant (mid-April to mid-May and mid-July to September) along rocky sections of coast. Rare (non-breeders) there in summer. Sometimes seen on beaches. Very rare in migration around San Francisco Bay. Accidental inland (fall) where recorded east of the Sierra Nevada at Mono Lake.

id you know? This species breeds mainly in Alaska and the Yukon Territory and winters widely on the Pacific coast from British Columbia to Peru as well as on many islands through the tropical Pacific. It and the Gray-tailed Tattler, an Asian species unrecorded in the region, were formerly placed in their own genus, *Heteroscelus*.

ate & Location Seen:

Greater Yellowlegs

Breeding

Juvenile

Lesser Yellowlegs

Breeding

Juvenile

Description: 14". A rather large shorebird **with long, slightly upturned bill, gray at the base** except in breeding plumage. **Long, bright yellow legs.** Plain wings and mostly white rump and tail in flight. BREEDING: Heavily spotted and barred with blackish above and below; bill all black. JUVENILE: Shows distinct streaks on neck. **Voice:** Loud, shrill three-noted descending whistle, *tew-tew-tew*. **Behavior:** Feeds quite actively, mostly on aquatic invertebrates, also on small fish. Often found individually; also in small groups, especially when roosting. **Similar Species:** See Lesser Yellowlegs (below). **Where, When to Find:** Fairly common migrant and winter visitor (mid-July to mid-May) nearly throughout. Juveniles typically arrive late August, sometimes earlier. Rare in summer. Very hardy; a few winter in the coldest interior areas where open water remains. Found in a wide variety of wetland habitats.

LESSER YELLOWLEGS *Tringa flavipes*

Description: 10". Smaller than Greater Yellowlegs, with **shorter, straight, all-dark bill.** NON-BREEDING: Slightly darker than Greater, especially on breast. BREEDING: Neck streaked, but rest of underparts whitish, unlike Greater. JUVENILE: Neck and breast grayish, not streaked like Greater. **Voice:** A mellow whistled tu-tu, often in a series. **Behavior:** A more relaxed feeding style than Greater, picking in shallow water for invertebrates, small fish; never runs to pursue prey like Greater. **Similar Species:** Quite similar to Greater Yellowlegs. Solitary Sandpiper (p. 151) is smaller and darker overall, with shorter, greener legs and bolder eye ring; in flight shows darker underwing and dark center to tail. **Where, When to Find:** Generally a rare spring (April to early May) and an uncommon (mid-July to September) fall (mostly juveniles, arrive early August) migrant throughout. A few winter in coastal regions and in the Central Valley.

Did you know? Although similar in appearance, the two yellowlegs are not each other's closest relatives.

Date & Location Seen: _____

Breeding
inornata

Non-breeding
inornata

Description: 15". A stocky **gray shorebird** with a **striking black and white wing pattern in flight**. The **legs are gray; medium-length** gray **bill is straight and fairly stout.** The plumage is mostly gray, becoming whitish on forehead and belly. In flight the rump and tail are mostly white, and the wings show a broad stripe bordered by black. In BREEDING plumage there is some barring and spotting on the underparts, back, and wings. JUVENILES are neatly marked with small buff-white spots on the back and wings.

Voice: Call is a reeling *kre-ree-reel*; also a nasal *yaah-yah* and a low *kip…kip*. On breeding grounds gives a loud whistled *pill-will-willet*.

Behavior: Non-breeders forage for invertebrates on sandy beaches, rocky shores and estuarine mudflats; breeders and migrants use a variety of wetland areas; may forage in dry fields. Large numbers roost together when not breeding, often with Marbled Godwits.

Similar Species: Slimmer Greater Yellowlegs (p. 155) has thinner, upturned bill, bright yellow legs, plain wings in flight.

Where, When to Find: Common migrant and winter visitor (late June to early May) along coast and throughout the San Francisco Bay area; winters north to Humboldt Bay. Uncommon (non-breeders) in summer. Generally a rare migrant (April to early May, late June to early September) in the interior lowlands and in the Sierra Nevada; a few winter in the southern San Joaquin Valley and at Owens Lake. Fairly common breeder in moist meadows, wetlands, and grasslands of the Great Basin.

Did you know? Our "Western Willet" (subspecies *inornata*) differs in breeding plumage, size, and bill shape and length from the "Eastern Willet" (*semipalmata*), which breeds on the Atlantic and Gulf coasts and winters in eastern South America. The numerous wintering willets on the south Atlantic and Gulf coasts are all western *inornata*, which breed east to the Great Plains.

Date & Location Seen: _____

Whimbrel

Long-billed Curlew

Description: 17 ½". A large mottled grayish-brown shorebird, **strongly decurved bill. Bold dark head stripes** diagnostic. All plumages similar. In flight, underwings are barred with dusky. **Voice**: Rapid series of high-pitched whistles on one pitch, *kee-kee-kee-kee-kee…* **Behavior**: Gregarious in migration. Probes in soft mud on mudflats, wet fields in migration; also picks for invertebrates on rocky shorelines. Similar Species: See Long-billed Curlew (below). **Where, When to Find:** Common migrant (March to May, July to September) along the coast and in the San Francisco Bay area, uncommon in winter. A few (non-breeders) summer. Common spring and rare fall (casual after mid-August) migrant in the Central Valley; rare migrant elsewhere in interior, not expected in winter.

LONG-BILLED CURLEW *Numenius americanus*

Description: 23". **Larger and more cinnamon** than Whimbrel, with a thinner and **longer bill**, especially in FEMALES; **lacks head stripes**. JUVENILE MALES have shortest bills. All plumages similar. In flight shows **cinnamon wing linings and flight feathers. Voice**: A loud upslurred whistle, *cur-leeee*, very different from Whimbrel. **Behavior**: Gregarious year-round; often with Whimbrels, Marbled Godwits, and Willets. **Similar Species**: Compare Whimbrel (above). A sleeping Marbled Godwit (p. 161) looks surprisingly like a Long-billed Curlew but is smaller, with darker legs. **Where, When to Find**: Fairly common in migration and winter (July to early May) along the coast and in interior valleys west of the Sierra Nevada, in large salt marshes, alfalfa fields, grasslands; sometimes on beaches. Rather rare in these areas in summer. Uncommon breeder in wetlands, moist meadows and grasslands in Great Basin. Favored grasslands in interior valleys now greatly reduced because of development, conversion to vineyards and nut farms.

Did you know? North American Whimbrels (subspecies *hudsonicus*) differ from Old World birds, lacking their whitish rump and underwings.

Date & Location Seen: _____

_____

escription: 18". A large **buffy-brown** long-legged shorebird with a **long, slightly upturned bill with pink-orange base, dark tip.** In flight, note **cinnamon-rufous wing lining and flight feathers.** BREEDING birds have dark barring on the underparts.

ice: Calls have a laughing quality; gives a nasal *kwa-ha* and a *goweeta-goweeta-goweeta* series.

havior: Probes into wet sand and soft mud with its long bill. Often found in large flocks in coastal bays, frequently mixed with Willets and other shorebirds; roosts on islands or patches of pickleweed at high tide. Migrants found in a wider variety of wetlands, as long as they are extensive.

milar Species: Whimbrel and Long-billed Curlew (p. 159) easily told by their decurved bills. Whimbrel is grayish-brown, not cinnamon. Beware of sleeping Long-billed Curlew, which is larger, with paler, bluish-gray legs.

here, When to Find: Common migrant and winter visitor (July to mid-May) along the coast and in the San Francisco Bay area. North of Sonoma County, winters regularly only on Humboldt Bay. Most numerous at the larger estuaries, with smaller numbers on beaches, especially in migration. A few non-breeders summer. Uncommon to rare migrant (April to mid-May, July to early October) throughout the interior; more numerous at Owens Lake. A few winter locally at large wetlands in the San Joaquin Valley.

id you know? In our godwits and curlews, the females are noticeably larger and longer-billed than the males. Marbled Godwits nest primarily on the northern Great Plains in the northern U.S. and southern Canada, also locally around the southwest portion of James Bay. A smaller subspecies (*beringiae*) is well isolated, nesting locally on the north side of the Alaska Peninsula and wintering from coastal Washington to San Francisco Bay; most winter at Humboldt Bay.

ate & Location Seen: _____

Ruddy Turnstone

Breeding Male

Non-breeding

Black Turnstone

Breeding

Non-breeding

Description: 9 ½". **Stocky, short-legged shorebird** with **stout, slightly upturned bill, harlequin plumage,** and a **striking pattern of dark and white in flight. Legs bright orange.** NON-BREEDING: Brownish overall with white belly, paler on head, throat, and sides of breast. BREEDING: Extensively rufous above, much white on head; MALES more extensively rufous, whiter headed. **Voice**: A rapid series of low-pitched guttural notes. **Behavior**: Forages on mudflats and beaches where they probe for prey and flip over small stones; also found along rocky shorelines, picking at mussels, barnacles, algae. Will feed on maggots on dead beached marine mammals. **Similar Species**: See Black Turnstone (below). Where, When to Find: Uncommon migrant (late April-early May, late July-early October) and rather rare winter visitor along coast and locally around San Francisco Bay, where formerly more numerous. Casual to very rare throughout the interior in migration. Juveniles appear late August.

BLACK TURNSTONE *Arenaria melanocephala*

Description: 9 ½. Shape, bill, and wing pattern like Ruddy Turnstone. **Overall darker and more uniform than Ruddy;** legs dull orange to dusky-red. BREEDING: White spot in front of eye and white spotting on sides of chest. **Voice**: Rapid trill notes; higher pitched, much less guttural than Ruddy. **Behavior**: Much like Ruddy, but more confined to rocky areas, jetties. **Similar Species:** Larger Surfbird (p. 167) much paler and grayer with thick yellow-based bill, greenish legs; in flight very different wing and tail pattern. **Where, When to Find:** Common winter visitor (a few non-breeders summer) in rocky areas along coast (mid-July to early May); scarcer and more local around portions of San Francisco Bay. Accidental migrant in Central Valley and east of the Sierra Nevada.

Did you know? Unlike Black Turnstone, which is confined to the west coast of North America, Ruddy is a circumpolar breeder.

Date & Location Seen:

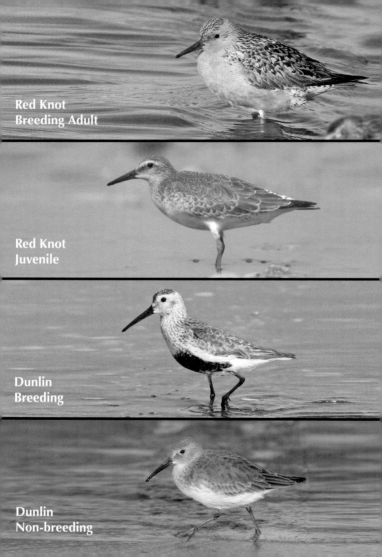

Red Knot
Breeding Adult

Red Knot
Juvenile

Dunlin
Breeding

Dunlin
Non-breeding

Description: 10 ½". Stocky, **pale gray sandpiper, medium-length straight bill,** short legs; whitish underparts have diffuse faint spotting. In flight, barred whitish rump, indistinct wing pattern. BREEDING: **Rufous on face and most of underparts**. JUVENILES: Variably buffy across breast, upperparts feathering shows dark subterminal markings and pale fringes. **Voice:** Mostly silent in our region; sometimes a *ka-whit* is given in flight. **Behavior:** Feeds on sandy beaches and mudflats, sometimes with dowitchers and Dunlin. **Similar Species:** Non-breeding plumaged Dunlin (below) darker and less chunky; bill is longer and decurved. Non-breeding dowitchers (p. 177) overall darker (especially Long-billed) with longer greenish legs, longer bill. **Where, When to Find:** Rare to uncommon migrant (April to early May, late July to early October) along coast and around San Francisco Bay. Juveniles arrive late August. Uncommon and local in winter around San Francisco and Humboldt bays. Casual migrant inland.

Description: 8 ½". Medium-sized sandpiper with a **long, drooping bill; blackish legs**. NON-BREEDING: Plain gray-brown above, **brown wash across breast**. BREEDING: **Reddish back, black belly patch. Voice:** Call a rough *jeeeev*, lower and harsher than Western Sandpiper's call. **Behavior:** Joins other shorebirds; wades belly deep into shallow water; also feeds on mudflats. **Similar Species:** See Western Sandpiper (p. 175), Rock Sandpiper (p. 167). **Where, When to Find:** Common migrant and winter visitor (late September to mid-May) to coastal estuaries. Uncommon spring and fall migrant elsewhere. Large numbers winter around San Francisco Bay and locally in the Central Valley.

Did you know? East Asian- and North American-breeding Dunlins, including our subspecies (*pacifica*), are among the few shorebirds that molt in the Arctic after breeding; immatures and adults arrive relatively late in fall, already in their drab non-breeding plumage.

Date & Location Seen: _____

_____

Surfbird
Breeding

Surfbird
Non-breeding

Rock Sandpiper
Non-breeding

Surfbird
Non-breeding

Description: 10″. **Medium sized, chunky, with short yellowish legs and a stubby, yellow-based bill.** White wing stripe and tail base visible in flight. NON-BREEDING: Overall lead gray, white belly, spots on flanks. BREEDING: Extensive spotting on head, breast and sides; rufous on scapulars. **Voice:** Largely silent in our area, unlike Black Turnstones with which they associate. **Behavior:** Probes intertidal rocks, algae for invertebrate prey. **Similar Species:** Thickish yellow-based bill diagnostic. Color paler, grayer than Black Turnstone; yellowish, not dark reddish legs. **Where, When to Find:** Fairly common migrant (late March to early May, August-September) and winter visitor along rocky sections of coast; scarce inside San Francisco Bay. Migrants also utilize sandy beaches, mudflats. Large numbers stage in fall at Bodega Bay. Accidental (spring) in Central Valley.

ROCK SANDPIPER *Calidris ptilocnemis*

Description: 9″. Rare winter visitant along the coast. Long, decurved bill has yellowish base, legs yellowish. NON-BREEDING: Dark slaty-gray above and on breast, streaks of spots on sides and flanks. In BREEDING plumage (acquired by April), rufous-edged feathering above, blackish patch on upper belly. All records are of subspecies *tschuktschorum*. **Voice:** Mostly silent in our area, gives a sharp *kwit* and chattering calls. **Behavior:** In our area strictly found along the rocky coastline, including jetties, where it always associates with the more numerous Surfbirds and Black Turnstones. **Similar Species:** Dunlin structurally similar but plainer; does not frequent rocky coastline. Larger Surfbird is paler gray with very different bill shape. **Where, When to Find:** Quite rare, local, and declining, along rocky sections of coast. Casual south of Sonoma County.

Did you know? The Surfbird breeds on windswept ridges of Alaskan mountains; winter range has greater latitudinal extent than nearly any other bird species: from southern Alaska to Tierra del Fuego.

Date & Location Seen:

_____

Non-breeding

Breeding

Juvenile

escription: 8″. The familiar medium-sized **pale gray and white sandpiper** of our coastal beaches. Shows **darker area at "wrist" of wing,** and a **prominent white wing stripe in flight.** Black bill is fairly short, straight and blunt-tipped; legs and feet are black (hind toe lacking). In BREEDING plumage, acquired late (May) in spring, there is an extensive, but variable rusty wash on the head, upperparts and chest. JUVENILE: Much darker on crown and upperparts that are extensively speckled with white.

oice: Call is hard *kip;* similar to call of Red-necked Phalarope, but lower pitched, not as sharp.

ehavior: Runs rapidly back and forth on sandy beaches with advance and retreat of waves; picks and probes for invertebrates, eggs. Usually found in small flocks. Also frequents mudflats, sometimes other wetland habitats that attract shorebirds.

imilar Species: Western (p. 175) and Least (p. 173) sandpipers are smaller, thinner billed, darker above (especially Least), and have hind toes; they tend to occur in estuaries and on mudflats, rather than on open, sandy beaches. Breeding plumaged birds that are much less familiar to observers have many times been confused with the smaller and casually occurring (to our area) Red-necked Stint (C. *ruficollis,* 6 ¼″).

here, When to Find: Common migrant and winter visitant from mid-July through May along coastal beaches. Juveniles arrive late August. Some (non-breeders) remain through the summer. Locally fairly common around San Francisco Bay. Rare migrant (late April-May, late July-September) throughout the interior, including the Sierra Nevada.

id you know? Sanderlings breed farther north than virtually any other shorebird (mainly on islands in the high Canadian Arctic); their extensive winter range extends south to Chile. The species is found worldwide, primarily on coasts.

ate & Location Seen: _____

Baird's Sandpiper
Juvenile

Pectoral Sandpiper
Juvenile

BAIRD'S SANDPIPER
Calidris bairdii

Description: 7 ½". A medium-sized, **buffy** sandpiper with **very long wings** that extend beyond the tail tip; stands with horizontal stance. Legs dark; thin bill is longish, straight. JUVENILE: Gray-brown back and wings have buff fringes to all feathers, yielding a **scaly appearance above**. The finely streaked breast is **strongly washed with buff**. ADULTS (much scarcer in our region) in BREEDING plumage are much less scaly above than juveniles, have black spotting above. **Voice**: Call is a harsh, dry *kreeee*. **Behavior**: Feeds slowly in shallow water and on flats well away from water. Sometimes found on beaches. **Similar Species**: See Pectoral Sandpiper (below). Least Sandpiper (p. 173) much smaller, darker with shorter wings (primaries do not extend beyond tertials, unlike Baird's and Pectoral). **Where, When to Find**: Rather rare but regular (overwhelmingly juveniles) fall (early August to early October) migrant throughout; most numerous east of the Sierra Nevada. Adults occur very rarely in spring and a few pass through fall, as early as July.

PECTORAL SANDPIPER *Calidris melanotis*

Description: 8 ¾". Similar in structure to Baird's, but larger, much more patterned above, **strong band of streaks across chest**. Legs yellowish; some yellowish-orange at base of bill. **Voice**: Call note is a low, rich *churk*, often repeated. **Behavior**: Feeds deliberately in shallow water and mud, often in or near vegetation. **Similar Species**: Sharp-tailed Sandpiper (*C. acuminata*, 8 ½"), an Asian species, is a very rare fall migrant (mid-September-October), mostly along coast. Brighter than Pectoral above, orangish-buff breast unmarked. **Where, When to Find**: Rare to uncommon fall (late August-October) migrant (mostly juveniles) throughout; more numerous on coast. Casual in spring.

Did you know? Most adult Baird's migrate through Great Plains, adult Pectorals through Mississippi and Ohio valleys; both winter in South America.

Date & Location Seen:

_____

Breeding

Non-breeding

Juvenile

Description: 6". The small *Calidris* sandpipers are collectively known as "peeps". This is the world's smallest sandpiper, but one of the hardiest. **Short-winged** in flight; tips of wings (primaries) are not visible at rest. **Bill is short, thin, and slightly arched**. Legs dull yellowish, sometimes discolored by mud. NON-BREEDING: **Brownish above**, with **brown wash across breast**. BREEDING: Breast strongly streaked; back feathers have black centers and some rufous fringes. JUVENILE: Rufous fringes to back and wing feathers, buffy wash across lightly streaked breast.

Voice: Call is a high *treep* or *tree-treep*.

Behavior: Forages on wet mud, lakeshores; usually does not wade into shallow water. Often in flocks.

Similar Species: Western Sandpiper (p. 175) is larger and grayer with longer, more decurved bill. In non-breeding plumage much whiter across breast, grayish above. In breeding extensively rufous on crown, face and upperparts; underparts extensively streaked with arrow-shaped spots. Legs dark, not greenish-yellow, but mud discolors legs. Compare p. 171. Rather rare Baird's is larger and paler (buffier) with horizontal stance, long wing tip projection, dark legs. Pectoral larger still with longer, yellowish-based bill and much longer wings (primary tips extend well beyond tertials and tail).

Where, When to Find: Common migrant and winter visitor (July through April) both in coastal estuaries and creek mouths and at wetlands, lakes, creek channels throughout the interior, west of the Sierra Nevada. Rare (non-breeders) in summer. Juveniles arrive by early August. Large numbers winter at Owens Lake, otherwise a common to uncommon migrant, rare in winter, in the Great Basin. This is our hardiest peep, wintering in many colder interior locations.

Did you know? Least Sandpipers have the most southerly breeding range of all our peeps; they nest extensively through the taiga regions rather than being restricted to high Arctic tundra.

Date & Location Seen: _____

Breeding

Non-breeding

Juvenile

Description: 6 ½". **Our most common peep; bill relatively long** (longer in FEMALES) **and slightly drooped, with fine tip.** Blackish legs. NON-BREEDING: Brownish-gray above, whitish underneath. BREEDING: **Rufous on crown, cheeks and upperparts**; breast and flanks marked with dark arrow-shaped spots. JUVENILE: Cleanly marked gray and chestnut above, clean white below (buffy wash on breast when fresh).

Voice: Call is a high, scratchy *djeeet*.

Behavior: Forages on mudflats and in shallow water, picking and probing for small invertebrates. Often found in flocks of thousands.

Similar Species: Least Sandpiper (p. 173) is smaller and browner (darker) in all plumages; non-breeding birds show brown wash across breast. Bill slighter and thinner, legs (if clean) greenish-yellow. Semipalmated Sandpiper (*C. pusilla*, 6 ¼"), a casual spring (May) and rare but regular fall (July to mid-September; mainly juveniles in early to mid-August) migrant throughout, is similarly colored, but in breeding plumage lacks Western's bright rufous tones and breast is streaked, not marked with arrow-shaped spots. Juveniles are more uniformly colored and darker above than juvenile Westerns. Semipalmated's bill is shorter, thicker and of more even thickness. Legs similarly dark. Call lower pitched.

Where, When to Find: Common to abundant migrant along coast (April to mid-May, late June to mid-October) nearly throughout; uncommon in the Sierra Nevada and Great Basin. Winters commonly at large coastal estuaries and around San Francisco Bay. Rather rare in winter in the Central Valley, mostly in the southern San Joaquin Valley. Also winters at Owens Lake. Rare (non-breeders) during a short period in early summer along the coast.

Did you know? Along with a few other North American species (e.g., Semipalmated Plover, Baird's and Pectoral sandpipers, Long-billed Dowitcher, and Gray-cheeked Thrush) its breeding range extends west into the Russian Far East.

Date & Location Seen: _____

Short-billed Dowitcher

Non-breeding

Juvenile

Breeding

Long-billed Dowitcher

Non-breeding

Juvenile

Breeding

scription: 11″. Dowitchers are long-legged medium sized shorebirds with **long straight bills, white triangular patches up backs, tails barred black and white. Best distinguished by voice**. NON-BREEDING: Grayish above and across chest with faint spots, whitish belly. BREEDING: Upperparts dark with extensive bright buff, rufous, and white markings; underparts cinnamon with **blackish spots on sides of breast, lower belly and vent paler.** JUVENILE: Colorful, with **rufous-buff internal markings on tertials, greater secondary coverts, and scapulars. Voice:** A distinctive mellow *tu-tu-tu*. Both species give aggressive *ju-ju-ju-jeeee-da*. **Behavior**: Feeds in shallow water with "sewing-machine" motions. Gregarious. **Similar Species:** Red Knot (p. 165) is smaller, with shorter bill and legs, paler above. See Wilson's Snipe (p. 179). **Where, When to Find:** Locally common migrant (late March-April, July-early October; juveniles arrive early August) along the coast and at large coastal estuaries. In winter, common visitor in San Francisco Bay, rare farther north, no interior records. Some in non-breeding plumage summer. Uncommon migrant in the Central Valley and at Owens Lake; rare elsewhere in interior.

LONG-BILLED DOWITCHER *Limnodromus scolopaceus*

scription: 11 ½″. Plumages like Short-billed. **Bill averages longer, tail darker**. NON-BREEDING: Darker, browner overall; breast unspotted. BREEDING: Darker above; **white tips to scapulars, barring on sides of neck**; more extensively colored below. JUVENILE: Duller; **lacks internal feather markings above. Voice**: A sharp *"keek"*, rapidly repeated when disturbed. **Behavior**: Prefers fresher water than Short-billed. **Where, When to Find:** Common migrant and winter visitor (late July to early May) in the coastal region and Central Valley. Common migrant (April to mid-May, late July-October) in Great Basin (uncommon elsewhere); some winter at Owens Lake. Juveniles don't arrive until mid-September.

d you know? *Limnodromus* means "marsh dwelling" in Greek.

te & Location Seen:

•scription: 10 ½". A dumpy brown short-legged shorebird with a **long, straight bill.** The crown and face are striped, and the **back has long creamy stripes**. The breast and sides are barred with dusky, contrasting with the white belly. The orange tail can be seen when the bird is flying away.

•ice: When flushed gives a raspy *scaip*. On breeding grounds males give a territorial winnowing sound in flight display; also loud *wheet* notes from perches, often fence posts.

•havior: Secretive; roosts by hiding motionlessly within short marshy vegetation and forages only infrequently away from the cover of vegetation. Usually found singly, but in good habitat small loose groups may be found. Flushes with zigzag flight, sometimes towering into the air, and then dropping.

•nilar Species: Dowitchers (p. 177) have longer legs, a white patch on their back, and lack the snipe's long pale back stripes. The rapid bill-jabbing feeding action of dowitchers differs from the snipe's more methodical probing.

•here, When to Find: Fairly common migrant and winter visitor (late September to mid-April; a few from mid-August and into May) throughout the coastal region and in all interior valleys. Somewhat local. Presence depends upon appropriate habitat (non-tidal marshy areas, flooded fields after rains); can be common. Common breeder in the Great Basin (a few winter); uncommon and local breeder in the Sierra Nevada. Has been suspected of nesting in the northern portion of the Sacramento Valley.

•d you know? Formerly known as the Common Snipe, but the mid-1940s lumping of New World and Old World groups has recently been reversed; Old World birds are still called Common Snipe (*Gallinago gallinago*). They occur regularly in the Aleutians and Bering Sea Islands; in 2011 one was collected in southern California's San Jacinto Valley, east of Riverside.

•te & Location Seen: _____

Breeding Female

Molting Juvenile

Juvenile
in more advanced molt

Description: 9 ¼". Phalaropes are unique swimming sandpipers with lobed toes and short legs; FEMALES are larger than MALES and brighter in breeding plumage. Wilson's is plump with a **long needle-like bill.** In flight plain wings, **white rump and tail**. NON-BREEDING: Uniformly pale grayish above; greenish-yellow legs. BREEDING: Females have a broad dark stripe through eye and down sides of neck; the hindneck is white, bordered by deep maroon; foreneck is apricot; male with similar pattern but duller. JUVENILE: Dark above with buffy edges; buff wash across front of neck in fresh plumage; plumage rapidly molted.

Voice: Call is a low grunting *wump*, often given in a short series.

Behavior: Swims, spinning to bring prey to the surface. More likely than other phalaropes to feed on mudflats, walking with forward-lunging gait, picking for brine flies and other prey.

Similar Species: Other two phalaropes (p. 183) smaller and shorter-billed, with dark legs and dark eye patch in non-breeding plumage; also a white wing stripe and a dark centered tail. Lesser Yellowlegs (p. 155) has much longer legs; feeds by picking at water surface.

Where, When to Find: Fairly common migrant and breeder in the Great Basin. Arrives after mid-April; most have departed by mid-September. Locally abundant (e.g., at Mono and Owens lakes) in fall migration (mid-June through August). Uncommon and local breeder in the Sierra Nevada. Rather rare spring (mid-April to early May) and uncommon to fairly common fall (mid-July to early September) migrant in coastal regions and interior valleys; more common in the Central Valley. Has nested on north coast; occasionally nests in Central Valley. Partial to marshes, ponds, especially wastewater and salt ponds.

Did you know? This is our earliest fall migrant (by second week of June); it crosses paths with northbound Willow Flycatchers!

Date & Location Seen: _____

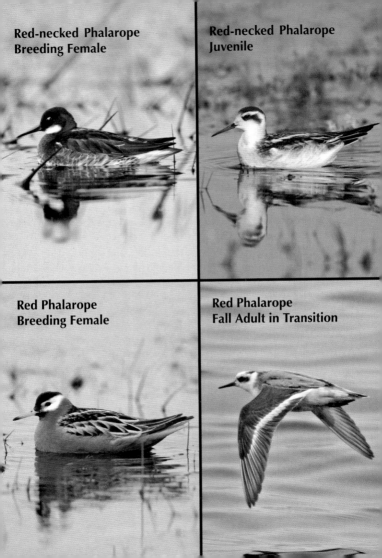

Red-necked Phalarope Breeding Female

Red-necked Phalarope Juvenile

Red Phalarope Breeding Female

Red Phalarope Fall Adult in Transition

escription: 7 ¾″. The smallest phalarope, with a **thin bill, white wing stripe, dark centered tail.** NON-BREEDING: **Dark patch through eye; back striped slaty and white**. BREEDING: Slaty head and sides of breast, white patch on sides of throat, red neck sides, gold back stripes; males are duller. JUVENILE: Like non-breeding adult but with dark cap, black upperparts with buff stripes. **Voice**: Sharp *kip* recalls Sanderling's call, but a bit sharper. **Behavior**: Feeds by spinning rapidly, bringing prey to the surface. **Similar Species:** See Red Phalarope (below). **Where, When to Find:** Most frequently seen in coastal waters, estuaries, and inland saline lakes. Common migrant (late April to late May, mid-July to mid-October, a few later); spring migration more rapid, somewhat irregular. Uncommon to common, even abundant (e.g., Owens and Mono lakes) migrant throughout much of the rest of the region. Most numerous at wastewater and salt ponds. Juveniles arrive early August.

RED PHALAROPE *Phalaropus fulicarius*

scription: 8 ½″. Larger with shorter, thicker bill (often with yellow at base) than Red-necked Phalarope; more conspicuous white wing stripe; swims with tail higher off water. NON-BREEDING: **Plain gray back**; face and tail pattern like Red-necked. BREEDING: **Bill yellow-based with dark tip, cheeks white, underparts red**; males duller, some white on belly. Blotchy plumage often seen on returning adults in mid-summer. Full juvenal plumage is not seen in our area. **Voice**: A sharp, high-pitched *keet* call. **Behavior**: Like Red-necked Phalarope. **Where, When to Find**: A migratory pelagic species, most frequent late July-October; irregularly, sometimes commonly, into December when closer to shore. Less numerous (May to early June) in spring, sometimes onshore after high winds. Casual (primarily fall) throughout the interior.

d you know? Food items within water drops are drawn up into the mouth from the bill tip by surface tension.

te & Location Seen: _____

Common Murre
Breeding Adult

Common Murre
Non-breeding

Pigeon Guillemot
Breeding Adult

Pigeon Guillemot
Juvenile

COMMON MURRE
Uria aalge

Description: 17 ½". Alcids (murres, auklets, murrelets, etc.) are diving seabirds with small wings and rapid whirring flight. BREEDING ADULT of this species, our largest alcid, is **blackish-brown above, including head, white below**. In winter shows white throat and neck sides, black streak behind eye; JUVENILES similar. **Voice**: Generally silent, except in nesting colonies. **Behavior**: Dives in pursuit of small fish. Lays a single egg; father accompanies juvenile during first month or more at sea. **Similar Species:** Murrelets (p. 487) have somewhat similar plumage patterns, but are much smaller and shorter-billed. **Where, When to Find:** Common year-round in offshore waters, can often be seen from shore; a few seen within San Francisco Bay in late summer. Nests (May-July) in large colonies; state's largest is on the Farallon Islands; large colonies also on Green Rock and Flatiron Rock, Humboldt County; smaller colonies exist on offshore rocks and coastal cliffs south to Big Sur.

PIGEON GUILLEMOT *Cepphus columba*

Description: 13 ½". Distinctive BREEDING ADULTS are **black with large white wing patch, bright red feet**; ADULTS in winter whitish below, mottled gray above; JUVENILES similar but with smaller white wing patch. **Voice**: Very rapid, high-pitched whistles and twitters heard when breeding. **Behavior**: Dives in pursuit of small fish. Juveniles self-sufficient at sea. **Similar Species:** Compare juvenile with non-breeding Marbled Murrelet (p. 487). **Where, When to Find:** Common summer resident in near-shore ocean waters, March-September; most migrate north to the Puget Sound region in winter. Nests (May-August) solitarily and in loose colonies, in burrows and on predator-free offshore rocks and coastal cliffs. Readily seen at many nesting locations, e.g., piers along Monterey's Cannery Row. Scarce just inside San Francisco Bay.

Did you know? Common Murres nest in densely packed colonies, with up to twenty pairs occupying one square meter at peak season.

Date & Location Seen: _____

Breeding Adult

Non-breeding Adult

First-year

Description: 13 ½", wingspan 33". A **small tern-like** gull with a **slender black bill** and pink legs. NON-BREEDING: Pale gray above, white head and underparts with **black spot behind eye. White triangle on outer wing, bordered by black**. BREEDING: In April adults acquire **complete slaty-black hood**. IMMATURE: Differs from adult in black tail band, dusky bar across upperwing, dark border along trailing edge of wing.

Voice: Buzzy, raspy calls.

Behavior: Feeds on small fish and invertebrates while swimming or dipping to surface in flight; also walks along mudflats, picking at surface. Flies with rapid, shallow wing beats. Can occur in large flocks.

Similar Species: Tern-like (compare with Forster's Tern, p. 209). Several other small to medium-small gulls with dark hoods can occur in the region, of which the Franklin's (p. 471) is the most regular onshore. Also, the Sabine's Gull (p. 491) is a fairly common to common migrant species offshore.

Where, When to Find: Common spring (mid-March to mid-May) and fall (late October-December) migrant in coastal regions (some farther offshore), uncommon (rare north of Sonoma County) in winter. Can be locally fairly common at some foothill reservoirs (e.g., Black Butte Reservoir, Tehama and Glenn counties) in migration and winter, yet scarce at others. Generally fairly common in the Central Valley at sewage ponds, rare to uncommon elsewhere in the Valley. Uncommon to rare migrant at lakes in the Sierra Nevada and the Great Basin. Some, mostly non-breeding immatures, summer locally throughout. Juveniles (usually already in molt) typically don't arrive until mid-October, but have appeared by August. Numbers may have declined somewhat in recent decades.

Did you know? The English name of this species honors Charles Lucien Bonaparte, an ornithologist and nephew of Napoleon.

Date & Location Seen: _____

_____

Breeding Adult

First-year

escription: 19", wingspan 51". A distinctive dark-bodied medium-sized gull. ADULT: **Gray overall** (darker above) with a **black tail** with white terminal band, **bright red bill, black legs**. In breeding plumage (late December to July) the head is **white**. IMMATURE: Juvenile is solidly dark brown; pale fringes to feathers of back and wings have mostly worn away by fall. Bill dull pink at base, dark at tip; legs blackish. Older immatures are progressively grayer; bill is extensively orange-red by second winter.

ice: Vocal when squabbling for food in groups; calls have a nasal, barking quality.

havior: Flocks occur around piers, on beaches, and where food is concentrated offshore; habitually follows boats. Often associates with feeding Brown Pelicans, seeking fish spilled from pouch. Also forages along the beach tide line like sandpipers, mainly for mole crabs.

milar Species: Distinctive, but beware dark juvenile gulls such as Western (p. 195) and California (p. 197). A few adults show bold white patches on upperwing; these can be mistaken for jaegers (p. 485), a similarity compounded by Heermann's habit of chasing terns in jaeger-like fashion. Various species of dark shearwaters (pp. 481, 483) have coloration like juvenile Heermann's Gull, but have longer, thinner wings and fly with stiff flaps and glides.

here, When to Find: Common along the immediate coast and offshore waters. Arrives in the region from more southerly breeding grounds, mostly in the Gulf of California, by late June; most remain into January. A few (mostly immatures) remain through the spring. Rare in mid-winter on the north coast. The species has nested on Alcatraz Island in San Francisco Bay and near Monterey.

id you know? The species was named for Adolphus Lewis Heermann, a mid-19th century U.S. explorer and field naturalist.

ate & Location Seen: _____

Non-breeding Adult

First-year

escription: 16", wingspan 43". A medium-small gull with a rounded head, large dark eye, and **short slender bill**. ADULT: **Small bill** is yellowish, faintly smudged with dusky near tip in winter; legs yellowish. **Mantle color medium gray** (like California, darker than Ring-billed). **Black wingtips** have **large white terminal spots** visible at rest and **subterminal spots** (often called "mirrors") **visible in flight**. In winter head and neck **washed with brown**. IMMATURE: First-winter birds are washed pale brown (by December with soft gray back), brownish underwing, almost entirely brown tail; legs pinkish, dull pink bill has dark tip. In second winter much like adult but less white in wingtips, some black near tail tip, black tipped bill, greenish legs.

oice: High squealing, mewing notes.

ehavior: Often forages by flying over inshore waters, bays, and sewage ponds, dipping to surface for food items, or by foraging while swimming in such waters. Also feeds on beaches.

imilar Species: Ring-billed Gull's (p. 193) thicker bill always has dark at or near tip, adult's eye yellow, mantle paler gray; white terminal and subterminal spots on primaries smaller. Immature (first winter) paler above and much paler below than Mew with white underwings, blackish tail band. Larger California Gull (p. 197) has longer, thicker bill with red and black spot, adults with more black in the wingtips.

here, When to Find: Common winter visitor along coast and coastal regions (mid-October to mid-April). Very rarely summers. Abundance diminishes with distance from the coast; generally rare in the Central Valley, but may be slightly more numerous/regular at favored locations (e.g., Nimbus Fish Hatchery). Accidental in the Great Basin.

id you know? Our region's Mew Gulls are of the subspecies *brachyrhynchus*, which is restricted to western North America; slightly larger subspecies in the Old World are often called the "Common Gull."

ate & Location Seen: _____

Breeding Adult

First-year

Non-breeding Adult

Description: 17 ½", wingspan 48". A medium-sized gull with a fairly short bill. ADULT: **Pale gray above**; black wingtips with white terminal spots, plus two white mirrors are sharply set off from pale gray wing. Winter birds get limited brown flecking on the head and neck. **Bill yellow with black ring near tip; eye yellowish-white**, legs yellow. IMMATURE: First-winter is pale gray on mantle, wings mottled brown above, whitish below; the head and breast are spotted with warm brown, tail white with darker mottling and blackish band at tip. Bill pink with black tip, legs pinkish, eyes dark. In second winter similar to adult but wingtip solidly black, variable small black band on tail tip, often broken; legs greenish-yellow.

Voice: High squealing notes, often with a slightly raspy quality.

Behavior: Feeds on fish, marine invertebrates; also scavenges along beaches and for refuse in parks, parking lots (though only infrequently at landfills).

Similar Species: California Gull (p. 197) is larger and longer-billed; adult has darker mantle, red spot on bill, dark eye. Sub-adults of many gull species show blackish ring on the bill; in particular second-winter California can suggest first-winter Ring-billed (but note the darker mantle, size and shape differences, greener legs). See Mew Gull (p. 191).

Where, When to Find: Common in coastal regions and in the Central Valley, although usually scarce and very local on the immediate coast (especially where rocky coastlines prevail) and very rare offshore (where seen mainly during fall migration). Fairly common migrant (some winter) on mountain lakes. Some (non-breeders) summer throughout, but are out-numbered by California Gulls. Common breeder mid-March to November in Siskiyou, Modoc, and Lassen counties.

Did you know? Populations of this species have skyrocketed around the Great Lakes; the North American (and World) population now probably exceeds four million birds.

Date & Location Seen: _____

Breeding Adult
occidentalis

Non-breeding Adult

First-year

Juvenile

escription: 25", wingspan 58". An abundant **large coastal gull**, usually the most common species in summer. **Robust bill is thick near the tip. Pink legs and feet.** ADULT: **Dark slaty gray back and upperwings** blending into black wingtips; in flight from below note extensive dark trailing edge to wing. Bill yellow with red spot. Winter adults remain mostly white headed. IMMATURE: First-winter is overall sooty with variable white mottling on rump and belly; underwings dark. Bill black. With molt, wear, and bleaching, feathering becomes progressively whiter on head and underparts and more slaty above through second and third winters.

oice: Typical gull calls, deeper than our other species; "long-call" is a series of *aah aah aah aah* notes.

ehavior: Scavenges on beaches, etc.; also forages for fish, squid and other prey offshore. Increasingly these gulls are moving inland to scavenge for garbage.

milar Species: Adults of all other regularly occurring large gulls have paler upperparts. First winter Westerns resemble Herring Gull (p. 199) overall but are more sooty in coloration and less scaly, lack pale window on inner primaries, and show a contrasting white rump. Hybrids with Glaucous-winged Gull are frequent; these are paler above than pure Westerns, often more like Glaucous-winged but with blackish wingtips as adults.

here, When to Find: Common resident along the coast and around San Francisco Bay, breeding locally, mainly on the Farallon Islands. Formerly rare, but increasingly frequent in the Delta Region of the Central Valley. Scarcer further inland, but recorded as far from the coast as Eagle Lake, Lassen County.

id you know? Two subspecies breed in the region. Paler mantled *occidentalis* (meaning "western") is found along most of the coast. Darker mantled *wymani* breeds north to Monterey County. The latter was named for Luther Wyman, the first Curator of Birds at the Natural History Museum of Los Angeles County.

ate & Location Seen: _____

Breeding Adult

Non-breeding Adult

First-year

Description: 21", wingspan 54". A common medium-large gull with a fairly long, slender bill. ADULT: **Medium gray mantle** and upperwings; in flight, note extensively black wingtips with large white mirrors. Head densely streaked with brown in winter. **Eyes dark, legs greenish** (deep yellow in breeding birds), **bill** yellow **with red and dusky spots near the tip.** IMMATURE: Mottled gray-brown; tail mostly dark, bill pale pink with black tip, legs pink; second-winter birds have gray mantle, pale gray bill with black ring near tip, pale gray-green legs.

Voice: Similar to Ring-billed but lower pitched, harsher.

Behavior: Large numbers commute between nighttime roosts off coast (or reservoirs) and feeding areas; the most common gull over urban lowlands in winter.

Similar Species: Ring-billed adult (p. 193) is paler gray above, shorter bill has black ring; first-winter mainly white below. Herring Gull adult (p. 199) also paler gray above, has pale eye, pink legs; first winter bird has all black bill in early winter, first and second winter birds have pale windows in outer wing.

Where, When to Find: Very common winter visitor and migrant (mainly August to early May) throughout including offshore to about 25 miles; Herring Gulls predominate farther offshore. Local in the Central Valley, but avoids the rice country. Nesting birds in south San Francisco Bay have increased from a few dozen in the early 1980s to more than 50,000; a few nest near Santa Cruz as well. The largest, best known colony nests on islands in Mono Lake; also nests at other Great Basin lakes. Uncommon to fairly common in the Great Basin in winter.

Did you know? Los Angeles began diverting water from Mono Lake feeder streams in 1941; over time lake level dropped enough that predators had land bridges to some islands. A 1983 California Supreme Court decision lessened diversions, and mandated that the lake level be allowed to rise.

Date & Location Seen: _____

**Herring Gull
Non-breeding Adult**

**Herring Gull
Juvenile**

**Iceland Gull
Non-breeding Adult**
thayeri

**Iceland Gull
Juvenile *thayeri***

**Iceland Gull
Juvenile *thayeri***

Description: 25", wingspan 58". A large pink-legged gull with a long, fairly thin bill. ADULT: **Upperparts pale gray; limited black in the wingtips. Eyes pale yellowish, legs pink.** In winter adults are streaked with brown on the head and neck. IMMATURE: Variable. First year birds mottled brown; head often noticeably paler. Immatures in flight show a pale window near the wing tip. **Voice:** Typical gull squeals and cackles. **Behavior:** Readily associates with other gulls. Partial to landfills and nearby water for bathing and resting. **Similar Species:** See first winter Western Gull (p. 195), California Gull (p 197) and Iceland Gull (below). **Where, When to find:** Fairly common winter visitor (October-April) generally throughout, fewest in the Great Basin; it is the most common gull far offshore. Very rare in summer. Like Ring-billed, but unlike California, it is numerous in the Central Valley rice country.

ICELAND GULL *Larus glaucoides*

Description: 23", wingspan 55". **Similar to larger Herring Gull.** Description pertains to the westerly wintering subspecies *thayeri*. ADULTS: Deeper pink legs (than Herring) are shorter, smaller bill is slightly greenish at base; eye often dark; orbital ring purplish, not red (Herring); wing tips show more white, especially on outermost primary; almost no black on underwing in flight. IMMATURE: First winter birds are frosty; primaries are brown (not blackish) with white fringes. Highly variable; paler birds resemble Glaucous-winged Gull (p. 201) in flight. **Where, When to Find:** Less numerous than Herring Gull; often associates with them. Uncommon to locally fairly common winter visitor (mid-October to March) in coastal regions, rare to uncommon in the Central Valley, rare to casual elsewhere.

Did you know? The "Thayer's Gull" (*Larus glaucoides thayeri*) has a checkered taxonomic history: Described as a species in 1915, lumped with Herring in 1931, split as a species in 1973, and lumped with Iceland in 2017.

Date & Location Seen: _____

Glaucous-winged Gull
Non-breeding Adult

Glaucous Gull
First- winter

Glaucous-winged Gull
First-year

Description: 26", wingspan 58". **Large, pale** Pacific Northwest **gull**. Winters commonly along the coast. Very similar structurally to Western Gull, with **long heavy bill** (often appears longer than Western), **deep pink legs**. ADULT: Gray above; grayish wingtips (**same shade as mantle**) with white spots. Dark eye with purplish orbital ring. Extensive gray-brown washing on head in winter. IMMATURE: First winter is mottled pale gray-brown throughout, including. Heavy **all black bill**. Worn immatures late in winter can be very pale.

Voice: Much like Western's.

Behavior: A marine gull, usually found along the immediate coast, offshore, and around San Francisco Bay. Often feeds in intertidal areas.

Similar Species: Widespread (along our coast) *occidentalis* subspecies of Western Gull (p. 195) similar, but much darker on mantle with black wingtips, head whiter in winter. First winter Glaucous-winged similar to young Iceland (p. 199), but larger, and larger billed; less patterned overall, and wingtips even with rest of upperparts, not darker. Slightly larger (on average) **Glaucous Gull** (*L. hyperboreus*, 27") is a fairly rare, but increasingly regular, winter visitor (late December to early April) mainly along the coast and to San Francisco Bay (a few to the Central Valley; casual elsewhere). Most are first winter birds with chalky white coloration, at least some limited buffy mottling, white wing tips; black tip to evenly proportioned pink-based bill.

Where, When to Find: Common along coast and the San Francisco Bay Area from October through April. uncommon (non-breeders) through summer. Many commute daily from tidal waters to inland landfills. Rare to locally uncommon in the Central Valley, casual to rare elsewhere.

Did you know? Glaucous-wingeds hybridize extensively with Western Gulls in the Pacific Northwest, and with Herrings Gulls in parts of southern Alaska; hybrids are intermediate between their parent species in mantle and wing tip color.

Date & Location Seen: _____

Breeding Adult

Juvenile

escription: 9″, wingspan 20″. A **tiny tern** with short yellowish legs and a short, slightly forked tail. BREEDING ADULT: **Bill yellow with small black tip. Distinct white forehead patch** contrasts with black crown and line through eye. Outermost flight feathers of wing blackish, contrasting with pale gray wing. IMMATURE: Juvenile has long dark patch behind eye, streaked crown, brownish barring on back. Older immatures and winter adults, rarely seen in our region, have black bills.

ice: A *ki-deek* or *k-seek*, often in a series.

havior: Hovers over the water surface, plunging in for tiny fish. Wing beats are very fast and shallow. Aggressive around nesting colonies, chasing after intruding gulls, crows, and other birds. Typically nests in loose colonies on sandy islands or (where fenced or otherwise protected from predators) in upper beach areas.

milar Species: Fairly unmistakable. Other terns are much larger, but Least can be confused with an immature or winter plumaged Forster's Tern (p. 209).

here, When to Find: Uncommon local breeder (late April-July) around the San Francisco Bay area; about 550 pairs in 2012 (~10% of the state's total). Largest colonies are in Alameda County (decommissioned airfield at Alameda Point, Hayward Regional Shoreline); much smaller colonies in Contra Costa, Napa, and Solano counties. Post-breeding (mid-July to mid-August), a little more widespread around south San Francisco Bay, where it stages before migrating (apparently over the Santa Cruz Mts.) to the coast and southward to winter. Rare to casual along the coast in spring and summer; recorded north to Del Norte County. Casual in the Central Valley (has nested in Kings County); accidental elsewhere in the interior. Formerly a more numerous and widespread nesting species.

id you know? Our "California" subspecies, *browni*, is classified as Endangered (state and federal), owing mostly to human use of beaches suitable for nesting, and receives intensive management.

ate & Location Seen: _____

Breeding Adult

Breeding Adult

escription: 21", wingspan 50". The **largest tern**, with a **deep red to red-orange bill**. Tail slightly forked. Always shows **blackish on underside of wingtips** in flight. BREEDING: Black crown, square at rear (not crested); pale gray above, otherwise white. NON-BREEDING: **Crown is peppered black and white, including forehead**. JUVENILES show brown mottling on back and wings, more extensively dark on the upper side of wingtips. Bill duller with more extensive dark.

ice: Call is a deep, raucous *kraa-aay-ow*. Young birds give a high, insistent whistle through the first fall and winter.

havior: Like most terns, feeds by plunging into the water to catch fish; also dips to surface to catch prey. Stands on beaches, mudflats in loose groups when not feeding, habitually facing into the wind. Nests in mixed tern colonies. Young accompany their parents into the fall.

milar Species: Much smaller Elegant Tern (p. 211) has pure white forehead in non-breeding plumage, and lacks black on underside of wingtips; very slender and long bill lacks black tip.

here, When to Find: Fairly common migrant and summer visitor along the coast (April into October). Fairly common, but local, nester in the San Francisco Bay Area and at Elkhorn Slough, northern Monterey County. Rare in winter along the coast (most regularly in Humboldt Bay). In the interior, including lakes and reservoirs on the coastal slope, the Central Valley, the Sierra Nevada, and the Great Basin, uncommon to fairly common migrant (April-May, late July-September); nesters visit nearby coastal slope reservoirs through the summer. Also nests locally in the Central Valley, the Great Basin, and at Clear Lake, Lake County.

id you know? This species is found nearly worldwide, yet despite its vast range it is quite uniform in appearance throughout and is regarded as monotypic (i.e., there are no recognized subspecies).

ate & Location Seen: _____

_____

Breeding Adult

Juvenile
surinamensis

Description: 9 ¾", wingspan 24". A **small, short-tailed dark tern**, found mainly in the interior. BREEDING: **Mostly black**, paler on back and wings, and **with white undertail**. NON-BREEDNG ADULTS: **Back and wing slaty gray**, white underparts with gray patch on sides of breast, distinct black markings on head. JUVENILES: shaded brown on nape, back, sides, flanks.

Voice: Calls include a metallic *kik* and a slurred *k-seek*.

Behavior: Flies with steady and rather slow (for its size) wing beats. Catches prey at water surface and in the air.

Similar Species: Non-breeding adults and juveniles are distinctive with their dark dorsal coloration, mostly white underparts with dark side patch, and black head patches. Breeding adults are unmistakable.

Where, When to Find: An uncommon to locally fairly common breeder in inland marshes and in the Central Valley's flooded rice fields. More numerous and widespread in the Sacramento Valley; scarcer in the San Joaquin Valley. Also breeds in the Great Basin and locally in marshes in the mountains. Arrives late April, mostly May, remains into September. More widespread in migration (May and mid-July to early September) in the interior. Abundant in late summer and early fall, if water conditions are appropriate, at Tule Lake National Wildlife Refuge in Siskiyou and Modoc counties. It is thought to be a major staging area; these terns appear to be attracted by the large numbers of damselflies. Formerly much more common; nested coastally at least once, in Monterey County. Coastally, now casual to very rare in May and late August to October. Casual well offshore in migration (mostly spring). Accidental in winter.

Did you know? Our North American subspecies, *surinamensis*, winters mostly in South America. Juveniles are easily identified to subspecies by their brownish-gray flanks. The other subspecies, *niger*, breeds in the Western Palearctic and winters in western Africa. A state Species of Special Concern.

Date & Location Seen: _____

Forster's Tern
Breeding Adult

Forster's Tern
First-winter

Common Tern
Breeding Adult

Common Tern
First-year

scription: 13", wingspan 31". Our common medium sized tern; **long tail is deeply forked**. ADULT: pale gray above; **wings frosted silvery-white**. Breeders (until mid-August) have all black crown; orange bill with black tip; in winter crown white, bill black; **eye patch black**, hindcrown grayish. IMMATURE: similar, but wingtips slightly darker; juveniles with rusty wash on back.

ice: Calls include a prolonged buzzy *keeeurr* and sharp *kit* notes.

havior: Hovers briefly, then plunges into water for small fish. Roosts on beaches, tidal flats. Often sits on low pilings in water. Nests are often in more vegetated areas of salt marshes than those of other terns, though in San Francisco Bay often on bare dredge spoil islands.

nilar Species: The **Common Tern** (*S. hirundo*, 12") is a rare spring (May) and uncommon fall (mostly September to early October) migrant along the coast (and offshore) and in San Francisco Bay. It is a rare (uncommon on Great Basin lakes, Lake Tahoe) but regular fall migrant (late August to early October) throughout the interior. Adults in breeding plumage (retained well into fall) have darker gray mantle and underparts, contrasting with shorter white tail and dark wedge in outer wing; immatures have dark bar on leading edge of wing, dark secondaries and nape. Calls differ slightly.

here, When to Find: Fairly common migrant and summer visitant (mid-April to mid-September) on coast (north to Sonoma County; rare farther north), the San Francisco Bay area and throughout the Central Valley. A very local nester, uncommon to fairly common in winter on coast and Bay Area. Uncommon migrant and summer visitor to large lakes in mountains.

d you know? The species was named for Johann Reinhold Forster, an 18th century naturalist who accompanied James Cook on his second Pacific voyage. The Great Gray Owl, the White-crowned Sparrow, and the presumed extinct Eskimo Curlew are amongst the species Forster described from the Hudson Bay region.

te & Location Seen:

Breeding Adult

First-year

Description: 17", wingspan 34". Much smaller than Caspian Tern with very long, slender orange-red bill, becoming yellow-orange near tip. BREEDING BIRDS have **black crowns, shaggy black crests**, often show pink wash below; from August to February rear crown and crest are black, forehead is white. Tail is rather deeply forked. IMMATURE has dusky markings on wings and tail, bill shorter, often yellower.

Voice: Call a very sharp *keer-rick*. Very vocal, especially when in flocks.

Behavior: Plunges into water to catch fish. Often roosts in large, tight flocks.

Similar Species: Much larger Caspian Tern (p. 205) has much thicker blood red bill (orange-red in juveniles) with a black tip, broader wings with blackish on the underside of the primaries (visible in flight), shorter tail. Another large tern, the Royal Tern (*T. maximus*, 20") is found regularly in fall and winter north to Pt. Piedras Blancas, near the Monterey County line. It occurred regularly to the San Francisco Bay Area until about 1910, but is now a very rare visitor (e.g., to Monterey County in winter). Notwithstanding a well-documented April 2014 Royal in Humboldt County, many (most?) northerly Royal reports likely apply to Elegant Tern. The Royal is plumaged like Elegant, but is larger, with a stouter bill. In non-breeding plumage (acquired earlier in the summer than Elegant) it averages whiter on the head. Calls slightly differ.

Where, When to Find: Common to locally abundant post-breeding summer and fall visitor (July to late October) along the entire coast, including around San Francisco Bay, arriving from southerly breeding grounds; partial to bays and harbors. Rare earlier in the spring (to late April); casual in winter. Much more common in recent decades than earlier in the 20th century.

Did you know? This Mexican species started breeding in southern California in the 1950s.

Date & Location Seen: _____

_____

Breeding Adult

Breeding Adult

escription: 18", wingspan 44". An unmistakable **black and white** seabird with a bizarre **orange-red bill with black tip**. On bill, **lower mandible longer than upper mandible**. ADULT: Black above, white on forehead and underparts; winter adults have broad white color. Legs orange-red. JUVENILE: Gray-brown with white scaling above; legs pale orange; base of bill duller orange-red, black feathering on back and wings is attained through first winter. Males larger and longer billed than females.

ice: Calls low pitched, include a barking *oww* or *arr*, and shorter *yip* notes.

havior: Feeds (largely at dusk and into night) by skimming low over water, dragging long knife-thin lower mandible through the water to catch small fish. Flocks roost on beaches, tidal flats, islands, during the day, often sleeping and sunning in bizarre positions. Nests with terns on isolated beaches and low islets within San Francisco Bay.

nilar Species: Unmistakable.

here, When to Find: Uncommon resident in San Francisco Bay (perhaps slightly less numerous in winter), primarily in the South Bay, but north as far as Brooks Island, Contra Costa County. Small numbers of migrants are regularly recorded around Monterey Bay. Casual wanderer northward along the coast to Bodega Bay, Sonoma County; accidental farther north, to Del Norte County, and well inland (Kings County, Yolo Bypass in Yolo County, Clear Lake in Lake County). Rare in winter away from San Francisco Bay. A state Species of Special Concern.

d you know? A recent arrival from Mexico, first recorded in southern California in 1962 (Orange County); it now breeds fairly commonly at the Salton Sea and locally along the coast there. The first northern California record was in 1971 at Bodega Bay, Sonoma County. The first San Francisco Bay record was in 1978 (Santa Clara County); the first nests were discovered there, and in Alameda County, in 1994. Other skimmer species occur in Africa and the Indian subcontinent.

ate & Location Seen: _____

Rock Pigeon

Rock Pigeon

Eurasian Collared-Dove

Description: 12 ½ ". The familiar domestic pigeon. "Wild type" birds are mainly gray with **white rump band, black wing bars, white wing linings,** and iridescent neck sides; tail has a black terminal band. Bill black, legs pink. An **array of other plumages** noted in city flocks. **Voice:** Gruff cooing notes; wingtips often make a clapping sound on takeoff. **Behavior:** Tame. Feeds for scraps on ground, nests on building ledges, under bridges, on other structures. **Similar Species:** Native Band-tailed Pigeon (p. 217) shows little plumage variation, has orange-yellow legs and bill base, white hindneck crescent, uniform gray plumage with darker flight feathers; tail has a pale gray terminal band. **Where, When to Find:** Ubiquitous introduced resident in towns, industrial and agricultural areas, and nearly all other areas of human habitation.

EURASIAN COLLARED-DOVE *Streptopelia decaocto*

Description: 12 ½ ". Common and increasing introduced species. **Pale gray-brown** with **black hindneck collar,** grayish undertail, squared tail with white corners. Dark flight feathers contrast with pale coverts, wing linings. **Voice:** Clear or slightly gruff *coo-COO-coo,* often repeated for long periods; also grating *grrroww.* **Behavior:** Feeds mainly on the ground, roosts and nests in trees; often perches on wires, rooftops. Display flights involve quick climb with rapid wing-beats followed by long, curving glide. **Similar Species:** Smaller Mourning Dove (p. 219) lacks black hindneck collar, has long, tapered tail. **Where, When to Find:** Resident throughout the region; most numerous in semi-rural inhabited areas, but increasingly seen in more natural areas as well.

Did you know? Captive Eurasian Collared-Doves in the Bahamas accidentally escaped in the 1970s, reached Florida by 1982, and became established in southeastern California by 2001. Now present in all 58 counties, the species spread through the state more rapidly than any other non-native species.

Date & Location Seen: _____

_____

Description: 14". Our native pigeon, the large and relatively long-tailed Band-tail is nearly uniform gray, highlighted by a **white crescent** and iridescent green scalloping **on the hindneck** (both absent in JUVENILES), and a **dark gray median and pale gray terminal tail band**. Underparts tinged with purple; **legs, feet and base of bill yellow-orange.**

Voice: Deep, owl-like cooing notes: *hoo–whooOOOoo*; grating call given in display flights which cover long arcs with rapid, shallow wing beats. Wingtips often make a clapping sound on takeoff.

Behavior: Forages by picking seeds or berries (such as acorns, elderberries) from trees and shrubs; flocks may wander nomadically in search of these resources. Also visits seed feeders. Flocks congregate around water seeps in the mountains.

Similar Species: Citified Rock Pigeon (p. 215) usually shuns natural, wooded habitats. Rock Pigeon flocks show a variety of plumages and color morphs, unlike more uniform-appearing Band-tailed Pigeons. The Band-tail's deep hooting calls (given only in daytime) can be mistaken for those of owls.

Where, When to Find: Fairly common resident in all types of oak and mixed oak-conifer woodlands west of the Cascade/Sierra Nevada crest. Uncommon to rare east of the crest, mostly in the Lake Tahoe area and southern Great Basin region. Mountain populations descend to lower elevation oak belts in fall; wintering populations swelled by migrants from the Pacific Northwest, but seasonal migratory movements not well known overall. If acorns are not available, flocks wander nomadically in search of toyon, madrone, and other berries; also resort to orchards, grain fields, and vineyards.

Did you know? Band-tailed Pigeons are the closest living relative to the extinct Passenger Pigeon. Some believe it may be possible to 're-create' a Passenger Pigeon by selectively modifying the Band-tailed Pigeon's genome.

Date & Location Seen: _____

Description: 12". One of the most widespread and abundant native birds in our region, the Mourning Dove is a slender **gray-brown dove** with a **pointed, white-edged tail**, a black facial spot, and a few **black spots on the wing coverts.** Legs pinkish, bare orbital ring pale bluish. JUVENILES show scalloped plumage due to whitish feather fringes.

Voice: Familiar song is a soft, cooing *hoo-OOOoo, hoo, hoo-hoo* with a distinctive rhythm. Wings make whistling sound in flight.

Behavior: Abundant and tame, often visiting seed feeders. Mated birds travel in pairs during the breeding season. Nests may be placed in trees, shrubs and even planters or hanging baskets adjacent to houses. Often gathers in large flocks in fall and winter. Forages for seeds on the ground.

Similar Species: Smaller than pigeons and slimmer than Eurasian Collared-Dove (p. 215), with pointed tail.

Where, When to Find: Fairly common to locally abundant summer resident and breeder wherever open spaces provide the seeds of grasses, forbs, or cultivated grains. There is a general movement from the northwest coast, the mountains, and the Great Basin during fall and winter, with return in spring. Patchily distributed in the northwestern counties in summer; locally rare to uncommon in winter. Absent only from the driest regions, the highest mountains, and pure coniferous forests.

Did you know? The species is named for its melancholy-sounding song, not because of a preference for early daylight hours.

Date & Location Seen: _____

Yellow-billed Cuckoo

Greater Roadrunner

YELLOW-BILLED CUCKOO
Coccyzus americanus

Description: 12". **Grayish brown above, white below;** long tail boldly patterned black and white below. Yellow orbital ring, **decurved bill with yellow lower mandible.** Rufous primaries prominent in flight. JUVENILE'S undertail less boldly marked, bill may be all black. **Voice:** One song a hollow, wooden *kuk-kuk-kuk* usually slowing and descending to a *kakakowlp-kowlp* ending. Also a series of *coo* notes. **Behavior:** Furtive, retiring, slow moving; forages for caterpillars, other large insects in mature riparian forests along larger streams. **Where, When to Find:** Very rare summer resident (June to early September); numbers drastically reduced by habitat loss, perhaps also pesticide use; state Endangered, federally Threatened. Probably still breeds in very small numbers along Sacramento River in Butte and Glenn counties, perhaps sporadically along Eel River in Humboldt County; casual elsewhere in migration.

GREATER ROADRUNNER *Geococcyx californianus*

Description: 23". An unmistakable large **ground bird** with **streaked breast** and upperparts, **long** green-glossed **tail, bushy crest,** and (at close range) bare red and blue facial skin. **Voice:** Call (delivered from atop a fencepost or shrub) is a slow, descending series of mournful cooing notes, suggesting a whimpering dog. Also gives a clacking rattle with the bill. **Behavior:** Terrestrial, usually flies only when chased. Runs or walks, then raises and lowers tail slowly after stopping. Eats small reptiles, large ground insects, even small birds. **Similar Species:** Might confuse with Ring-necked Pheasant (p. 71). **Where, When to Find:** Rare to uncommon but widespread year-round resident in open brushy habitats in foothills fringing the Central Valley, the inland side of coastal mountains south of San Francisco, and the Great Basin region south of Crowley Lake.

Did you know? Roadrunners are ground-inhabiting cuckoos, and their footprints show the typical cuckoo pattern of two forward- and two backward-directed toes.

Date & Location Seen: _____

_____

Snowy Owl

escription: 16″. A medium-sized, very **pale buffy, gray and white** owl of open country, with **dark eyes** and a **heart-shaped face**. FEMALES usually deep buff on underparts, MALES usually white. Large, rounded head shows no "ear" tufts.

ice: Commonly heard territorial call is a long, rasping screech, often uttered in flight in the evening. Young birds beg with a short screech.

havior: Active at night, when it hunts for rodents, often with long, coursing flights. Sits quietly during the day in trees or within structures (old barns and outbuildings, bridges). Nests in large tree cavities, ledges, old buildings, stacks of hay bales, or suitably large nest boxes, such as in vineyards.

milar Species: No other owl in the region combines dark eyes and very pale plumage. Among regularly occurring owls, only Short-eared Owl (p. 235) is nearly as pale. Much larger **Snowy Owl** (*Bubo scandiacus*, 23″) has yellow eyes; can be all white, white with dense blackish barring, or intermediate. This casual winter visitor from the Arctic has occurred in our region in only seven winters since 1900.

here, When to Find: Fairly common (but secretive) year-round resident throughout much of the region in low- to mid-elevation grasslands, agricultural areas, and open forests and woodlands. Scarcer away from these low-elevation habitats and in colder areas, from which it may withdraw in winter. Resides also in urban areas, often nesting in palm trees or artificial structures. Avoids dense forests, rare at higher elevations. Road-killed birds are often seen along major highways, especially I-5 in the San Joaquin Valley.

d you know? On average, Barn Owls breed more frequently, and have larger clutches and shorter life spans, than other owls in our region.

ate & Location Seen: _____

Description: 8 ½". A **small**, finely marked **grayish** owl with **yellow eyes,** short "ear" tufts (often not visible), **white spotted scapulars and coverts.** Like most of our small owls, it is best found and identified by voice.

Voice: Territorial song is an accelerating "bouncing ball" series of short, low whistles *hoo hoo hoo-hoo-hoo-oo-oo-oo.* When more excited, birds utter a "double trill" – a short, low-pitched trill followed after a moment's pause by a longer trill. When very agitated – for example by humans imitating their song – birds may utter short, sharp barks, usually transitioning into "bouncing ball" or "double trill" songs after a while.

Behavior: A nocturnal perch hunter of small rodents and large insects; almost never seen during the day, when it retreats to tree cavities (where it also nests). Usually found in pairs. Can often be lured into view at night by imitating its vocalizations.

Similar Species: Flammulated Owl (p. 459) of mountain forests is smaller, with dark eyes and different voice. Buff and brown Northern Saw-whet Owl (p. 237) lacks "ear" tufts and fine plumage patterning. Compare with larger Long-eared Owl (p. 235).

Where, When to Find: Widespread year-round resident in riparian strips and lowland, foothill, and mountain woodlands west of the Cascade/Sierra Nevada crest. Most common in oak-dominated forests. Fairly common locally in Inyo County in tracts of pinyon pines, riparian woodlands, and planted trees at towns and ranches. Fairly common in oak-dominated forests in southwestern Modoc County, less so in juniper woodlands and other habitats elsewhere in the county.

Did you know? Western Screech-Owls residing in humid north coast areas are browner than those in drier parts of the region. Owls' "ear" tufts are feather tufts that signal species identity and behavioral state. They have no connection with owls' well-developed auditory capabilities.

Date & Location Seen:

_____

_____

Description: 22". Our familiar **large, tufted** owl. Size of a Red-tailed Hawk, with **yellow eyes** set in a **broad facial disk** whose color varies geographically; finely barred and streaked brown, gray and white plumage. Conspicuous **white throat.** FEMALES are larger than MALES.

Voice: Often heard rhythmic hooting, especially near dawn and dusk: *hoo-HOO, HOO, HOO* or *hoo-hoo-HOO, HOO-HOO;* higher-pitched in females than males. Fledged young give a rising shriek.

Behavior: Hunts nocturnally from a perch for rodents, snakes, large ground insects (such as Jerusalem crickets), and sometimes even smaller owls. Calling birds often sit conspicuously atop tall trees, utility poles. Pairs often sing duets.

Similar Species: Far larger than our other common resident owls. Compare with Long-eared Owl's (p. 235) longer and more closely spaced "ear" tufts, rufous facial disk, more streaked underparts. Forest-dwelling brown Barred Owl (p. 233) and dark brown Spotted Owl (p. 233) both have large, round heads and dark eyes, and lack "ear" tufts.

Where, When to Find: Widespread resident throughout the region, nesting from sea level to 7000' elevation. Found in nearly all habitats that provide suitable nest sites (cliff ledges, broken tree trunks, old hawk nests), but avoids dense coniferous forests. Found in many residential areas and large urban parks, but absent from the most heavily urbanized areas.

Did you know? Except for Barn Owl – which may nest during any month of the year, Great Horned Owl is our earliest nesting owl, with females often on eggs by mid-January.

Date & Location Seen: _____

Description: 6 ¾". A **very small grayish-brown owl** with **yellow eyes** that is **boldly striped below.** It has a **relatively small head** that's dotted with small white spots, **prominent "false eyes"** on its nape, **no "ear" tufts**, and a relatively **long tail.**

Voice: Call (given in early morning; less often later in day and at dusk) is a series of piping *toots*, given at 2-3 second intervals; also a rapid trill that may transition to normal tooting. Imitating its call will often attract small woodland birds intent on "mobbing" their potential predator. Its call can be confused with similar sharp call notes uttered by Mountain Quail, and by some chipmunk species.

Behavior: An aggressive, mainly diurnal predator; most active in the morning and early evening. Hunts rodents and lizards from a perch, and captures perched birds with quick, shrike-like flights. Can take prey much larger than itself.

Similar Species: Western Screech-Owl (p. 225) is larger and grayish overall, has "ear" tufts and a short tail, and lacks "false eyes." Northern Saw-whet Owl (p. 237) is larger, has a big head, a prominent facial disk, and a short tail; lacks "ear" tufts and "false eyes."

Where, When to Find: Absent from the floor of the Central Valley, otherwise widespread although sparsely distributed throughout the region. Resident along riparian strips, in foothill oak and pine woodlands, and in mixed conifer forests and along mountain meadow edges to at least 7000' elevation.

Did you know? In *The Distribution of the Birds of California*, Grinnell and Miller describe its status as "Usually, where detected at all, 'common,' for an owl." Translation: it can seemingly pop up anywhere within the habitats described above.

Date & Location Seen:

Description: 9 ½". A **pigeon-sized, long-legged, ground-dwelling** owl of dry open country. **Yellow eyes,** broad white chin and **white "eyebrows"** are distinctive; lacks "ear" tufts. Body plumage spotted and barred, brown and white.

Voice: Rasping, barking notes, such as *kwik-kwik-kwik*.

Behavior: Often visible during the day, perching on earthen levees, fence posts, concrete cisterns, or on the ground; perched birds bob up and down when agitated. Nests in dis-used mammal burrows or artificial holes in the ground. Flight is low, with quick flaps and a glide. Forages mainly at dusk and at night, hunting insects and small mammals from a perch or in low, ranging flight; often hovers when foraging.

Similar Species: Unmistakable; other small, yellow-eyed owls dwell in woodlands or forests, and are much shorter-legged. Short-eared Owl (p. 235), also of open country and partly diurnal, is much larger and buffier, with long streaks below; its characteristic slow, mothlike flight much different than Burrowing Owl's.

Where, When to Find: Uncommon year-round resident in the Central Valley's grasslands, mostly on private land. More scarce in the valleys of Modoc, Lassen, and Plumas counties, and in Inyo County. Small numbers persist in urbanized former agricultural areas around San Francisco Bay and nearby counties. In fall and winter a few birds are found along the coast in areas where breeding is not known; some reach the Farallon Islands. These may represent migrants from the Great Basin or from other breeding areas outside the state that are snowed over in winter.

Did you know? Loss of grassland habitat due to urbanization and changing agricultural practices are ongoing threats, as is the poisoning of ground squirrels whose burrows these owls depend upon for nesting. A state Species of Special Concern.

Date & Location Seen: _____

Spotted Owl
occidentalis

Barred Owl

Description: 18". A midsized **plump brown owl, spotted whitish above and below. Large, round head, no "ear" tufts, dark eyes, brownish facial disk. Voice**: Common territorial call a barking *hoo, hu-hu, HOOO*; other vocalizations include barks and rising whistles. **Behavior**: Forages nocturnally on wood rats, flying squirrels, other small mammals. **Similar Species**: Closely related to Barred Owl (below), but tamer and strictly nocturnal. **Where, When to Find**: Fairly common resident in shady mature coniferous and mixed forests and wooded canyons in coastal mountains south through Marin County (federally Threatened subspecies *caurina*); also (state Species of Special Concern *occidentalis*) from 3000' to 5500' mostly on the west side of the Cascade/Sierra Nevada range south through Tulare County, and in Monterey County. Declining due to forest management practices and competition from Barred Owls.

BARRED OWL *Strix varia*

Description: 21". **Chunky brown owl** with a **barred breast** and a **streaked belly**; whitish spots on head and back. **Large, round head, no "ear" tufts, dark eyes, pale facial disk. Voice**: Common territorial call a rhythmic series of loud *whoo's: who-cooks-for-you, who-cooks-for-you-all*. More likely than other large owls to call during the day. **Behavior**: Preys upon small mammals, also on amphibians, reptiles, and invertebrates. More aggressive than Spotted Owl, with strong circumstantial evidence of preying upon them. Displaces them from prime habitat; also hybridizes, producing "Sparred Owls" with intermediate appearance and vocalizations. **Where, When to Find**: Habitat and range same as Spotted's (except absent from Monterey County); much less numerous. Scarce south of Plumas County.

Did you know? Barred Owl, formerly limited to eastern forests, reached Washington by 1965, Oregon by 1972, California by 1981, Marin County by 2002, Tulare County by 2004, and Inyo County by 2016.

Date & Location Seen: _____

Long-eared Owl

Short-eared Owl

Long-eared Owl

Short-eared Owl

Description: 15″. **Slender**, with **yellow eyes, long "ear" tufts, rusty facial disk, bold blackish streaks and crossbars on underparts. Voice:** Generally silent except when breeding. MALE'S territorial song a series of 10 or more soft *whoo* notes, 2-4 seconds apart; FEMALE's version more nasal, higher-pitched. **Behavior**: Preys nocturnally on small rodents, coursing low over open country. Nests in nearby woodlands, using other species' old stick nests. **Similar Species:** Larger, chunkier Great Horned Owl has more widely spaced tufts; underparts differ. **Where, When to Find:** Uncommon resident throughout the region except nearly absent from the Central Valley floor and more urban areas; perhaps most numerous in the northeastern part of the region. Winter visitors augment numbers somewhat. Roosts mainly in dense willows, conifers, or broad-leafed trees, sitting vertically near the trunk. Small groups gather in winter roosts, e.g., at Mercey Hot Springs, Fresno County.

SHORT-EARED OWL *Asio flammeus*

Description: 15″. A **plump-looking** owl with **yellow eyes, short "ear" tufts** rarely visible, long **brownish stripes on buffy breast, whitish belly. Voice:** Generally silent. Male hoots and claps wings in display flight; both sexes bark, scream, or whine in nest defense. **Behavior**: Courses low over marshes and grasslands with moth-like wing beats, foraging for small mammals. May hunt at any hour, but mainly crepuscular. In flight, differs from Long-eared Owl (above) in underwing and underpart patterns, flight style. Nests and generally roosts on the ground. **Where, When to Find:** Uncommon. Breeding largely limited to wildlife refuges, most regularly in the northeastern part of the region and in Suisun Marsh. Winter visitors may augment residents many-fold, might then be seen over marshes or grasslands anywhere in the region.

Did you know? Because of apparent population declines, both of these owls are listed as state Species of Special Concern.

Date & Location Seen:

235

Juvenile

Description: 8". A small nocturnal forest owl with a **puffy head, no "ear" tufts, yellow eyes**, white eyebrows, white spotting on wings, and **broad reddish-brown streaks below**. Distinctive JUVENILE plumage is seen about May-September: **dark reddish brown above, tawny rust below.**

Voice: Territorial song is a long, monotonous series of low, whistled *toot* notes, about two per second. Also utters sharp squirrel-like squeals and barks, and a chilling, rising wail.

Behavior: Strictly nocturnal. Hunts rodents from a perch, nests in woodpecker holes, readily uses nest boxes. In breeding season, roosts in or near nest cavity; in winter, roosts in dense vegetation. Once found it can often be approached quite closely.

Similar Species: Western Screech-Owl (p. 225) is grayish overall, has "ear" tufts; Flammulated Owl (p. 459) is smaller, rusty-brown overall, has seldom visible "ear" tufts; both have very different calls. Northern Pygmy-Owl's tooting is much slower, one toot every 2-3 seconds.

Where, When to Find: Uncommon resident in mixed and coniferous forests from near sea level to at least 8,000'. Some move downslope from northerly or snowed-over areas in winter, when they may occasionally be found as well in willow thickets, brushland and other unlikely-looking habitats. Casual in the Central Valley.

Did you know? Reportedly gets its name because a vocalization (likely the juvenile's begging call) resembles the sound made by whetting a saw with a file. Another suggested origin is a corrupted pronunciation of the French word *chouette*, meaning "small owl."

Date & Location Seen: _____

**Lesser Nighthawk
Male**

**Common Nighthawk
Male**

LESSER NIGHTHAWK
Chordeiles acutipennis

Description: 8 ½ ". Nighthawks are aerial feeders, mainly at dusk and dawn. They have long notched tails and **long, pointed wings** with a **prominent whitish band across the primaries near the tip; throat patch white** in MALES, **buffish** in FEMALES. Like Common Nighthawk (below), but **inner wing** ("arm") **broader, outer wing** ("hand") **shorter, wing tip rounder. Voice:** A quiet, low seconds-long trill given in flight and while perched. **Behavior**: Hides on ground or low branch by day; foraging flights with erratic swoops and flutters. Nests on the ground in gravel washes. **Similar Species:** Smaller Common Poorwill (p. 241) has short, rounded tail and unbanded round wings. **Where, When to Find:** Uncommon and local summer resident (April to August) mainly around the fringes of the southern Central and Salinas valleys, and in the Great Basin region from Fish Slough, Mono County, southward.

COMMON NIGHTHAWK *Chordeiles minor*

Description: 9 ½ ". **White wing band** is broad on MALES, thinner on FEMALES, and **close to the base of the primaries.** Male shows white tail bar. **Voice:** Diagnostic nasal *peent* call is given even in migration. In steep courtship display dive, male's wings make a hollow booming sound. **Behavior:** Roosts by day on ground, fence post, or lengthwise on a tree's branch. Foraging flight graceful, with continuous deep flapping and sporadic gliding. Nests on the ground. **Where, When to Find:** Uncommon summer resident (late May to August) in Humboldt and Del Norte counties, eastward to Modoc County and south through the Sierra Nevada (mainly east side) and Great Basin region.

d you know? Nighthawks and poorwills are in the family Caprimulgidae (from the Latin *caper*, a goat, and *mulgere*, to milk); derived from an incorrect legend that they fed on goat's milk, hence their historical name "goatsuckers."

te & Location Seen:

Male

scription: 7 ¾ ". A small goatsucker with a **large, flat-topped head** and **short, rounded tail**. Intricate **"dead-leaf" pattern** of brown, tan, gray, black and silver; throat black with white band below. **White** (MALE) **or buffy** (FEMALE) **tail corners**.

ice: Distinctive, plaintive *poor-will* (*poor-will-ip* heard at closer range) is given repeatedly (about once every 1.5 sec), often for minutes on end. Gruff *wuk* or *wep* given in flight.

havior: Most vocal and active at dusk and dawn, and on moonlit nights, but may feed and call much of the night when the air is warm. Roosts and nests on the ground; sallies up from ground in erratic, floppy flight to catch moths, beetles, etc. Capable of entering a state of torpor daily, apparently in response to low ambient temperature and/or food shortage.

milar Species: Lesser and Common Nighthawks (p. 239) both have longer tails, wing bands, and spend much time in flight (often in daylight).

here, When to Find: Common summer resident (May to August) in chaparral, dry woodlands, steep mountain slopes, and rocky areas throughout, to about 6,000' elevation. Often seen along roads or roadsides after dusk or before dawn. Nests usually on bare ground, often somewhat shaded. Populations migratory at higher elevations and from northerly areas, but timing and routes poorly known; a few may hibernate, but probably most leave the region. Sometimes found in coastal locations during winter months.

d you know? Meriwether Lewis was apparently first to write of Common Poorwill's ability to become torpid. In North Dakota on October 16, 1804, the temperature about 30°, he wrote, "This day took a small bird alive of the order of the ... goat suckers. It appeared to be passing into the dormant state."

ate & Location Seen:

scription: 4 ¾". A tiny, dark gray-brown **aerial bird** with rapid twinkling wing beats; like a "cigar with wings." **Dusky**, with **paler grayish throat**, **breast** and **rump**. **Short squared tail** has spiny tips to all feathers.

ice: A very high, rapid chippering, often running into an insect-like trill. Very vocal around roost sites, on breeding grounds, and within foraging flocks; migrants are usually silent.

havior: On the wing all day, with frantic flight consisting of rapid, stiff wing beats and short glides. Large evening roosting concentrations may occur in redwood snags and urban and suburban chimneys and building shafts in both spring and fall. Roost gatherings in towns such as Arcata, Garberville, Healdsburg and San Rafael may contain several hundred birds. The sight of these swifts swirling over and then dropping into roost cavities is unforgettable!

ilar Species: White-throated Swift (p. 245) is larger, with longer wings and longer pointed tail; plumage more contrasting blackish and white. Swallows have looser flight on more flexed wings, are usually contrastingly pale on underparts.

ere, When to Find: Common and widespread migrant from mid-April to mid-May, and again from late August through September. Most often seen in numbers during inclement weather, when flocks often concentrate over lakes and reservoirs with swallows. Breeds (May through August) in north coastal and montane coniferous forests, mainly from Santa Cruz Mts. north in coastal regions and locally on the west slope of the central and northern Sierra Nevada; a few breed locally in Ft. Bidwell and in southwestern Modoc County. Breeding mainly in mature forests, it is listed as a state Species of Special Concern.

l you know? Although spectacular roosts may occur in some of our urban buildings, this species may also "roost" on the wing at night.

te & Location Seen: _____

White-throated Swift

Black Swift

Description: 6 ½". An accomplished scythe-winged aerialist with bold patterning. **Blackish-brown with white throat** coming to a point on the lower breast, **white flanks and rump-sides. Long tail** has a shallow fork, but is **usually carried in a point.** White markings often hard to see, so distinctive shape (long, thin wings, elongated rear body and tail) help identify it.

Voice: A long, descending series of rapid notes, *jee-jee-jee....*

Behavior: On the wing all day, often at great heights. Flight combines rapid wing beats and glides. May fly low over freshwater ponds, lakes. Roosts throughout year and nests in spring, summer in crevices in cliff faces, also crevices and weep holes in highway overpasses and bridges.

Similar Species: Black Swift (*Cypseloides niger*, 7 ¼") is **entirely blackish**, with **broad and only slightly notched tail**, broad wings angled at wrist; flight mainly long glides. A scarce migrant (mainly late May-early June and September), with small numbers nesting in coastal cliffs and canyons of Monterey and Santa Cruz counties and behind waterfalls in rugged canyons from Siskiyou, Trinity and Shasta counties south locally through the Sierra Nevada; foraging birds can range great distances from the nest. A state Species of Special Concern.

Where, When to Find: Uncommon to fairly common (but local) summer resident in mountains, canyons, and cliffs in coastal regions mostly from the San Francisco Bay area south, and at lower elevations on the Sierra Nevada's west side; also on the east side and in mountain ranges of eastern Mono and Inyo counties. Has adapted to highway structures in urban areas, including several (e.g., Stockton) in the Central Valley. Forages widely. More localized in winter.

Did you know? The Black Swift's wintering grounds were recently found to be in the western Amazon region of South America.

Date & Location Seen: _____

Adult Male

Immature

escription: 3 ¾″. A spring and summer hummingbird, **bill long** and slightly decurved, head small and squared. MALE: **Chin black, lower throat bordered violet** (looks black in most lighting); **white spot behind eye; broad white collar** below throat; sides and flanks olive, upperparts deep green; tail blackish, slightly forked. FEMALE: **Chin and throat whitish,** slight buff wash on flanks, tail with white corners.

oice: Soft, squeaky *hew* or *tew* notes; soft, sputtering rattle. Male's wings make dry reeling buzz in flight.

ehavior: Wags tail vigorously when hovering. Male's display flight is a rapid series of low, shallow arcs with an audible dry wing buzz. Distinctive nest is soft and smooth, often built from straw-colored fuzz from undersurface of sycamore leaves.

milar Species: The gorget (iridescent area on chin, throat) of males of other species may look black under poor lighting conditions; sides of gorget of Anna's (p. 249) and especially Costa's are more elongated. Female Anna's is larger, dingier on underparts; Anna's does not bob tail. Female Costa's has shorter bill and tail, lacks buff on flanks, has long grayish white eyeline connecting with pale gray neck sides. All differ in calls.

here, When to Find: Summer visitor (mid-April to August) in foothill and valley woodlands (cottonwoods, alders, and especially sycamores), oak woodlands, well-wooded residential areas and parks. Mainly away from the immediate coast, north to the south and east San Francisco Bay area, and throughout the Central Valley. Fairly common in the Owens Valley; scarcer farther north, east of the Sierra Nevada. More widespread in migration, but rare after mid-September; winters in Mexico.

d you know? The Black-chin's closest relative is the Ruby-throated Hummingbird – the familiar eastern North America species which has occurred in Northern California only about a dozen times.

te & Location Seen: _____

Anna's Hummingbird
Adult Male

Anna's Hummingbird
Female

Costa's Hummingbird
Adult Male

Costa's Hummingbird
Female

Description: 4". An abundant year-round resident and our largest hummingbird (though still diminutive). MALE: **Crown, chin,** and **throat brilliant rose red;** whitish ring around eye; upperparts iridescent green, underparts mostly olive-gray. FEMALE: Color on head is limited to **variable red patch in center of throat;** underparts dingy grayish; tail corners white. JUVENILES lack red on throat.

Voice: Soft *chip* notes and scratchy *chicka-chicka-chika* series. Male song is a scratchy, squeaky series in a distinctive rhythm.

Behavior: Males perch conspicuously; display consists of slow, steep climb to 50-100', then a high-speed dive with a loud *peek!* sound as the bird pulls out.

Similar Species: Costa's Hummingbird (*C. costae,* 3 ½") is smaller, male's gorget purple, more elongated at sides. Relatively short-billed and short-tailed; female has long whitish supercilium that extends down behind ear coverts and connects with grayish white throat sides. Calls are high, soft *pit* notes (suggesting a Bushtit) and a high, sputtering *pit-it-it-trrrrrr* series. Male gives very high-pitched, prolonged *ziinngggggg,* rising then falling in pitch. Uncommon breeder, mainly in inner Coast Ranges of Monterey County, foothills on the San Joaquin Valley's western fringe, arid areas of southern Mono County, and Inyo County; rare winter visitor on coast.

Where, When to Find: Common throughout the year in the coastal lowlands and foothills (scarce east of the Sierra Nevada, but fairly common in southwestern Modoc County); more widespread in the higher mountains April to September. A few remain in the coldest areas in winter where feeders or sufficient ornamental flowers are available. Found in urban areas, parks, chaparral, and woodlands; can be especially abundant around groves of winter-flowering eucalyptus.

Did you know? Recent studies confirm that the explosive popping sound at the bottom of the male's display dive is made by the spread tail feathers.

Date & Location Seen: _____

Rufous Hummingbird
Adult Male

Allen's Hummingbird
Adult Male

Female

Rufous Hummingbird
Selasphorus rufus

Description: 3 ¾". Migrant hummingbird with much rufous in the plumage. MALE: Gorget bright red to orange-red; crown green; **back, rump, tail, sides and flanks rufous.** FEMALE: Throat and breast whitish; **sides and flanks washed cinnamon;** some **rufous at base of tail.** IMMATURE male has some red on throat, more rufous on body and tail than female. **Voice:** Hard *tewk…tewk* calls and an excited *zeeeee-chuppity-chuppity.* Wings of adult male make a musical trilling sound. **Behavior:** Very aggressive; dominates feeders. **Similar Species:** Allen's (below) nearly identical, but adult males extensively green above; pin-like outer tail feathers are narrower than in Rufous. See also Calliope (p. 461) and Broad-tailed (p. 471). **Where, When to Find:** Fairly common spring (mid-February to early May) and fall (late June to mid-September) migrant; spring passage mainly in lowlands and foothills, in fall many move through the high elevations. Breeds just north of our region (Oregon to Alaska), winters in Mexico.

Allen's Hummingbird *Selasphorus sasin*

Description: 3 ¾". Fairly common coastal hummingbird with rufous in the plumage. MALE: Gorget bright red to orange-red; crown and **back green; rump, tail, sides and flanks rufous.** Females, immatures almost identical to Rufous. **Voice** and **Behavior** like Rufous, but display dive of male preceded by several shallow arcs ("pendulum display"), and dive is steeper and not repeated in rapid succession; breathy *pfvvvvvvvv* sound at bottom of dive. **Where, When to Find:** Summer resident (mainly February through June) in gardens, urban parks, coastal sage, and willows along the entire coast within, and for a short distance east of, the humid fog belt. Southbound migrants (mainly late June and July) pass rarely through the southern Sierra Nevada. Allen's and Rufous casual from October to early January.

Did you know? Complicating the identification issue, a few adult male Rufous (above) have green backs like Allen's.

Date & Location Seen: _____

Male

Female

Description: 13″. A distinctive, boldly plumaged water-bound bird with a **bushy crest** giving a large-headed appearance. Male is **blue-gray above, white below,** with a blue-gray band across the upper breast; white patch on primaries shows in flight. Female is similar to male, but with additional **rusty band across lower breast** and onto sides and flanks. JUVENILES of both sexes have single band (mixed blue and rust) across chest and rusty on flanks.

Voice: Loud, harsh staccato rattle frequently announces the kingfisher's presence.

Behavior: Perches with very short legs on branches of waterside trees, shrubs (as well as utility wires). Flies with quick, irregular rowing wing beats; when foraging hovers over water, then plunges in to catch fish, crayfish, and other prey. Nests in long burrows it excavates in friable earthen riverbanks (and occasionally in artificial drainage holes).

Similar Species: Our only kingfisher. Superficially suggests a jay, but behavior utterly different. Other plunge-diving birds, such as terns, are very different in shape and plumage.

Where, When to Find: Rare to uncommon breeding resident along rivers, streams, and the banks of some reservoirs to about 6,000′ throughout the region, except nearly absent from the southern San Joaquin Valley. More numerous and widespread in migration and winter (late July to April), southward and downslope from areas of hard freezing. In winter, found also in coastal wetlands and along the coast.

Did you know? Both sexes help excavate nest burrows. Active burrows that have been measured range from 32 inches to 14 feet long; 3 to 6 feet long seems most common.

Date & Location Seen:

Acorn Woodpecker
Male

Lewis's Woodpecker
Adult

Description: 9″. A noisy and social inhabitant of oak woodlands, this medium-sized woodpecker is **glossy black above** with a **clown-like black, yellow and white face,** black chest, white underparts, and bold **white patches on the wings and rump.** MALE has white forehead, red crown; similar FEMALE has black bar on forecrown in front of the red patch.

Voice: Noisy. A repeated *ja-cob, ja-cob…*or *ratch-et, ratch-et…*along with a variety of grating or cawing calls.

Behavior: Social; nests in small communal groups. These groups harvest and store acorns in conspicuous "granary" trees (or utility poles), returning through the year to consume them. They also sally after flying insects and forage for ants on the ground or tree limbs.

Similar Species: Lewis's Woodpecker (*M. lewis*, 10 ¾″) is an irregular fall and winter visitor (migrates from northern/eastern portions of breeding range, resident elsewhere) to open country with large oaks. Uncommon and local breeder in the Great Basin, Sierra Nevada (especially in burns), and inner Coast Ranges; occasional elsewhere. Rare near the coast. **Glossy greenish black** above with a red face and **pinkish belly; no white** in its plumage. Lewis's flight is direct, crow-like; other woodpeckers' flight is undulating.

Where, When to Find: A conspicuous year-round resident in live oak woodlands and valley oak savannas throughout, and in mountain forests and riparian woodlands where oaks are present. Even urban areas with oaks, such as Sacramento, can host Acorn Woodpeckers, though they've declined in some areas. Found in only a few places on the east side of the Sierra Nevada, and largely absent from extensive areas without oaks (e.g., most of the Modoc region and San Joaquin Valley).

Did you know? Long-running studies at the Hastings Reserve in Monterey County's Carmel Valley and elsewhere have made Acorns one of the best-studied woodpeckers in the world.

Date & Location Seen: _____

Red-breasted Sapsucker
Adult *daggetti*

Hybrid Red-breasted X
Red-naped Sapsucker

Red-naped Sapsucker
Adult Male

escription: 8 ½". A mottled black and white woodpecker with **mostly red head** and **pale yellow belly.** Like all sapsuckers, it shows a long white strip on the wings. The back and central tail feathers are barred with white and the rump is white. Many birds, especially when worn, show some black and white markings on the face.

oice: A querulous, descending *mew* or *kwirr*, but rather silent for a woodpecker. Territorial males of all sapsucker species "drum" in a unique, broken rhythm.

ehavior: Drills distinctive circumferential rows of small holes in tree trunks and limbs, returning to eat sap that collects in these wells (as well as trapped insects). Look for wells on Brazilian peppers, eucalyptus, various orchard trees, and oaks. Quiet and unassuming.

milar Species: Red-naped Sapsucker (*S. nuchalis*, 8 ½") is uncommon in the southeast edge of the region in fall and winter, rare elsewhere. A few (perhaps tens of pairs) likely still breed in the Warner Mts., possibly also in the White Mts. and on the east slope. At the western edge of its range often pairs with Red-breasted, which it closely resembles, but Red-naped has **black bordering the red throat** and a **black bar from behind the eye across the hindcrown** (with a red patch behind this on the nape). Female Red-naped usually shows much white on the chin. Red-breasted x Red-naped hybrids are frequently seen.

here, When to Find: Fairly common resident in mixed deciduous-conifer woodlands in the northwest and throughout the Cascades, Sierra Nevada, and Great Basin mountains (withdrawing from the highest elevations in winter); widespread from October through March in lowlands and foothills, even in residential areas and city parks.

id you know? Despite the apparent damage sapsuckers inflict on trees, there is little evidence to suggest they are an important cause of tree death.

ate & Location Seen: _____

Male

Female

Description: 7 ½". This common small woodpecker has a **zebra-striped back**, black **spotting and barring on the sides, white spotted wings**, and thick black bars on the sides of the head. MALE has a red patch on the rear of the crown, lacking in FEMALE. As in all our woodpeckers of this genus, juveniles of both sexes have some red atop the crown.

Voice: Call is a short, staccato *p-r-r-t*, often drawn out as a long rattle *prt-prt-prrrrrrrrrrrt*; also a loud *quee-quee-quee* when birds interact. Birds on territory give a long steady drum with bill.

Behavior: Forages on trunks, limbs and small branches of a variety of trees (but especially oaks) and chaparral shrubs. Nest cavities are drilled in dead or dying limbs of oaks, sycamores, and other trees.

Similar Species: Ladder-backed Woodpecker (p. 471) is closely similar, limited to desert woodlands of Inyo County. Ladder-backed has relatively wider white bars on the face and back, lacks the solid black uppermost back of Nuttall's, shows buffy cast on underparts, more black barring on outer tail feathers, and male has red extending farther toward forehead. Ladder-back's calls differ.

Where, When to Find: Year-round resident in oak and riparian woodlands, low to middle-elevation mountain forests, tall chaparral, and occasionally suburban neighborhoods; found from the northern fringes of the Sacramento Valley and the western foothills (rare higher) of the Sierra Nevada southward, and in coastal counties from Mendocino County south. Fairly common resident in the Owens Valley.

Did you know? This species is nearly endemic to California, extending a short way south into northwestern Baja California. It is known to hybridize with Ladder-backed and, very rarely, with Downy Woodpeckers.

Date & Location Seen: _____

Downy Woodpecker
Male

Downy Woodpecker
Female

Hairy Woodpecker
Male

Hairy Woodpecker
Female

Description: 6 ¾″. Our **smallest woodpecker**, with **long white back stripe**, buffy-white underparts, and white-spotted wings; outer tail feathers with some black barring. **Bill very short**. MALE has red bar on nape, lacking in FEMALE. **Voice:** Call is a soft *pik*; another distinctive call is a descending whinny, *dee-dee-dee-dee…* Territorial birds give a single drum roll, quieter than that of larger woodpeckers. **Behavior:** An acrobatic woodpecker, foraging on small branches and twigs as often as on larger limbs. **Similar Species:** Compare Hairy Woodpecker (below). Nuttall's Woodpecker (p. 259) has black-and-white barred back and is more heavily marked below. **Where, When to Find:** Year-round resident in lowland and foothill riparian woodlands, as well as in groves of other deciduous trees (including ornamental birches, liquidambars, plane trees in some urban areas). Scarce or absent in the highest mountains, much of Inyo County, and much of the San Joaquin Valley.

HAIRY WOODPECKER *Dryobates villosus*

Description: 9 ¼″. Like a **large version of the sparrow-sized Downy Woodpecker;** note especially the relatively **longer and stronger bill**. Outer tail feathers pure white. Like Downy, only male shows red on nape. **Voice:** Call is a loud, piercing *peek* or *pee-ik*, sharper than Downy's call. These calls may run into a long whinny, louder than Downy's and more nearly on one pitch. Drum is a loud, strong roll. **Behavior:** Bores into bark and wood with strong bill; often concentrates foraging on dead and dying trees. **Where, When to Find:** Conifer-dominated woodlands in foothills, mountains and coastal woodlands throughout; casual non-breeding visitor to floor of Central Valley.

Did you know? Both species have subspecies in our damp north-coastal forests that are strongly washed with brown on the underparts, unlike birds in the rest of our region.

Date & Location Seen:

"Red-shafted"
Male

"Red-shafted"
Female

Description: 12 ½". A large woodpecker. Our "Red-shafted" birds are generally **brown to gray-brown above** with thin black crossbars and **white rump**; buffy white with **round black spots below. Black crescent across chest.** In flight shows **salmon-pink color in underwings** and tail. MALE: Red "whisker" marks, lacking in FEMALE. A few birds seen in late fall and winter show yellow underwing color, red nape crescent, and (in males) black whisker mark; these are "Yellow-shafted" flickers. Intergrades between red- and yellow-shafted birds – far more numerous than "pure" yellow-shafteds – show some "yellow-shafted" characters.

Voice: Common call is a piercing *keeeew* or *kleeew*; also gives a muffled *wur-wur-wur* in flight and a *wick-a wick-a wick-a* series. Territorial birds in breeding season give a long *wik-wik-wik-wik...* series, sometimes followed by a drum.

Behavior: In "unwoodpecker-like" fashion, often forages on the ground for ants, but also forages on trunks and limbs. Flashy underwing color shows prominently in undulating flight.

Similar Species: Unmistakable, but see female Williamson's Sapsucker (p. 461), a smaller, uncommon species of high elevation conifer forests.

Where, When to Find: Resident in woodlands of foothills, mountains, and coastal regions throughout, but has decreased as a breeder in many urban areas. Many migrants move into the area from late September through March, when seen almost anywhere.

Did you know? Eastern/boreal "Yellow-shafted" and western "Red-shafted" flickers intergrade extensively where their ranges overlap on the Great Plains, and birds showing intermediate or combined characters are often seen in our region outside the breeding season.

Date & Location Seen: _____

_____

Male

Female

Description: 16 ½". A **huge**, impressive **black woodpecker** with **red crest, white neck stripe,** white underwing-linings and patch at base of flight feathers. MALE with red forehead and whisker; these areas are black in the FEMALE.

Voice: Common call is a long series of slightly tinny *hee-hee-hee-hee...* notes or coarser *wuk wuk, wuk...* notes, given in flight and while perched. Male's territorial drumming is loud, slow, and powerful; can be short or up to three seconds long, accelerating and then trailing off at the end.

Behavior: Forcefully and audibly flakes bark and wood from dead and dying trunks and branches, working from near the ground on fallen logs to high on trunks of the tallest sequoias and firs.

Similar Species: Its large size and crest distinguish it from all of our other woodpeckers; the white wing linings are also distinctive in flight. Size and flight are suggestive of the American Crow (p. 305); note the white in the wing.

Where, When to Find: Coastal and coast range conifer and conifer-oak woodlands, south to the Santa Cruz Mts. (where expanding), and mature forests at middle elevations in the mountains from Mt. Shasta and Lassen Peak south through the west side of the Sierra Nevada (with a few eastward into the Tahoe Basin and Modoc County). This species is most at home where the tallest redwoods, sequoias, pines and firs grow.

Did you know? With the extinction of the Ivory-billed Woodpecker, this is the largest extant woodpecker in North America.

Date & Location Seen: _____

Adult Male

Adult Male

Female

escription: 9", wingspan 22". A small, **dainty** falcon with slender, pointed wings, a long tail and buoyant flight. Note **two** distinctive **black stripes on sides of head.** MALE: Blue-gray wings, **rusty back, rusty tail** with black tip; buff below with black spotting (immature has brown streaks). FEMALE: Larger, with barred rusty back, wings and tail; underparts with reddish streaking.

oice: High *killy killy killy killy* in a series. Most vocal during the breeding season.

ehavior: Perches openly on wires, antennas, treetops. Flight is buoyant, with rapid, shallow wing beats. Often hovers to spot prey, including insects, lizards, small rodents and birds. Nests in tree cavity or hollow within palm fronds.

milar Species: Merlin (p. 269) is a stockier falcon with more powerful, direct flight; usually shows white eyebrow, heavily streaked underparts, solid gray or brown upperparts; lacks two distinct face stripes. Sharp-shinned Hawk (p. 115) has short, rounded wings, solid gray or brown back, very different hunting behavior and habitat.

here, When to Find: Fairly common to common resident throughout the region. Numbers are reduced in coastal regions in summer and in the Great Basin and especially the Sierra Nevada in winter. Over much of the region it is most numerous in winter. An early spring migrant (late March through April). Fall migration begins in August.

id you know? Various subspecies of kestrels live from Alaska all the way to the southern tip of South America. Other related species are found in the Old World. One, the larger Eurasian Kestrel (*F. tinnunculus*, 13 ½"), a casual visitor to North America, was once caught and photographed in fall at Hawk Hill, Marin County. It has only a single facial stripe.

ate & Location Seen:

suckleyi

Adult Male
richardsoni

Juvenile
columbarius

escription: 10", wingspan 24". A **small** but **powerfully built** falcon. Variable. ADULT MALE is a variable shade of gray and FEMALES and JUVENILES vary from pale to nearly blackish-brown, depending upon the subspecies. Head shows thin white eyebrow (lacking in darkest birds) but no strong markings. All ages and sexes are streaked below. Taiga breeding *columbarius* is our most common subspecies. Its plumage is intermediate (individually variable) between pale *richardsoni* breeding on the northern Great Plains, and darkest *suckleyi*, with indistinct tail bands, breeding in humid forests from western British Columbia to southeast Alaska.

oice: Rather harsh calls are heard around the nest, not in our region.

ehavior: Primarily hunts flocking birds (e.g., larks, pipits, small shorebirds) in open areas with its fast, powerful flight. Perches most frequently near tops of trees, but will sit on posts, occasionally poles and even on the ground. Does not hover. Often quite approachable.

milar Species: Peregrine Falcon hunts and flies in a manner similar to Merlin; it is much larger and broader winged, with a broad dark moustachial stripe. Compare American Kestrel (p. 267).

here, When to Find: Uncommon migrant and winter visitor (mid-September to mid-April, a few earlier and later) nearly throughout the region. All three subspecies occur throughout; *columbarius* is most numerous in all regions. Pale *richardsoni* is most frequently encountered in large open areas, mirroring its haunts on the northern Great Plains. Darkest *suckleyi* (some *columbarius* also quite dark) is the scarcest subspecies; most probably occur in the western portions of our region.

id you know? Merlins have notably increased their numbers in recent decades. This Holarctic species was described by Linnaeus, the Swedish botanist, in 1758, interestingly from a winter-taken specimen from South Carolina. Six other subspecies occur in the Old World (including Sweden!).

ate & Location Seen: _____

**Peregrine Falcon
Adult**

**Peregrine Falcon
Juvenile**

Prairie Falcon

Prairie Falcon

Description: 16", wingspan 41". A heavy falcon with amazingly fast and powerful flight. At rest, wingtips reach or nearly reach tail tip. Always shows **thick black moustache** on side of the face. ADULT: **Slate-gray above;** creamy buff underparts, **black barring on lower breast and belly.** Tail gray with narrow black bars; underwing barred with black. JUVENILE: Sooty-brown above, heavily streaked below. **Voice:** A loud and harsh *ray ray ray* series and softer *ee-chup* calls heard near nest. **Behavior:** Hunts for birds by stooping upon them in rapid dive and hitting them with large, powerful feet. Perches on bare limbs, cliff faces, utility poles and building ledges. **Similar Species:** Compare with smaller Merlin (p. 269) and especially Prairie Falcon (below). **Where, When to Find:** Uncommon but widespread resident nearly throughout region, but quite rare in the Sierra Nevada and Great Basin in winter. Hunts over wetlands; routine now in cities (where often hunts Rock Pigeons).

PRAIRIE FALCON *Falco mexicanus*

Description: 16", wingspan 40". A large pale brown falcon of open areas, including rocky hills (especially for nesting) and grasslands. Like immature Peregrine, but paler brown; face stripe thinner; long pale eyebrow. In flight, **blackish "armpits" continue into broad bar on underwing. Voice:** Generally silent except around the nest; calls are higher-pitched than Peregrine's. **Behavior:** More apt to be found away from wetland areas than Peregrine, preferring vast open areas. Readily sits on poles, rock piles, isolated treetops, etc. **Where, When to Find:** Uncommon resident in the Great Basin, Inyo County, and western fringes of the Central Valley; otherwise, mainly an uncommon to rare winter visitant (late August to April; few through summer); scarcest on coast.

Did you know? Through intensive management, including captive breeding and bans on certain pesticides, Peregrine Falcons have recovered from severe declines in the mid-20th century.

Date & Location Seen: _____

271

Olive-sided Flycatcher

Western Wood-Pewee

scription: 7 ½". A **bull-headed** flycatcher. Faintly streaked olive sides, **distinct white stripe down center of underparts; white patches** may show above wings when perched. Wings long, tail short. **Does not flick wings or tail. Voice:** Song heard on breeding grounds, a loud, whistled *what PEEVES you!* with the middle note higher. Call a series of *pip* notes. **Behavior**: Sits conspicuously atop tallest available perch, often a snag. Undertakes long aerial pursuits of flying insects, often returning to same perch. **Similar Species:** See Western Wood-Pewee (below). **Where, When to Find:** Fairly common summer resident (late April-September) in coniferous and mixed woodlands of the coast and the mountains. A rare migrant (May, late August-September) away from breeding areas; more numerous in the Great Basin. A state Species of Special Concern.

WESTERN WOOD-PEWEE *Contopus sordidulus*

scription: 6 ¼". A **drab peak-headed flycatcher,** olive above, grayish below; wings long and pointed; tail moderately long. **Does not flick wings or tail.** Lacks eye ring, wing-bars not bold. **Voice**: Common call a burry descending *breeeur*. "Dawn" song more complex, repeated monotonously, e.g., *breeeur pur-dil-ip*. Also gives a clearer, slightly descending, *PEE-ur* note. **Behavior**: Perches rather upright, often conspicuously. Foraging sallies usually not as high as Olive-sided Flycatcher's; often returns to same perch. Usually in trees but migrants sit on fences, etc. **Similar Species:** Larger Olive-sided has shorter tail, blockier head, distinct white stripe down underparts. See Willow Flycatcher (p. 275). **Where, When to Find**: Fairly common to common summer resident (May to early September) in wooded sections throughout region. More widespread in migration (mid-May to early June, mid-August to mid-September).

d you know? Although considered monotypic, eastern (and northern) Olive-sided Flycatcher populations give a distinctly different song from western birds, accenting the last rather than the middle note.

te & Location Seen: _____

Spring

Fall Immature

Description: 5 ¾". The small look-alike *Empidonax* flycatchers can all be separated from similar appearing pewees by their distinctive tail movements while perched; all but Gray flick their tail initially up. Within the genus they are identified by their calls, subtle plumage differences, bill size, and wing and tail length. Willow **lacks an eye ring**, and has a relatively **long, broad bill** (all orangish underneath). Throat whitish, upperparts washed olive; underparts mostly pale; dull whitish wing-bars (in western subspecies, bolder in eastern birds). JUVENILE: Wing-bars buffy (dull whitish in adults).

Voice: Call is a rich *whit*. Song (often heard in spring migration and sometimes in early fall) is a snappy, burry *WITZ-beeeur!*, also a rough *breeet*.

Behavior: Flicks tail up like nearly all other *Empidonax*. Migrants are often found in somewhat open areas perching on fence lines, etc. Birds on breeding territory spend most of their time foraging within willows.

Similar Species: All of our other *Empidonax* have strong eye rings. Pacific-slope and Cordilleran (p. 281) are more green and yellow; Hammond's (p. 277) has a tiny, dark bill; Dusky (p. 279) is grayer overall; Gray (p. 279) dips tail downward. Most misidentifications involve the generally much more numerous Western Wood-Pewee. Willow Flycatchers are a little more olive above, their lower mandible lacks a strongly dark tip, and they have much shorter wings. Always watch for the diagnostic (compared to pewees) tail flicking: if over time the bird has not flicked its tail, it's probably a pewee.

Where, When to Find: Uncommon spring (mid-May to mid-June) and fairly common fall (August-September) migrant throughout region, though scarcer along the coastal slope. Local, uncommon, and declining breeder in the mountains (mid-elevations) and the Great Basin in scrubby wet willows.

Did you know? Breeding populations have catastrophically declined in California over the last century; state listed as Endangered.

Date & Location Seen: _____

Hammond's Flycatcher

Hammond's Flycatcher
Fall

scription: 5 ½". Our smallest *Empidonax*, with **small, dark tipped (often mostly dark) lower mandible,** relatively short tail, **olive-gray breast, sides and flanks, grayish head, long wingtips.** White eye ring gives it a kinglet-like appearance. Fresh fall birds much more yellow and olive overall, but always with a gray chin.

ice: Call, a soft *peep*, unlike our other *Empidonax*; migrants often silent, especially in fall. Song (heard only on the breeding grounds) is a series of three phrases, the second one being low pitched and rough.

havior: Often sings and forages at upper levels of canopy and can be hard to view well. Migrants often forage low, but within densely forested habitat; can also be found in more open areas.

nilar Species: Dusky Flycatcher (p. 279) is larger, with a longer bill and tail, paler head, and a short primary projection; it gives a soft whit call. Bright fall Hammond's can easily be confused with Pacific-slope Flycatcher (p. 281); note Hammond's gray chin and upper throat. Least Flycatcher (*E. minimus*, 5 ¼") is a rarely occurring eastern species, primarily from along the coast and in fall. It is structured like Hammond's (big head, short tail) and has a conspicuous eye ring. Its bill is broader at base; underparts, especially the flanks, are paler; the call note, a sharp *whit*, is delivered rather frequently.

here, When to Find: A fairly common but rather local breeder at mid-elevations in dense coniferous (usually) forest in the mountains, including the Coast Range south to Lake County; rare to absent as a breeder in Modoc County. Otherwise a rather rare spring (April to mid-May) and fall (mid-September to mid-October) migrant; uncommon in the Great Basin. Very rare in winter, with scattered records west of the Sierra Nevada.

d you know? Unlike our other *Empidonax*, Hammond's molts on the breeding grounds, resulting in a later fall migration.

ate & Location Seen: _____

_____

Dusky Flycatcher

Gray Flycatcher

Description: 5 ¾". Like Hammond's (p. 277), but **slightly paler, longer billed and longer tailed; short primary projection.** Underparts (spring and summer) paler, more uniform; belly more yellowish; eye ring less contrasting; some pale in lores. **Voice:** A soft *whit*. Song, delivered on the breeding grounds, a series of short phrases: *see-pit, gr-reep, seet!*; lacks burry low note of Hammond's; also gives *dee-hic!* notes. **Behavior:** More sedate than Hammond's; lacks wing flicking. Tail flicked up. **Similar Species:** Gray Flycatcher (below) similarly structured and colored but always dips its tail initially down, like a phoebe. **Where, When to Find:** Fairly common summer resident (May to mid-August) throughout the mountains (usually below and above Hammond's elevation range) including the northern Coast Ranges; isolated population in the Santa Lucia Mts., Monterey County. A rare, likely over-reported spring migrant (late April to mid-May) in the lowlands west of the Sierra Nevada; fairly common spring and uncommon fall migrant (late August-September) east of the Sierra Nevada.

GRAY FLYCATCHER *Empidonax wrightii*

Description: 6". Like Dusky Flycatcher, but averages grayer; always easily told by **habit of dipping its tail down first** like a phoebe. **Voice:** Common call a *whit*, like Dusky but slightly louder. Song two-parted, *chi-bit, greep!*. **Behavior:** Rather sedate in its foraging behavior, always dipping tail down, especially after landing. Found in a variety of habitats, but avoids dense woodland. **Where, When to Find:** Fairly common summer resident (May to mid-September) in a variety of arid and open woodlands in the Great Basin and ranges east of the Sierra Nevada; isolated population on San Benito Mtn. Rare but regular spring (mid-April to mid-May) and casual fall migrant west of the Sierra Nevada. Very rare in winter.

Did you know? The famous taxonomist Allan R. Phillips first noted the diagnostic downward tail bobbing of the Gray Flycatcher.

Date & Location Seen: _____

Description: 5 ½". The common *Empidonax* west of the Sierra Nevada. **Yellowish** underparts (**including throat**), olive upperparts; **bold teardrop shaped eye ring**. Tail longish, lower mandible entirely orange. Some fall birds are quite dull, almost whitish below; compare the photographs.

Voice: Male gives a high, upslurred *psee-eee*, both sexes give a high *seet*. Song, heard mostly in the early morning on breeding grounds, is a measured *psu-weeet, pit-ik, seep!*

Behavior: Forages within the canopy in shady canyon woodlands. Flicks tail up.

Similar Species: The high-pitched call differs from *whit* or *peep* calls of other *Empidonax*. Hammond's (p. 277) and Dusky (p. 279) have smaller, narrower bills, grayer heads, and less yellowish plumage (throat never yellow), though fall Hammond's are bright. The Cordilleran Flycatcher (*E. occidentalis*, 5 ½") has been identified as the breeding population in the Warner Mts. of northeastern California and perhaps the high eastern Sierra Nevada. It is separated with difficulty only by vocalizations, especially the two-parted *wheet-seet* call of males. Recent studies indicate that in parts of the western U.S., within range of Cordilleran, birds give intermediate vocalizations. Migrants have sensibly not been identified in California.

Where, When to Find: Fairly common migrant (late March – May, mid-August – early October) and summer resident over much of the region from the lower west side of the Sierra Nevada west. Prefers heavily wooded areas, which can include residential areas. East of the Sierra Nevada, an uncommon spring (mid- to late May) and rare fall (mostly September) migrant; on the basis of male calls, it is believed that these are mostly, maybe entirely, Pacific-slope, not Cordilleran.

Did you know? Vocalizations of Pacific-slope and Cordilleran Flycatchers are intermediate in a wide area of the western U.S.; some argue to re-lump them as the "Western Flycatcher."

Date & Location Seen: _____

escription: 7". This familiar, perky flycatcher is **blackish on the head, breast and sides,** with dark gray upperparts and pale-edged blackish wings and tail. The **lower breast and belly are contrastingly white.** JUVENILE: Differs from adult in having cinnamon-tinged wing-bars.

ice: Quite vocal. Call is a sharp *chip*; song is a prolonged series of *fee-BEEE, fee-BEER* phrases.

havior: A conspicuous, confiding species often found around water (streams or ponds), also in close proximity to our dwellings, even in heavily urban areas. Frequently moves and spreads its tail in a strong arc while perched. Makes short sallies to the ground from an open perch to catch insect prey. Builds its mud-lined nest beneath building eaves, bridges, or natural sheltered sites.

milar Species: Unmistakable, but note that plumage pattern can resemble some juncos (p. 419), which are very different, sparrow-like birds. An eastern relative, the Eastern Phoebe (*S. phoebe*, 7") is a rare late fall migrant and winter visitor to our region, primarily west of the Sierra Nevada. It is olive above with a darker head and no eye ring, and pale below with a yellow wash on the belly in fresh plumage. Its habits are like the Black Phoebe.

here, When to Find: Generally common over most of the region, including lower elevations of the Sierra Nevada; rare at higher elevations there. It is much scarcer and more local in the Great Basin and is rare in the northeastern corner of the state, but has nested at Adin, Modoc County. Small numbers winter in Inyo County.

d you know? Black Phoebes have a wide range, from s. Oregon to n. Argentina, but in the U.S. are mainly limited to the Southwest.

te & Location Seen: _____

scription: 7 ½". An open-country flycatcher that is **grayish** above with a **salmon-colored belly** and contrastingly **blackish tail**. The wings and tail are longer than on Black Phoebe. JUVENILE has cinnamon wing-bars.

ice: Call is a rich downslurred whistle, *peeew*. Song, usually heard only on breeding territories, alternates downslurred *pdeeew* and rising *pi-di-reee?* phrases. Not as vocal as Black Phoebe.

havior: Perches openly on fences, weed stems, and often even on bare ground. The tail is dipped and spread in a broad, shallow arc when perched. Most foraging takes place at ground level. Mud-lined nest are built under rock or building ledges.

milar Species: Ash-throated Flycatcher (p. 287) is more crested and whiter below with a pale yellow, not salmon-buff, belly. The longer tail and the wings show extensive rufous. The Western Kingbird (p. 289), another open-country flycatcher, is larger, with a pale gray head and chest and a yellow belly. Neither species dips its tail.

here, When to Find: Fairly common fall migrant and winter visitant through much of the region from mid-September to February; uncommon migrant in northeastern California. Fairly common year-round resident in southeastern Mono County; elsewhere in Great Basin an uncommon and local breeder and migrant (March, September). Breeds locally around the fringes of the Central Valley north to Contra Costa County. Rare on the coast north of Sonoma County.

id you know? Say's Phoebes have a huge latitudinal breeding range, from near the Bering Sea shore on the Seward Peninsula of w. Alaska south to central Mexico. Our region hosts breeding residents as well as migrants and winter visitants from well to the north.

ate & Location Seen: _____

Description: 8 ½". This medium-large, slender, bushy-crested flycatcher shows **rufous flashes in the wings and the long tail**, gray-brown upperparts, a **pale gray chest** and **pale yellow belly**. JUVENILE differs in its nearly entirely rufous tail (migrates south in this plumage).

Voice: Common calls include a sharp *bik* or *pip* and, on the breeding grounds, two-noted *ki-brick* and playground whistle-like *pip-preeer*.

Behavior: Usually perches within the canopy of shrubs or trees, sometimes more openly (e.g., territorial calling males). Does not dip or flick tail, but may crane its neck and bob head when agitated. Nests in natural or woodpecker-excavated tree cavities or in open-topped posts.

Similar Species: Western Kingbird (p. 289) is often found in more open situations. It is paler headed with a brighter yellow belly; shorter tail is black, with white-edged outer tail feathers. Brown-crested Flycatcher (p. 471) nests at only one location in Inyo County.

Where, When to Find: Common summer resident mid-April to mid-August over much of the region in open woodland. Absent from densely forested areas. Much more local in coastal regions, mostly on drier eastern slopes of Coast Ranges. Generally rare as a migrant away from nesting areas. A little more numerous in fall (late July-August) when migrants are noted rarely in the higher mountains (breeds at lower elevations in the Sierra Nevada). Casual in winter from coastal areas.

Did you know? Two other closely similar *Myiarchus* species are casual or accidental visitors to our region. Dusky-capped (*M. tuberculifer*, 7 ¼") is actually more likely than Ash-throated in winter (all records near coast); Great Crested (*M. crinitus*, 8 ¾") is noted almost annually on the coast in fall.

Date & Location Seen:

Western Kingbird

Cassin's Kingbird

Tropical Kingbird

Eastern Kingbird

Description: 8 ¾". Our only widespread kingbird in the region. **Head, chest and upperparts pale gray; black tail edged white**. JUVENILE paler below, sometimes almost white-bellied. **Voice**: Call is a sharp *bik*. Territorial song is a *pik pik peek PEEK-a-lo* crescendo; also sputtering notes. **Behavior**: Like all kingbirds, pugnacious; often seen harassing crows, ravens, hawks. Forages from fence lines, telephone wires, weeds and shrubs in open areas. **Similar Species:** Cassin's Kingbird (below). **Tropical Kingbird** (*T. melancholicus*, 9 ¼"), a rare fall and winter visitant mainly to coastal areas (casual in Central Valley), has a much longer bill, yellow breast, brownish tail, and greener back. **Eastern Kingbird** (*T. tyrannus*, 8 ½"), a casual to rare (mostly fall) visitor to the region has nested in northeastern California on many occasions. It is dark above and white below, with a white band on tail tip. **Where, When to Find:** Common in summer (late March – August) over much of region, except coast where generally rare (mostly spring) from mid-April to May and August to early October; has nested on northwest coast. Uncommon in higher mountains in fall (August).

CASSIN'S KINGBIRD *Tyrannus vociferans*

Description: 9". A boisterous and vocal flycatcher with a confined range in the region. Olive-gray above with a **yellow belly. Head and chest dark gray,** with contrasting white chin. Dull blackish tail has narrow buff tip. **Voice**: Quite vocal; distinctive call a loud *chi-BEER*. **Behavior**: Like Western; prefers less open areas. **Where, When to Find:** A rare to uncommon summer resident (late March – August) in dry areas west of the Central Valley north to Alameda County; has nested Marin and Solano counties. Casual elsewhere and in winter.

Did you know? Cassin's Kingbird is one of four North American bird species named for John Cassin, a renowned mid-1800s ornithologist.

Date & Location Seen:

Loggerhead Shrike

Northern Shrike Adult

Northern Shrike Immature

Description: 9″. A songbird turned bird of prey. Sleek but bull-headed; gray and white with a **bold black mask**. The black wings and tail show white patches. The thick **black bill is hooked at the tip**. JUVENILE: Like adults, but slightly barred brownish.

Voice: Generally quiet away from breeding territories, but sometimes gives a harsh scolding *jaahh jaahh jaahh*. The fairly unobtrusive song is a short series of gurgled or liquid two-note calls and musical bell-like notes.

Behavior: Perches openly on fence lines, wires, or the tops of shrubs or low trees, waiting to pounce on prey (large insects, lizards, small mammals and birds) with short flights. Flight is rapid and direct, often ending in a quick climb to a perch.

Similar Species: Northern Mockingbird (p. 359) similarly colored, but has thin bill, longer legs, lacks thick black mask, and shows more extensive white along the sides of its tail. **Northern Shrike** (*L. borealis*, 10″) is a scarce and irregular visitor (late October to March) to open habitats of northernmost counties, rarely farther south, including the Sacramento Valley south to the Delta region. Larger, with longer bill and tail than Loggerhead; our visitors are mostly immatures, washed brown and lightly barred below, with an indistinct mask.

Where, When to Find: Found in open fields, grasslands and agricultural areas with scattered shrubs and trees. Uncommon summer resident in the Great Basin areas and year-round resident through the Central Valley. Now breeds rarely nearer the coast from Sonoma County southward; a strong decline in coastal breeding populations has led to listing as a state Species of Special Concern.

Did you know? Many species of shrikes are declining worldwide; pesticides, loss of prey populations, and modification of open country habitat may be among the causes.

Date & Location Seen: _____

Cassin's Vireo

Plumbeous Vireo

Bell's Vireo
pusillus

Description: 5 ½". An **olive-gray** vireo with greenish back, white throat, **pale yellow sides**, gray head with **bold white spectacles**, and **white wing-bars**. Rather stocky and short-tailed, with a heavy bill.

Voice: Song consists of well-spaced, short slurred phrases, some fairly clear, others harsh and burry. Common call is a descending scold: *shep, shep, shep, shep.*

Behavior: Forages sluggishly in tall shrubs and trees, sometimes quite high. Tail is held straight; no tail or wing flicking.

Similar Species: Plumbeous Vireo (*V. plumbeus*, 5 ¾") is a close relative breeding in the Great Basin and Rockies; it is larger-billed, gray above, with little or no yellow tint to flanks. Uncommon breeder (late May through September) in arid montane woodlands of e. Alpine, Mono, Inyo, and se. Tulare counties; very rare fall and winter visitor, mostly near coast. **Bell's Vireo** (*V. bellii*, 4 ¾") is plain grayish above, whitish below, with tinge of yellow on flanks, single thin wing-bar, and indistinct pale eyebrow; long tail often held cocked. Breeds (April to August) in willow riparian thickets. Nearly extirpated from region. Small numbers breed regularly only at China Ranch, Inyo County; a few found recently in breeding season in the Owens, upper Salinas R., and Central valleys. These are the Endangered (state and federal) "Least" Bell's Vireo (*V. b. pusillus*). Also see Hutton's Vireo (p. 295).

Where, When to Find: Fairly common summer resident (April to August) in oak and conifer and mixed oak-riparian woodlands of the Coast Ranges and mountains mainly west of the Sierra Nevada crest. Uncommon spring migrant (late March to mid-May) and rather rare fall migrant through foothills and lowlands; rare winter visitor.

Did you know? Populations of all of these vireos, but especially Bell's, have been severely impacted by Brown-headed Cowbird brood parasitism. Trapping of cowbirds in vireo breeding habitat has contributed to recovery.

Date & Location Seen: _____

HUTTON'S VIREO
Vireo huttoni

Description: 5". A small, compact **olive-green** vireo, **pale olive below** tinged slightly yellow. **White wing-bars**; thick **off-white eye ring** (flared back behind the eye and broken by olive above the eye) extends forward to bill as a broad spectacle. Legs blue-gray.

Voice: Song is a monotonous repetition of well-spaced, burry, slurred phrases, such as *dzuwee, dzuwee, dzuwee…* or *zweeu, zweeu, zweeu…* Calls include a scolding *ree-dee-dee-dee*.

Behavior: An arboreal gleaner, taking caterpillars and other insects from leaves and twigs. May flick wings, kinglet-fashion, but behavior still fairly sluggish as is typical of vireos.

Similar Species: Ruby-crowned Kinglet (p. 343) is superficially closely similar, but more active and "nervous"; the kinglet has thinner blackish legs, a very thin pointed bill, and only one prominent wing-bar (bordered behind by blackish bar at the base of the flight feathers). These kinglets would not be expected in Hutton's habitat between mid-May and early September. See Cassin's Vireo (p. 293); Hutton's lacks contrasting gray head and white throat; spectacle of Hutton's is interrupted above eye (complete in Cassin's).

Where, When to Find: Fairly common to common year-round resident in oak woodlands and mixed oak-riparian or oak/chaparral interface, usually below 4500'. Although mainly a bird of live oaks, it breeds also in lowland riparian areas and second-growth conifer woodlands on the coastal slope, but is absent in most flat coastal lowlands except as scarce winter wanderer. Casual east of the Sierra Nevada and in northeastern California.

Did you know? In the mid-19th century, John Cassin named this species in honor of William Hutton, "a zealous and talented young naturalist," who collected one near Monterey, California.

Date & Location Seen: _____

_____

Description: 5 ½". A plain vireo **without wing-bars. Pale grayish olive** with a **pale eyebrow** and short pale line under the eye. Brighter birds in fresh fall plumage are tinged yellow on the sides. Bill and legs gray.

Voice: Song is a long rambling warble with many changes in pitch, e.g., *wilchee-weedee-whew-chewee-deewillchee*, usually incorporating high fussy notes. Calls include a short *vit* and scolding *eeah*.

Behavior: Typical deliberate vireo gleaning behavior, working slowly through foliage gleaning insects; sometimes briefly hovers to pick food off leaves. Like most vireos, can sing incessantly while foraging; sometimes even sings from the soft cup nest that is suspended from a thin branch fork.

Similar Species: Our other expected vireos have wing-bars (faint in Bell's). Vireos are told from warblers by their more sluggish behavior and heavier, hooked bills. Differ from small flycatchers in horizontal posture, gleaning behavior.

Where, When to Find: Rather common and widespread migrant March through May and mid-August to mid-October. Breeds (April to August) in streamside woodlands of sycamores, alders and cottonwoods, in shady oak woodlands from near the coast through the foothills, and in conifer forests and aspen groves in the Sierra Nevada and other high mountains. Our populations have declined in recent decades. Winters in Mexico and Central America.

Did you know? The Warbling Vireos in eastern and western North America likely represent two different species; eastern birds are larger and their songs differ.

Date & Location Seen: _____

Description: 11 ½". A familiar bold, **crested** jay of forested areas. Mostly **deep blue**, but **blackish-brown** on **head, crest** and back. Tail and wings with fine black cross-bars, forehead shows thin blue stripes. Heavier and shorter-tailed than scrub-jays.

Voice: Raucous calls include a *shook-shook-shook…* series and harsh *jeeahhhh*. Also produces a dry rattle, bell-like notes, and mimicked hawk screams.

Behavior: Travel in pairs or small groups, feeding on pine seeds, acorns, invertebrates and sometimes small vertebrate prey or birds' eggs. Can be tame and bold around mountain campgrounds, where their abundance is subsidized by food provided by humans. Loud calls and aggressive mobbing behavior by these jays often signals the presence of a perched hawk or roosting owl.

Similar Species: Distinctive, as it is our only crested jay, apart from the Blue Jay (*C. cristata*, 11"), an eastern North American species that has wandered on a few occasions to our region.

Where, When to Find: Common year-round resident in coniferous forests and coastal and foothill oak-conifer associations, from sea level (locally) to tree line; familiar in well-wooded residential areas of the Coast Ranges and Sierra Nevada foothills. Absent from the Central Valley and unforested coastal and Great Basin lowlands, though a few may rarely wander to these areas in fall and winter.

Did you know? Increasing human settlement and recreation in the highest elevations of the Sierra Nevada has promoted colonization of these areas by Steller's Jays within the past 100 years.

Date & Location Seen:

California Scrub-Jay

Woodhouse's Scrub-Jay
woodhouseii

escription: 11 ½". The familiar "blue jay" in the region's non-forested lowlands and foothills. Slender and long-tailed. **Deep blue above** with a **brown back patch**; whitish underparts separated from white throat by a **distinct partial blue collar. Lacks a crest**. JUVENILE: like adult but mostly gray-brown on head, collar gray and indistinct.

ice: Main calls are a harsh, upslurred *jreeee?* and (usually in flight) a rapid series of *sheelp, sheelp...* notes. Interacting birds may give a dry rattle.

ehavior: Bold and familiar, these scrub-jays are easily drawn to backyards with peanuts or sunflower seeds. Acorns form an important natural food, but these versatile omnivores also eat other seeds, insects, and often eggs and nestlings of songbirds.

milar Species: Woodhouse's Scrub-Jay (*A. woodhouseii*, 11 ½") is an uncommon, generally shy resident in arid Great Basin woodlands from the Mono Lake region south; has wandered once west to McGurk Meadow in Mariposa County. More slender-billed, less contrastingly patterned and paler blue above than California Scrub-Jay, with collar more obscure and sides and flanks brownish gray; voice somewhat higher pitched. Steller's Jay (p. 299) of forested habitats has a conspicuous crest and is entirely dark blue below. The gregarious Pinyon Jay (p. 463) of the Great Basin is entirely dull blue.

here, When to Find: Common resident through most of the region, absent only in the higher mountains and the Great Basin ranges from the Mono Lake region south (where replaced by Woodhouse's). Found in a variety of scrubby and woodland habitats from sea level to as high as 5,000', and quite adaptable throughout our urban areas.

id you know? "Western" scrub-jay was split in 2016 into California and Woodhouse's, the latter ranging from the interior West to south-central Mexico; they interbreed in the Pine Nut Mountains east of Lake Tahoe.

ate & Location Seen: _____

Yellow-billed Magpie

Variable skin patch

Black-billed Magpie

YELLOW-BILLED MAGPIE
Pica nuttalli

escription: 16 ½". Unmistakable **long-tailed** bird with boldly patterned **glossy black and white patterning**; in flight shows **large white wing patches. Bill yellow**, as is variably-sized bare skin patch below eye. **Voice**: Nasal *meg? meg?* calls along with other harsh scolds. **Behavior**: Found in loose flocks, foraging as they walk along ground or flying with deep buoyant wing beats. Nests, often in loose colonies, are deep stick piles high in trees. **Similar Species**: Can only be confused with the closely-related Black-billed Magpie (below) of the Great Basin region; the ranges of the two species do not normally overlap, but their ranges approach one another in Shasta County. **Where, When to Find**: Found only in California. Year-round resident within and on the fringes of the Sacramento and northern San Joaquin valleys (to northern Fresno County), locally in the inner Coast Ranges from Alameda County south. Now local in the Sierra Nevada foothills (below about 2000') from Nevada County south to Amador County. Numbers have declined with persecution, habitat loss, and (recently) mortality from West Nile Virus.

BLACK-BILLED MAGPIE *Pica hudsonia*

escription: 19". Like Yellow-billed, but slightly larger, **bill black**, lacks yellow facial skin. **Voice** and **Behavior** similar to Yellow-billed's. **Where, When to Find:** Fairly common year-round resident, mainly east of the Cascade/Sierra Nevada range in open sagebrush flats, riparian woodlands along creeks, and planted trees around small towns and ranches. Found from Scott Valley (Siskiyou County) east through the Fall River Valley area (Shasta County) and in the Great Basin southward to Lone Pine (Inyo County) in the Owens Valley; also in the south end of the Tahoe Basin.

id you know? Both of our magpies have shown high mortality rates from West Nile Virus, and surveys demonstrate moderate to severe declines through most of their ranges in California.

ate & Location Seen: _____

American Crow

Common Raven

American Crow

Common Raven

AMERICAN CROW
Corvus brachyrhynchos

escription: 17 ½". Familiar large **all black** bird, with rounded wingtips. **Heavy black bill, square or slightly rounded tail**. JUVENILE: Plumage dull sooty; recently fledged young show pink on the base of the bill. **Voice**: Harsh *cawwr* or *caw, caw caw* series, changing in quality with context. Interacting birds can give a loud dry rattle. **Behavior**: Intelligent and inquisitive, crows forage in a variety of ways including scavenging, exploiting abundant seed or insect crops, and preying on small vertebrates or even intertidal invertebrates. They gather into huge winter roosting flocks around groves of trees. **Similar Species**: Compare larger Common Raven (below). **Where, When to Find:** Common year-round resident in woodlands, orchards and towns throughout, mainly below about 2,000 feet; somewhat more local in the mountains and in the northeast part of the region, where some migrants pass through.

COMMON RAVEN *Corvus corax*

escription: 24". Our **largest songbird**, twice the weight of a crow, with long pointed wings. **All black, very heavy black bill, wedge-shaped tail**, and thin lance-like feathers on the throat. JUVENILE: Like adult, but duller black, and with variable pink on the bill. **Voice**: A deep, resonant croak, e.g., *craaaah* or *kronk*, lower pitched than crow. Also a hollow knocking call and higher gurgling notes. **Behavior**: Omnivorous, often seeking roadside carrion; many forage at landfills and dumpsters. Routinely soars high in the air, like hawks but unlike crows. **Similar Species**: Compare American Crow (above). **Where, When to Find**: Locally fairly common in the mountains, coast ranges, Great Basin, and San Joaquin Valley. More local on the immediate coast (scarcest in Monterey County).

id you know? Predation pressures from increasing populations of these two species have been implicated in the decline of many bird (and other vertebrate) species.

ate & Location Seen: _____

Male

Juvenile

escription: 7 ¼". A flocking sparrow-like bird of open country. Pinkish-brown to russet above, variably streaked; mostly white below. **Tail black with brown center and white edges.** MALE shows **black bib** on chest, black cheek patch, black bar across forecrown with small projecting feathers ("horns"). **Throat and eyebrow yellow.** Coloring varies geographically. FEMALE similar, but duller, with less contrasting pattern. JUVENILE is streaky, suggesting a sparrow or pipit.

ice: Song starts with short *terp* notes, followed by a rising, tinkling flourish; often given in sustained flight. Flight calls include *tseep, tew,* and *zip* notes.

havior: A ground bird, but will perch on low shrubs, fence lines. Walks or runs on the ground; does not hop. Found in pairs in the breeding season, but gathers into large flocks (sometimes thousands) in fall and winter that wheel about, low over open fields.

nilar Species: American Pipits (p. 363), which also flock in open country, are darker, more slender, streaked on breast, and habitually bob their long tails. Sparrows have thicker, more conical bills.

here, When to Find: Common breeder in open valley and foothill grasslands, preferring areas with bare or nearly bare ground. Locally common breeder in high elevation "bald" hills, mountain meadows, and above tree line; scarce near the coast. Large flocks, involving multiple subspecies, some of which breed outside the region, gather (October to February) on bare or closely cropped agricultural fields, airfields, and shorelines in lowlands.

d you know? A Horned Lark's "horns" – actually, occipital feather tufts – can be raised or lowered, but are usually erect in males.

te & Location Seen: _____

_____

Male

Female

Description: 8″. This and other swallows resemble swifts, with their slender bodies and long, pointed wings, but have more fluid flight. By far **our largest swallow.** ADULT MALE **dark glossy purplish blue overall.** Adult FEMALE and JUVENILE **sooty gray above, whitish below. Tail strongly notched.**

Voice: Male's song a low-pitched, loud, rich, gurgling chortle. Call notes include rich, low whistles, and a descending *churr*.

Behavior: Like all swallows, spends most of the day on the wing foraging for flying insects, often at greater heights than other swallow species. Nests in woodpecker holes, snags, and suitable cavities in man-made structures. Has nested in power pylons (e.g., along Red Hills Road, Lake County), and in weep holes beneath elevated freeways and overpasses in the Sacramento area.

Similar Species: In flight, male especially resembles European Starling (p. 361), but note martin's strongly notched tail and typical swallow flight. Tree Swallow (p. 311) is smaller, has white underparts, tail less strongly notched.

Where, When to Find: Uncommon to rare breeding summer resident (late March to September) in the western part of the region. Rarely seen in migration. Widely but locally distributed in low to intermediate elevation wooded areas. A few isolated pairs breed in the western foothills of the Sierra Nevada. The Sacramento area hosts the last remnant of a once widespread Central Valley population. Declines continue there; 2013's survey found only 46 nesting pairs (down more than 50% from ten years earlier), and a new threat: American Kestrels preying upon nestlings in weep holes.

Did you know? Purple Martin is a state Species of Special Concern, with a population estimated at about 1,000 pairs statewide. Nest site competition with starlings is the main threat to remnant lowland populations; re-colonization there is highly unlikely.

Date & Location Seen: _____

Tree Swallow Male

Male

Female First-year

Violet-green Swallow Male

Male

escription: 5 ¾". Bi-colored: **entirely dark above, white below**. Tail slightly notched. MALE is deep **iridescent steel blue** to blue-green above, pure white below; FEMALE usually much duller above than male. JUVENILE brown above, variable tinge of gray across breast. **Voice**: Calls have rich, liquid quality: *treep* or *chirp*. Song a series of liquid chirps and whistles. **Behavior**: Tied to water. Perches on wires, bare twigs, bulrushes, often over water. Nests in woodpecker holes, cavities in riparian trees; readily uses nest boxes. **Similar Species**: Compare Violet-green Swallow (below). Smaller Bank Swallow (p. 313) resembles juvenile Tree but has paler brown back and rump, more distinct breast band. **Where, When to Find**: Widespread migrant and breeding summer resident (February to October) throughout the region; abundant in lowlands, uncommon at higher elevations. Huge post-breeding flocks sometimes gather to feed and roost in Delta area marshes and fields. Rare in winter in lowlands.

VIOLET-GREEN SWALLOW *Tachycineta thalassina*

escription: 5 ¼". A small, **short-tailed, green-backed** swallow with white underparts, **white on face over eye,** and **white sides to rump**. Tail slightly notched. MALE has bright felt-green back and crown, violet rump. Plumages of FEMALE and JUVENILE duller; face pattern more obscure. **Voice**: Call a double-noted *tsew-tsip* or *chew-lip*. Song a rhythmic series of *chip, tseep*, and *chew* notes. **Behavior**: A swallow of wooded areas, spends more time perching in trees than other swallows. Nests in woodpecker holes, locally on cliff faces. **Similar Species**: Compare Tree Swallow (above); beware that white on flanks of Tree sometimes appears to be rump patches. **Where, When to Find:** Widespread migrant and breeding summer resident (February to October); common in forests and woodlands, also in drier regions where cliff faces provide nest sites. Rare in winter in lowlands.

d you know? Tree Swallow is the region's most prevalent wintering swallow.

ate & Location Seen: _____

Northern Rough-winged Swallow

Bank Swallow

NORTHERN ROUGH-WINGED SWALLOW
Stelgidopteryx serripennis

Description: 5 ½ ". A **dull brown** swallow with mostly white underparts; **dingy brownish throat and breast**. Tail squared or very slightly notched. JUVENILE resembles adults, but with cinnamon wing-bars. **Voice**: Calls are short, burry, e.g., *brrrt* or *prrrrit*. **Behavior**: Flight buoyant, with deep, slow wing beats. Often forages over water. Nests in holes in earthen banks, but in urban and suburban settings more typically in weep holes or drain holes in bridges or retaining walls. **Similar Species**: See Bank Swallow (below). Dullest female Tree Swallows (p. 311) are more slaty above, show more contrast between dark upperparts and whitish underparts. **Where, When to Find**: Fairly common migrant and breeding summer resident (March to early September) throughout the region except for heavily forested mountains.

BANK SWALLOW *Riparia riparia*

Description: 5 ¼". Our smallest swallow. **Distinct brownish gray breast band,** often extending in a line down center of the breast. Throat is white; **white curves around rear border of ear patch**. Pale brown above, wings darker. **Voice**: Call a series of buzzy, short *dzrrt* notes. **Behavior**: Flight is fast, with quick, shallow wing beats. Excavates nest burrows in steep, erodible riverbanks, gravel pits, road cuts. **Similar Species**: Northern Rough-winged Swallow (above). Juvenile Tree Swallow (p. 311) has incomplete gray breast band. **Where, When to Find**: Uncommon to fairly common migrant and summer resident (April to September). Highly local, owing to nesting requirements; state listed as Threatened. Colonies nest at Crowley Lake, along the Sacramento and Feather rivers, at Año Nuevo State Reserve, and at Fort Funston in San Francisco, with smaller colonies elsewhere.

Did you know? *Riparia riparia* is one of the most widely distributed swallows in the world; its English name is Sand Martin in the Old World.

Date & Location Seen: _____

At mud nest

Description: 5 ½". A **square-tailed** swallow; ADULTS with a **chestnut throat and cheek that contrasts with the white underparts. White forehead** contrasts with dark cap; upperparts with white back streaks and a distinct **deep buff rump** patch. JUVENILE is duller and less strongly patterned, with variable white spotting in dull brown throat.

Voice: Calls include rough *vrrrt* or *veer* notes, a more musical *veeew*, and a prolonged song of grating, creaking notes.

Behavior: Often found in large flocks. Typical flight includes circling and steep upward climbs. The distinctive gourd-shaped nest, made of mud pellets, is placed under a protective ledge, commonly on highway overpasses, bridges over rivers or aqueducts, on dam faces, or under eaves of houses; also on cliffs.

Similar Species: Distinct buff rump patch differs from all of our other swallows. Beware short-tailed juvenile Barn Swallow (p. 317); it has a dark forehead, noticeably forked tail. Wings broader and relatively shorter than Tree or Barn Swallows.

Where, When to Find: Common migrant and breeding summer resident (late February through August) throughout the Region's lowlands, foothills and open areas in the mountains; large flocks of these and other swallows are found in early spring around bodies of water. Winters mainly in South America; seen only very rarely after September in our region.

Did you know? Cliff Swallows are extremely social at all times, seeking out other individuals whenever away from their nests. Preening birds on wires are often spaced as closely as 4", and sometimes even with "shoulders" touching.

Date & Location Seen: _____

escription: 6 ¾". A large, slender swallow with a **very long, deeply forked tail**. ADULT MALE is deep **steel blue above**, with a **chestnut forehead and throat, orangish underparts**. White spots show on the spread tail. ADULT FEMALE resembles male, but tail shorter, underparts a bit paler. JUVENILE'S tail even shorter, but still strongly forked; underparts whitish-buff.

ice: Common call is a scratchy *vit*. Song combines *vit* calls and other scratchy notes; also a strong upslurred whistle, e.g. *vit-wheeet?*

havior: Often found near water. Reuses an old mud cup nest or builds a new one, on a ledge or against a vertical wall with a protective overhang. Uses human structures, bridges, overpasses, piers and other harbor structures. Nearby mud is required for nest construction. Forages at lower altitudes than most other swallow species (usually below 30 feet) over open areas such as ponds, grassy pastures, plowed fields, meadows, and farmyards.

milar Species: No other local swallow combines the orangish underparts and very long forked tail. Shorter-tailed juveniles can suggest Cliff Swallow (p. 315), but have dark rump and prominent tail notch.

here, When to Find: Common migrant and locally common breeding summer resident throughout the region, mainly from late March to September. Fall migrants pass widely and commonly through the region as late as October. Avoids densely forested areas and the highest mountains. Small numbers occur through winter in the San Francisco Bay area and Sacramento Valley, or appear as winter visitors along the coast.

id you know? Barn Swallow is the most widely distributed and abundant swallow in the world, breeding on all six temperate continents.

ate & Location Seen: _____

Chestnut-backed Chickadee
rufescens

Chestnut-backed Chickadee
barlowi

Mountain Chickadee

Black-capped Chickadee
occidentalis

CHESTNUT-BACKED CHICKADEE
Poecile rufescens

Description: 4 ¾". Active forest bird with **dark cap, black throat** contrasting with **white cheeks. Back and sides chestnut** (except sides grayish in *barlowi*, resident from the Golden Gate south). **Voice**: Vocal; flock members give high lisping notes and buzzy, rapid *see-dee-dee-dee*. **Behavior**: Travels through trees (often quite high) in loose flocks, often with other species mixed in; acrobatic forager at twigs, leaf clusters. **Similar Species**: Mountain Chickadee (below) has white eyebrow stripe, lacks chestnut; Black-capped (below) cleaner black and white, with gray back, buff-pink sides. **Where, When to Find:** Common in coastal and Inner Coast Range forests, especially where conifers dominate; local in conifers on west slope of Sierra Nevada south to Mariposa County.

MOUNTAIN CHICKADEE *Poecile gambeli*

Description: 5 ¼". **Gray and white** chickadee with **black cap and throat, black stripe through eye, white eyebrow.** Lacks chestnut or strong pink or buff tones in plumage. **Voice**: Husky *chick-a-dee-dee* call; also lisping and "gargling" notes, and song of two to five clear, haunting whistles. **Behavior**: Active core member of woodland bird flocks in higher mountains. Feeds acrobatically. Like other chickadees, nests in cavities and may visit seed and suet feeders. **Similar Species**: Black-capped Chickadee (*P. atricapillus*, 5 ¼") restricted to willows and other river valley scrub in Del Norte, Humboldt, and Siskiyou counties; casual to Trinity, Shasta, and Mendocino counties; lacks white eyebrow, washed pinkish on sides, and gives more nasal and rapid *ch-dee-dee-dee-dee* call. **Where, When to Find**: Coniferous forests throughout Sierra Nevada and other mountain ranges above about 5,000' (locally in highest Coast Ranges). Rare and irregular visitor to Central Valley and other lowlands.

Did you know? Various species of chickadees (called "tits" in the Old World) are conspicuous residents of forests and woodlands throughout the world's northern temperate areas.

Date & Location Seen: _____

Oak Titmouse

Juniper Titmouse

OAK TITMOUSE
Baeolophus inornatus

Description: 5 ¾". A small, fussy woodland bird. **Plain gray**, tinged slightly brown, and sporting a **short gray crest**. The bill is gray and wedge-shaped; the stout legs are gray. Sexes and age classes are similar.

Voice: Scolding calls include *si si cheeh* and high *tsee* notes. Gives a bewildering variety of simple songs, such as *pee-doo, pee-doo, pee-doo* or *tu-wee, tu-wee, tu-wee;* also a bubbly trill.

Behavior: Found in pairs or family groups. Gleans insects and seeds from twigs, branches and trunks of oaks and other trees, shrubs. Often hammers audibly with the bill. Nests in cavities in trees, and will sometimes take to nest boxes.

Similar Species: Juniper Titmouse (*B. ridgwayi*, 5 ¾") is found very locally in pinyon-juniper associations east of the Cascade/Sierra Nevada crest from central and eastern Modoc County south through Inyo County; purer gray than Oak Titmouse, and calls slightly more rapid. Bushtits (p. 323) are much smaller and longer-tailed, travel in large flocks. Chickadees (p. 319) have strong black and white head markings and lack crest.

Where, When to Find: Fairly common year-round resident in live oak woodlands, and where oaks are mixed with chaparral, conifers; also in riparian woodlands with oaks or cottonwoods.

Did you know? The closely-related Oak and Juniper titmice were formerly "lumped" as the "Plain Titmouse;" studies in overlap areas, such as the Modoc Plateau, showed genetic, plumage, size, and vocal distinctions.

Date & Location Seen:

Male (Coastal)

Male (Interior)

Female (Coastal)

Description: 4 ½". Bushtits are **tiny**, plump-bodied, **long-tailed, gray birds** that **travel in large, busy flocks**. Bill is short, stubby and black. MALE: eyes dark; FEMALE: eyes creamy white. JUVENILES of both sexes are dark-eyed. The brownish crown of widespread "Coastal" birds contrasts with grayish ear patch. Interior subspecies *plumbeus* (resident in pinyon-juniper woodlands along our eastern border) has gray crown and pale brown ear patch, and purer gray flanks; calls are lower-pitched.

Voice: Flocks keep up a constant light, rapid twittering *pit…pit…pit*, with a variety of other short notes such as *tsee* or *spik*. When a hawk or other aerial predator is sighted, many birds in the flock emit a high, trilling alarm call (often a birder's best hint that a hawk is in the vicinity).

Behavior: Acrobatic gleaning birds, often hanging upside down from small twigs. Flocks in non-breeding season may consist of a dozen to several dozen birds, moving frantically through shrubbery and crossing gaps in single-file flight lines. Birds travel in pairs or family groups during breeding season. The distinctive nest is a soft hanging pouch, 8-10" long, with a small entrance high on one side.

Similar Species: Unmistakable by virtue of tiny size, long tail, and flocking behavior. Chickadees (p. 319) are larger, with strong head markings; titmice (p. 321) are larger, with obvious crests.

Where, When to Find: A very common and familiar year-round resident in woodlands and chaparral below about 6,000'. Found in oak and riparian woodlands, chaparral, and urban parks and gardens; absent only from the higher mountain ranges.

Did you know? The two distinct subspecies groups come close to meeting in the vicinity of Lone Pine, Inyo County. Bushtits are found from sw. British Columbia to Guatemala; their closest relatives live in Eurasia.

Date & Location Seen: _____

Red-breasted Nuthatch
Male

White-breasted Nuthatch
Male
aculeata

RED-BREASTED NUTHATCH
Sitta canadensis

Description: 4 ½". Nuthatches creep acrobatically up and down on trunks, branches in wooded habitats. This species' **distinct white eyebrow** is lacking in other nuthatch species. MALE with **black crown** (**gray** in FEMALE), **black eye stripe. Underparts washed rusty** (male) **to deep buff** (female). **Voice**: Distinctive nasal "tin horn" notes with complaining quality; also softer squeaky notes. **Behavior**: Hammers at bark or seeds with wedge-tipped bill. **Similar Species**: Other nuthatches lack black eye stripe/white eyebrow combination, are mostly white or gray-buff below. **Where, When to Find**: Resident in coniferous forests throughout; locally resident in humid portions of coastal counties. Wanders irregularly to lowlands some falls and winters, sometimes in large numbers.

WHITE-BREASTED NUTHATCH *Sitta carolinensis*

Description: 5 ¾". A stubby-tailed gray and white climbing bird with a **dark crown, white face** and underparts, rufous area under the tail. **Bill is long, slender and chisel-like**. The gray and black tail shows white patches near the corners. Crown and hindneck black on MALE, dark gray on FEMALE. **Voice**: Song is a rapid series of rich *twhee, twhee…* notes. Call of widespread subspecies *aculeata* a nasal *airrhh* or *eehr*; call of interior montane *tenuissima* very different, a stuttering *eh-eh-eh*. **Behavior**: Like Red-breasted. **Similar Species**: Our only nuthatch with eye surrounded by white. **Where, When to Find**: Common year-round resident *aculeata* in foothill oak woodlands and oak/conifer forests; also in lowland valley oak savannas, riparian woodlands with mature cottonwoods and sycamores, and suburban parks. Interior montane *tenuissima* resident from Modoc County south in pines, firs of the eastern Sierra Nevada and south to the mountain ranges of Inyo County.

Did you know? Vocal differences and morphologic and genetic evidence suggest that three distinct White-breasted Nuthatch subspecies groups (including eastern *carolinensis*) may constitute separate species.

Date & Location Seen: _____

_____

Pygmy Nuthatch
Sitta pygmaea

Description: 4 ¼″. Our **smallest nuthatch**, and our only one that is **dark from crown to eye**. It has a blackish eye-line, a gray crown, and a buff tinge to its underparts. There is a distinctive small whitish patch on its nape.

Voice: Call is a high *peep*, often running into an excited series. Birds of coastal pines routinely give notes in rapid series.

Behavior: Hyperactive in small, noisy groups, feeding at tips of pine boughs or on small branches. Like Red-breasted, can be very responsive to "pishing" and imitations of small owl calls. All of our nuthatches nest in cavities, often those made by woodpeckers.

Similar Species: Red-breasted Nuthatch (p. 325) has a white eyebrow over the black stripe through its eye and pale rusty underparts; White-breasted (p. 325) is much larger, with a white face.

Where, When to Find: Fairly common resident (subspecies *melanotis*) mainly in ponderosa and Jeffrey pines from 6,000′ to 8,000′ primarily on the east side of the Cascade/Sierra Nevada range (uncommon and local at somewhat lower elevations on the west side) and in the high mountains of Inyo County. Fairly common to abundant local resident (*pygmaea*) in Bishop and Monterey pines north along the coast to central Mendocino County. Formerly absent from the San Francisco peninsula and the East Bay hills, now a locally fairly common resident there; apparently restricted in the East Bay hills to groves of Monterey pines. Casual around planted pines in lowlands away from breeding localities in winter.

Did you know? This species has a counterpart in the pine forests of the southern Atlantic and Gulf Coast states, known as the Brown-headed Nuthatch. The two species differ strikingly in their vocalizations.

Date & Location Seen:

Description: 5 ¼". A slender, cryptic **trunk-creeping bird** that uses its long stiffened tail as a prop. Streaked black and **brown above, with pale spotting; white throat** and breast, becoming grayish-tan on belly. Intricate light and dark markings on folded wing, and long **buffy wing-stripe visible in flight.**

Voice: Very high pitched *tseeee* note; song is a rhythmic *see-see-seee, seedly-see.*

Behavior: Unobtrusive, and remarkably well camouflaged against tree bark; usually found by high-pitched calls. Works upward on tree trunks and outward on large branches in spiral fashion, then flies down to a nearby trunk or branch to repeat the process. Its nest is often built behind a slab of bark or in another tree crevice.

Similar Species: Unmistakable once seen; high pitched calls can suggest some calls of Golden-crowned Kinglet (p. 343).

Where, When to Find: Widespread resident in pines, firs, incense-cedars in all mountain areas and locally in conifers along the entire coast. There is some irregular movement away from coniferous forests in fall and winter, when it may be found in small numbers in the Central Valley and other lowland areas.

Did you know? Several similar "tree-creepers" are found in Eurasian forests, but the Brown Creeper, though highly variable geographically, is the only one in the Americas; superficially similar but much larger woodcreepers found from Mexico through South America are unrelated.

Date & Location Seen: _____

_____

Rock Wren

Canyon Wren

Description: 6". A **pale gray-brown** wren with a **buffy belly**. Back speckled with white; whitish **breast finely streaked**. The barred tail with buffy corners is held in line with the body, not angled upward as in many wrens. **Bill long and thin. Voice:** Song a series of repeated cricket-like notes, *tr-ree, tr-ree, tr-ree...* or *jeer, jeer, jeer...* Calls include a trilled *pd-zeeee* and various scolding notes. **Behavior:** Perches almost exclusively on rocks, talus slopes, and rocky desert soils, forages for insects and spiders. Nests are built deep within rock crevices, entrances lined with pebbles. Bobs up and down when agitated. **Similar Species:** Canyon Wren (below) much rustier, with contrasting white throat. **Where, When to Find:** Local summer resident of rocky areas in arid foothill regions, at higher elevations, in the Great Basin, and locally along the coast north to Marin County. Winter visitors occupy similar habitats, sometimes ones unsuitable for breeding (e.g., riprap, debris piles) in warmer areas.

Canyon Wren *Catherpes mexicanus*

Description: 5 ¾". A "boulder wren" that craves shade. **Rich rusty**, with a **contrasting white throat** and **very long, slender bill**. Rusty areas dotted with black and white; **bright rusty tail** has thin black bars. **Voice:** Song is a beautiful cascade of clear whistled *tew* notes; call a loud, buzzy *zeep*. **Behavior:** Forages among boulders, in rocky stream beds, on cliffs in shaded canyons. Often sings from boulders, bobbing with quick "knee-bends" when agitated. Nests built within caves, crevices, outbuildings. **Where, When to Find:** Uncommon and local resident in shaded canyons with boulders or steep rock cliffs through most of the Sierra Nevada and the Great Basin (withdraws from higher elevations in winter); locally in the inner Coast Ranges.

Did you know? The Rock Wren is the only resident landbird on the Farallon Islands, 32 miles west of San Francisco.

Date & Location Seen: _____

House Wren

Pacific Wren

escription: 4 ¾". A **plain brownish** wren with **fine black barring** on the wings, flanks, undertail and tail. Shows only a thin, indistinct eyebrow. The moderately long tail is often held cocked upward. **Voice**: Calls include a rolling, trilled *aairrrrr*, a harsh, scolding *jihhhh, jihhhh*, a thinner *shhhihhh*, and mewing notes. Lively, bubbly song of trills, sputters and fussy notes is a characteristic spring sound in riparian and oak woodlands. **Behavior**: Sings energetically from an exposed perch, tail vibrating. Forages for insects, spiders, and grubs along branches, trunks, and in tangles. Nests in cavities, which may be aggressively commandeered from other birds. **Similar Species**: Bewick's Wren (p. 337) has bold white eyebrow. See Pacific Wren (below). **Where, When to Find**: Summer resident (late March to September) in oak and riparian woodlands and mountain thickets, locally to above 7,000' in high mountains. Uncommon in winter in thickets and well-planted parks and gardens in the Central Valley and coastal regions.

escription: 4". Like a tiny, **stub-tailed** House Wren with **deep rusty plumage tones.** Buffy supercilium; belly, wings and tail finely barred. **Voice**: Call, *timp-timp* (like Wilson's Warbler in quality); also a rapid thin rattle. Song very high-pitched, prolonged set of musical trills. **Behavior**: Skulks within vines, tangles, mossy logs and ferns in shaded forest understory, tail usually cocked. **Similar Species:** Compare House Wren (above). **Where, When to Find:** Resident in understory of shaded, dense forests (such as fir, redwood); widespread and common in humid coastal regions, more local near coast south of Marin County and along west (mainly) slope of Sierra Nevada. A few found in the Central Valley, other lowland areas in winter.

id you know? House Wrens are known to puncture the eggs of other songbirds and sometimes take over nest cavities.

ate & Location Seen: _____

MARSH WREN
Cistothorus palustris

Description: 5″. A small, busy denizen of extensive marshes of cattails and bulrushes (tules). Well-marked, with a dark crown, **whitish eyebrow, black and white striped back**, and **rusty rump**. Dull whitish breast, with tan sides and belly. The **short tail is often cocked vertically** or even forward over the back. JUVENILE: patterning more subdued than adult.

Voice: Common call is a hard *chet-chet*. The energetic song, given endlessly in the breeding season (and often even at night), is a variable set of rattles, gurgles and *tik* notes, such as *tuk, tik, jrrrrrrrr* – often a dominant sound in freshwater marshes.

Behavior: Perches on vertical reed stems, gleaning for insects. Often stays well hidden, but singing birds sometimes sit more openly. Nest is a woven structure attached to reeds. Males build many more nests than are used for breeding.

Similar Species: Bewick's (p. 337) and House (p. 333) Wrens lack rusty rump and have plain brown backs, also occupy very different habitats.

Where, When to Find: Common resident in freshwater and brackish marshes along the entire coast and adjacent lowlands, and through the Central Valley. Uncommon, patchily distributed resident in western foothills of the Sierra Nevada. Uncommon to locally common summer resident (rare in winter) to about 6,500′ in marshes of northeastern California, the south Lake Tahoe basin, and elsewhere in the more arid interior. Fall and winter migrants more widespread in the lowlands.

Did you know? The Marsh Wrens of eastern and western North America have different vocal repertoires (much more extensive in western birds) and differ slightly in appearance; they are considered separate species by some taxonomists.

Date & Location Seen: _____

escription: 5 ¼". A slender wren with a long tail that is often cocked upward at an angle and flipped from side to side. **Brown above** with a distinct **white eyebrow, grayish white below**. Undertail and upper surface of tail finely barred with black. White tail corners sometimes visible.

ice: Quite vocal. Common calls include a buzzy, scolding *bzzzzz* and a scratchy *vvit* or *jik*. The complex and varied song starts with short introductory notes and buzzes and ends in a musical trill; individuals have a variety of different songs.

havior: A curious and often confiding bird of dense brush, constantly moving about and waving its long tail. Feeds on insects and spiders, often probing into loose bark, root tangles and crevices in stone walls. The nest is placed in a crevice, among exposed roots, or in an artificial cavity.

milar Species: House Wren (p. 333) lacks the distinct white eyebrow, has a slightly shorter tail, and is more evenly gray-brown above and below. Marsh Wren (p. 335) has striped back, shorter tail, and rusty on wings and rump; usually only in marshes and damp tangles.

here, When to Find: Common year-round resident in coastal scrub, chaparral, and arid woodlands, and the brushy understory and edges of oak and riparian woodlands nearly throughout. Found also in suburban gardens and parks, and even in heavily urbanized areas so long as there is enough shrubby growth. Mainly found below 5,000'. Absent from the higher Sierra Nevada and Cascade ranges. In southeastern Inyo County, present only in winter.

d you know? This wren's name, pronounced like the car ("Buick"), honors British naturalist and engraver Thomas Bewick.

ate & Location Seen: _____

Breeding Male

Non-breeding

BLUE-GRAY GNATCATCHER
Polioptila caerulea

escription: 4 ½″. A small, slender, and very active songbird; **blue-gray above, whitish-gray below** with a **white eye ring**. Long **black tail shows much white along the sides** (looks mostly white from below). MALE: Black stripe on sides of forehead in breeding plumage, lacking in winter birds and immatures. FEMALE: Always lacks black forehead mark; tinged slightly brownish above.

ice: Call is a thin, peevish *speeeeee* or *speeee-peee*. Unimpressive song is a series of squeaky, wheezy notes and chips.

havior: Very active, flitting around low shrubs and mid-levels of trees while flipping its long tail from side to side. Makes frequent short sallies for flying insects as well as gleaning twigs and foliage. Often seen in pairs.

milar Species: Unmistakable; it is the only gnatcatcher in the region, except for southeastern Inyo County (see Black-tailed Gnatcatcher, p. 473). Thin scold notes can be similar to some calls of House Wren (p. 333).

here, When to Find? Uncommon to fairly common summer resident, mainly April to July, in open woodlands such as blue oaks and pinyon-juniper; also in chaparral, scrub-oaks, and riparian thickets. Most numerous in the inner Coast Ranges, Sierra Nevada foothills, and Great Basin; scarce to absent in the humid northwest coastal region. Rare in winter in the Central Valley and coastal lowlands; most birds winter south of our region.

id you know? Gnatcatchers (family Polioptilidae) form an exclusively New World group of about 17 species; they are perhaps most closely related to the wrens and creepers.

ate & Location Seen: _____

Description: 7 ½". A **chunky dark gray semi-aquatic songbird** of rushing streams with long pinkish legs and short tail (often cocked upward). JUVENILE is paler below, bill yellowish at the base.

Voice: Loud *zeet* or *zeet-zeet* call is audible about roaring of creek water. Loud song, often given in flight, includes paired whistles, buzzes.

Behavior: Perches on boulders along creeks, frequently bobbing up and down and "blinking" conspicuous white "eyelids." Submerges into flowing water to forage on aquatic invertebrates, small fish. Flight is rapid and whirring, close to water surface. Nest, a ball of mosses, is placed in spray zone of cascades, on a nearby ledge, or beneath a bridge.

Similar Species: Unmistakable. Black Phoebe (p. 283) also perches on rocks in creeks, but has white belly, very different shape. Juvenile European Starling (p. 361) is superficially similar, but behavior utterly different.

Where, When to Find: Uncommon and localized year-round resident along fast-flowing permanent streams throughout the region to at least 8,000'; also sometimes along high elevation lakeshores. Lowland sites include Lost Man Creek, Humboldt County; Alum Rock Park, San Jose; Pescadero Creek, San Mateo County; and the Big Sur River, Monterey County. Lee Vining Creek, Mono County and Foresta Falls in Yosemite National Park are among the many reliable mountain locations. Breeding sites and numbers vary with rainfall and stream conditions. Some disperse in winter to non-breeding streams, and to lower elevations.

Did you know? Adaptations for an aquatic existence include very dense plumage, extra-large oil glands for waterproofing, nasal flaps to keep water from entering the nostrils, and short, muscular wings for submergence and underwater propulsion.

Date & Location Seen: _____

Ruby-crowned Kinglet Female

Male Displaying Crest

Golden-crowned Kinglet Female

Male Displaying Crest

RUBY-CROWNED KINGLET
Regulus calendula

Description: 4 ¼". A tiny, plump "neurosis with feathers." **Olive** with a yellowish tinge; **white eye ring** (broken above), **one bold white wing-bar bordered behind by a black bar** at the base of the flight feathers. Tiny thin bill, short notched tail and slender black legs with yellow feet. MALE: bright red crest, hidden except when bird is agitated. FEMALE: lacks crest. **Voice:** Call a husky *ji-dit*, often run into an agitated series. Song starts with high, thin notes, then builds into rich, warbled repeated phrases, amazingly loud for a tiny bird. **Behavior:** Extremely active, constantly flitting about, often flicking its wings. Feeds by gleaning, also hovers briefly to pick insects off foliage. Often forms core of wintering mixed-species groups of small insectivores. **Similar Species:** Compare Hutton's Vireo (p. 295). **Where, When to Find:** Common winter visitor throughout except coldest northeast and high mountains, mainly late September to early April; found in woodlands, tall chaparral, thickets and gardens. Uncommon to rare breeder in lodgepole pine and fir forests in the high Sierra Nevada and other high mountains of the northern counties.

GOLDEN-CROWNED KINGLET *Regulus satrapa*

Description: 4". Kinglet with **orange and yellow crown bordered by black stripes**; white eyebrow. Underparts whitish with olive-gray tinge. **Voice:** Very high, thin *see see see* call notes. Song structure like Ruby-crowned's (above), but much higher pitched. **Behavior:** Typical active kinglet behavior. In winter usually found in small, loose groups, often with mixed-species flocks in conifers. **Where, When to Find:** Breeds mainly in fir forests of the higher mountains, and in coastal redwood/Douglas-fir associations south to Santa Cruz County. Most move to lower areas in fall, wintering on coast, foothill regions, and lower elevation forests. Rare in the Central Valley.

Did you know? Kinglets, a tiny family (6 species) of tiny birds, have no known close relatives among the songbirds.

Date & Location Seen: _____

Description: 6 ½ ". A **fluffy-bodied, short-winged and long-tailed brown bird** of dense brush, heard far more often than seen. **Breast is pinkish with indistinct thin streaks. Eyes whitish.** Bill short, stout, slightly curved. Birds on the humid northwest coast are darker and ruddier than those of interior and southern areas.

Voice: Song, a characteristic sound of chaparral and brushy riparian habitats, is a series of *peep* notes, accelerating into a rapid trill, *peep, peep, peep-peep-pee-pee-pee-prrrrr*. Song of female is slower, with notes often doubled and no terminal trill. Call is a dry purring *churr*.

Behavior: Flits about within dense brush, its thin, loose tail often angled upward. Gleans insects, also eats small berries. Found in closely associated pairs, the male and female frequently trading calls.

Similar Species: Wrens have thinner bills, dark eyes, and very different calls.

Where, When to Find: Common year-round resident in dense brushland, often of continuous chaparral type, as well as moist wooded riparian areas with lush understories, from the coast eastward through foothills and lower mountains (to about 4,500'). Absent from the Klamath Basin, Modoc County away from the southwestern area near Day, and east of the crest of the Cascade/Sierra Nevada range (except a few on the east slope of the Sierra Nevada in southwestern Inyo County). Very sedentary; rarely crosses tracts of unsuitable habitat.

Did you know? Current genetic studies suggest that the Wrentit's genetic affinities lie with the Old World sylviid warblers.

Date & Location Seen: _____

Western Bluebird
Male

Western Bluebird
Female

Mountain Bluebird
Male

Mountain Bluebird
Female

escription: 7″. A plump thrush with a short tail. **Head, wings, rump and tail blue. Breast, sides, and variable patch on back chestnut.** Blue areas deep and vibrant on MALE; paler and more subdued on FEMALE. JUVENILE is spotted white above and below. **Voice**: Calls include a musical *phew* (often given in flight) and a rough chatter. Song consists of short warbled phrases. **Behavior**: A versatile forager; hops on ground for insects, sallies upward for flying insects, picks berries from mistletoe, junipers, toyon, etc. A cavity nester; takes readily to nest boxes. **Similar Species:** Compare Mountain Bluebird (below). **Where, When to Find:** Common summer resident (March-October) in open woodlands, oak savannas, and large forest-margined meadows from the coast to about 5,000′ on the west side of the Cascade/Sierra Nevada range; sparsely localized breeder east of the crest. Small flocks are widespread in winter.

MOUNTAIN BLUEBIRD *Sialia currucoides*

escription: 7 ¼″. Slimmer than Western Bluebird, with longer bill, wings, primary projection, and tail. MALE: **Deep sky blue overall,** with whitish belly and undertail coverts. FEMALE: **Ashy-gray overall**, with white belly and undertail coverts, **pale blue primaries and tail**. JUVENILE is like female, but with spotted underparts. **Voice**: Call a thin, descending *vieuw*; song a warbled jumble of call notes. **Behavior**: Often hovers; forages on aerial and ground-dwelling insects. Nests in cavities, nest boxes, and rock crevices above tree line. **Where, When to Find**: Fairly common summer resident (March-October) in large, open mountain meadows or shrublands, dry grassy openings, and rocky fell-fields generally above 6,000′. Rare on high peaks in northern Coast Ranges. Highly migratory; in winter, fairly common in the Owens Valley, generally uncommon in the Central Valley and surrounding foothills, rare in coastal lowlands.

id you know? In winter in the lowlands Western Bluebirds often flock with Yellow-rumped Warblers and sparrows.

ate & Location Seen:

"Russett-backed" group

Description: 7". *Catharus* thrushes are plump, thin-billed birds with spotted breasts and buffy wing stripes which show in flight. Our "Russet-backed" Swainson's Thrushes (*ustulatus* subspecies group) are **uniformly russet brown on upperparts, wings, tail**. Broad **buffy eye ring; throat and breast buffy with brown spots**; sides and flanks brownish, belly white.

Voice: Song begins with querulous *queee*, followed by beautiful, fluty phrases that spiral upward. Calls include a liquid *whit* or *pwip*, and a rich *queee?* Calls differ in "Olive-backed" birds.

Behavior: Feeds on insects within shady woodland understory, less frequently on more open pathways, lawn borders. Migrants sometimes feed in small groups, often visit fruiting shrubs. Does not flick wings or cock tail. Territorial birds sing from mid-story. This nocturnal migrant is often heard overhead in spring and fall, giving a distinctive *queee?* flight call.

Similar Species: Hermit Thrush (p. 351) shows contrast between brown or gray-brown upperparts and rusty tail, has whitish eye ring, and blackish spots on creamy breast. Hermit frequently flicks wings and cocks tail, unlike Swainson's. Call notes differ.

Where, When to Find: "Russet-backed" birds are common spring migrants (mainly May) and generally uncommon, infrequently detected fall migrants (September, early October) mainly coastally; they winter on the Pacific Coast from western Mexico to Costa Rica. Fairly common breeder in riparian thickets and moist forests with dense understory in the coastal region's lowlands and foothills. Uncommon and declining breeder on the west side of the Sierra Nevada. Numbers of "Olive-backed" birds, *swainsoni* subspecies group, formerly common east side breeders, are apparently much reduced; reasons are unknown.

Did you know? Our Pacific Coast "Russet-backed" birds may perhaps constitute a separate species from "Olive-backed" birds east of the Sierra Nevada, which winter in South America.

Date & Location Seen: _____

HERMIT THRUSH
Catharus guttatus

escription: 6 ¾ ". Plain **grayish-brown** to **brown above, with rump and tail contrastingly reddish brown.** Buffy-white on **breast with blackish spots,** sides and flanks grayish, belly white. Complete, **thin white eye-ring.** Our breeding subspecies are grayer than our small, dark wintering birds; inland mountain breeders are large and long-billed, breeders in coastal counties are small.

oice: Beautiful song begins with long whistle, then cascading fluty phrases; successive songs on different pitches. Calls include *chup* or *chup-chup*, a clear descending whistled *tew*, and a wheezy, rising *zhweee*.

ehavior: Hops on ground for insects, usually remaining in shade; often visits fruiting shrubs in winter. Usually seen singly. Rapidly flicks wings and slowly raises and lowers tail when perched.

imilar Species: Swainson's Thrush (p. 349; absent in winter) is more uniform russet-brown above, with broad buff eye ring, brown breast spots, and buffy flanks; doesn't flick wings or cock tail. Thin bill separates thrushes from sparrows.

Where, When to Find: Common from October to early April in parks, gardens, chaparral and woodlands in lowlands and foothills. Fairly common to common breeder through most mountain ranges (absent from more arid portions of the inner Coast Ranges), favoring dense or well-shaded coniferous forests from sea level to mid elevation, and more open, drier forests near tree line, but shunning pinyon pines and Jeffrey pine woodlands.

id you know? Stand on the edge of a moist mountain meadow in a dense coniferous forest as dusk approaches on a calm evening. Experience the Hermit Thrush's haunting, ethereal song, and you will probably join those who consider this species the finest songster in North America.

ate & Location Seen: _____

Male

Juvenile

escription: 10". A familiar large, plump thrush with gray-brown upperparts, **rufous-red breast**, and **white markings around the eyes**. MALE'S head is blackish, breast deep reddish-orange; FEMALE is paler and duller, with gray-brown head. JUVENILE is heavily spotted with dusky on the breast, and with whitish on the wings and back.

oice: Song is a pleasing carol of two- or three-noted rich whistled phrases. Calls include a hard *pup-pup*, a squealing *kli-kli-pup*, and a high, lisping flight call.

ehavior: Much of the time feeds mainly on the ground, often probing into moist soil for earthworms and grubs. Runs on the ground, with sudden stops. The nest is a mud-lined open cup. Winter flocks seek sources of berries, including toyon, manzanita, mistletoe, juniper, and planted fruiting trees and shrubs such as pyracantha and olives; they often flock with waxwings.

milar Species: Varied Thrush (p. 355) is more furtive than robins, and differs in long orange eyebrow, gray or black breast band, and orange patterning on wings. See Spotted Towhee (p. 393) and Black-headed Grosbeak (p. 423).

/here, When to Find: Robins breed commonly in moist woodlands of the foothills, in the mountains to 10,000', and also in well-watered residential areas and urban parks in the valleys and lowlands. In winter they travel in nomadic flocks and can be very common where fruits and berries are available; numbers vary greatly from winter to winter.

id you know? The robin's song is perhaps more familiar to birdwatchers and non-birdwatchers alike than that of any other songbird.

ate & Location Seen: _____

Male

Female

escription: 9 ½". A striking thrush with **predominantly orange underparts**, a dark breast band, an orange eyebrow, **two orange wing-bars**, and an **orange wing-stripe** that's **prominent in flight**. MALE has rich blue-gray nape and back, broad black breast band; FEMALE has a narrow dusky breast band, and browner upperparts. JUVENILE resembles female, but belly is white, breast scalier-looking.

oice: Song is like a high whistle on a single pitch superimposed upon a low buzz, which it repeats on different pitches. Call is a soft, low *tschook*; in winter a single song phrase is sometimes heard.

ehavior: Forages on or near the ground in dark forests with a wet, mossy, almost completely shaded floor. Breeds (April – August) in heavy mature stands of conifers, principally redwoods and Douglas-firs near the coast; in winter seeks similar features in lesser degree: shaded ground and dense trees, along ravines in warmer and more arid areas.

milar Species: American Robin (p. 353) has a black head, lacks a breast band, and lacks an orange eyebrow and wing markings.

/here, When to Find: Common year-round in coastal redwood parks and other suitable habitat from about Garberville, Humboldt County, northward; rare in the Santa Cruz Mts. Winters from the ocean eastward to the Cascade/Sierra Nevada range (to 5,000' on the west slope); in the Central Valley largely limited to wooded areas in the central and northern portion. Wintering numbers vary greatly from year to year. Scarce migrant through the Great Basin, though it can appear almost anywhere in spring and fall migration.

id you know? Its generic name, *Ixoreus*, comes from the Greek words *ixos*, which means mistletoe – one of the species' favored wintertime berries, and *oreos*, which means mountain.

ate & Location Seen: _____

Description: 12". A large, long-tailed **brown** bird with a remarkable **long, decurved bill**. Its brown plumage is enlivened only by a whitish chin, faint dark "whisker marks," and **tawny-buff undertail coverts** and suffusion on belly.

Voice: Song is rich and varied, with phrases (including mimicry) repeated 2-3 times; it is choppier than a mockingbird's song, with harsher phrases and less repetition. Calls include a harsh *chelk* and a gurgling *gr-lik*.

Behavior: Terrestrial, scratching through the leaf litter with its long, curved bill for seeds, insects. Runs on the ground; flight is labored, low. Hard to see except when vocalizing, when it often perches atop a shrub or low tree.

Similar Species: California Towhee (p. 397) has similar plumage, but a very different short, conical bill. In Inyo County, the California Thrasher's range approaches that of the sandy gray LeConte's Thrasher (p. 475), but is well separated from that of the grayish, pale-eyed Crissal Thrasher (p. 475).

Where, When to Find: Fairly common year-round resident on brushy mountain slopes, and in chaparral and brushy riparian thickets through most of the region to about 5,000′ elevation. Range extends around the Central Valley, through the Coast Ranges north to San Francisco Bay, and inland in scattered locations further north to the Shelter Cove area, Humboldt County, and Yreka, Siskiyou County. Small numbers reside on the east side of the Sierra Nevada south of Lone Pine, Inyo County.

Did you know? This thrasher is almost exclusively found in California, extending just a short way into northwestern Baja California, and with only a few records in interior southwest Oregon.

Date & Location Seen: _____

Description: 10″. This familiar large and long-tailed songster is **gray** above and grayish-white below, with **large white patches on the wings and extensive white along the sides of the tail.** Eyes yellowish. The slender bill is slightly curved. JUVENILE differs from adults in brown spotting on the underparts, dark eyes.

Voice: Famous song is rich, loud and varied; it consists of a huge variety of simple notes or phrases, each usually repeated 3-6 times. Many of these phrases are copied from other birds, or other familiar ambient sounds. Frequently sings at night in spring and summer. Calls include a harsh *chack* and a drawn-out scolding *shrrrrr*.

Behavior: Feeds on insects and berries. Often runs a few steps on the ground, then stops and flashes wings open in jerky fashion (which may serve social functions as well as flush up insect prey). Aggressive when protecting nest and fledglings.

Similar Species: Much scarcer Loggerhead Shrike (p. 291) has thicker, hooked bill, bold black mask. See female Phainopepla (p. 367), Townsend's Solitaire (p. 465).

Where, When to Find: Fairly common year-round resident in urban areas, suburbs, orchards and ranch yards at low elevations along the coast north to the San Francisco Bay area, and north through the Central Valley. Scarce around towns further north along the coast and inland, and east of the Sierra Nevada, mainly in winter. Absent from the higher mountains.

Did you know? Mockingbirds have thrived in human-modified landscapes, benefiting from irrigation and the planting of fruiting trees and shrubs that can sustain the species year-round. They moved north through California over the last century from their original stronghold in the southwest, and first nested in Oregon in 1993.

Date & Location Seen: _____

Juvenile

Breeding Male

Non-breeding

Description: 8 ½". A stocky **blackish** songbird with a **short, squared tail** and pointed brown wings. **Straight, pointed bill**; dull pinkish-orange legs. Body plumage **iridescent black, bill bright yellow** (base bluish in MALES, pinkish in FEMALES) when breeding. In winter, plumage **heavily spangled with whitish** spots, bill blackish; white spotting wears away in late winter to reveal breeding dress. JUVENILE is gray-brown throughout, with dark bill and lores, but shows distinctive starling shape.

Voice: Extremely varied; song incorporates much mimicry (including entire songs of species such as Western Meadowlarks and California Quail). Buzzes, clicks, rattles and high squealing characterize the prolonged song. Calls include a buzzy *dzeeer*, harsh *shurrr*, and sharp *vit* predator alarm call.

Behavior: Waddles on ground, using gaping motion of bill to probe lawns, soil. Flocks also exploit fruit (grapes, olives, palm fruits, etc.), grain, and even tidal wrack and estuarine mudflats. Flies with rapid wingbeats, flight silhouette appearing triangular. Nests in cavities in trees or structures, often aggressively usurping cavities from native species such as Purple Martin and Lewis's Woodpecker.

Similar Species: Blackbirds have longer tails, never show yellow bills.

Where, When to Find: Very common year-round resident throughout the region. Most numerous in urban, suburban and agricultural areas, but also invasive in natural riparian and conifer forests, to about 7,500' on the east side of the Sierra Nevada. Large flocks gather in the winter in open parks, fields, and agricultural areas.

Did you know? This species was introduced from Europe to New York in the late 1800s; it first appeared in California near the town of Tulelake, Siskiyou County, in January 1942.

Date & Location Seen: _____

Non-breeding

Description: 6 ½". A slender ground bird with a **thin bill,** gray-brown upperparts, pale, **buff-tinged underparts** with **streaks on breast,** and **white edges to the tail. Walks** on the ground, **constantly bobbing the tail up and down**. BREEDING birds are grayer above and richer buff below, with breast streaks reduced or absent. NON-BREEDING birds more heavily streaked below, faintly streaked on back.

Voice: Calls include a thin *tseep*, and a doubled *tsi-sip* given in flight. Song, a rapid series of jingling *chee* or *cheedle* notes, is often given in flight on the breeding grounds.

Behavior: Usually seen on the ground, but sometimes sits on fence lines, wires, or tree branches. In winter, gathers in large flocks in open fields, sometimes mixing with Horned Larks.

Similar Species: Many sparrows are superficially similar but have short, conical bills and do not bob tails. Red-throated Pipit (*A. cervinus*, 6") of Eurasia is seen regularly along the coast in fall; it has a boldly streaked back and breast, pink legs, high-pitched *speee* call.

Where, When to Find: Common winter visitor, mainly from October to April, in lowlands throughout the region, although rare in midwinter in northeastern California. Favors open terrain with sparse stubble or grass, also shorelines and river flats. Rare and highly localized breeder in moist meadows (10,000' – 12,000') in the Sierra Nevada, from near Mt. Whitney north to the Lake Tahoe region.

Did you know? Known in the Old World as "Buff-bellied Pipit." California's first nest was found near an alpine lake at 10,500' in the Hall Natural Area, on the eastern edge of Yosemite National Park, on August 1, 1975. Breeders there are the Rocky Mountain subspecies *alticola*, with unstreaked, rich buff underparts.

Date & Location Seen: _____

Adult

Juvenile

Description: 7 ¼". A **sleek, crested** bird that travels in tight flocks. **Soft brown, tinged yellow on the belly. Black chin and mask.** Lower back and rump gray. Blackish **tail has yellow band** at the tip. Small **wax-like red spots** are found on the tips of the secondaries of many adults. JUVENILE is duller, with broad indistinct streaking below.

Voice: Call is a soft, very high-pitched *sreeee*, unimpressive if uttered by a single bird, but amounting to quite a din when a flock chimes in.

Behavior: Nomadic winter visitors, descending on fruiting trees and shrubs such as toyon, elderberries, mistletoe, and pyracantha to consume berries. Flies in tight flocks, often of dozens or hundreds of individuals; sometimes flocks with American Robins. In warmer weather often sallies from treetops for flying insects. Within flocks birds may perch in close proximity, sometimes even passing berries to one another.

Similar Species: Flocking behavior and triangular flight shape can suggest European Starling (p. 361). Bohemian Waxwing (*B. garrulus*, 8 ¼") is a rare and irregular winter visitor, sometimes in flocks, to the northeastern corner of the state and east of the Sierra Nevada. It is larger and grayer than Cedar, and shows white wing markings and chestnut (not white) undertail coverts.

Where, When to Find: Irregularly common visitor from September through May, with the largest numbers often occurring in late winter and spring. Found throughout the region where berry crops can be found, including urban parks, residential areas, and native woodlands. Uncommon breeder in moist coastal lowlands mainly from Humboldt County northward; rare breeder locally in northeastern Modoc County.

Did you know? No other local wintering species remains so late in spring; Cedar Waxwings sometimes linger into early June.

Date & Location Seen: _____

Adult Male

Female

Description: 7 ¾". A sleek, long-tailed, **crested** bird with **red** eyes, short thin bill. The MALE is **shiny black**, with **large white wing patches** (usually visible only in flight). The FEMALE is **dark gray**, with indistinct **pale gray wing patches**. JUVENILES resemble adult female, wing patches virtually lacking; male acquires black plumage by first winter.

Voice: Common call is a soft, upslurred *pooee*; also a harsh *churr*. Song consists of disjunct, scratchy warbles. Captured birds expertly mimic a variety of other birds' calls when handled.

Behavior: Perches upright atop shrubs, low trees. During warmer months sallies after flying insects; in fall and winter feeds mainly on mistletoe and other berries. Often found in small loose flocks.

Similar Species: Northern Mockingbird (p. 359) is larger, lacks crest, and has much white in the tail.

Where, When to Find: Fairly common spring and summer resident (mainly April to October) subject to much seasonal movement, in foothill oak and sycamore woodlands and chaparral ringing the San Joaquin Valley and the southern Sacramento Valley, and east of the Sierra Nevada north to Big Pine, Inyo County. Breeding distribution not well known. Winters irregularly in the Central Valley and surrounding foothills. Rarely found to the coast in winter.

Did you know? The species' generic name affirms that the adult male wears a "black, shining robe," from the Greek *phainos*, shining, and *peplos*, a robe; *nitens*, from the Latin *nitere*, to shine, emphasizes the appellation.

Date & Location Seen: _____

_____

Non-breeding

Description: 6 ¼". Longspurs were formerly included with the sparrows, but are taxonomically distinct. Lapland Longspur occurs in small numbers annually, in late fall and winter. Tail deeply notched; in flight, note **outermost pair of tail feathers mostly white**. In winter, **bold dark bar outlines plain buff ear patch, reddish edges on greater coverts and tertials**. White throat, dark whisker, white underparts with brown streaks on flanks. MALE shows broad, smudgy black chest band; FEMALE shows a thin buff band.

Voice: Flight call a dry mechanical rattle, mixed with whistled *tew* notes.

Behavior: Picks seeds off the ground in pastures and fields with open ground and short, sparse grass, often with flocks of Horned Larks or American Pipits. May hunch down and "freeze" or run when approached; when flushed, swirls into often lengthy flight, calling occasionally. May return to the same spot or choose similar habitat some distance away.

Similar Species: Even rarer fall and winter visitor Chestnut-collared Longspur (*C. ornatus*, 6") is plainer brown above; tail is white with a dark triangle at its tip; repeated *kit-tle* flight call differs from Lapland.

Where, When to Find: Rare to uncommon fall migrant and winter visitor (late September to March) to shores, grassy coastal headlands, agricultural grasslands, and bare fields in the coastal region, Sacramento Valley, and more northern valleys. Mostly seen in late fall; scarcer in winter. Specific spots to seek longspurs in winter include Hayward Regional Shoreline in Alameda County, outer Point Reyes in Marin County, agricultural areas around Tule Lake and Alturas in Siskiyou and Modoc counties, and the grasslands of Yolo County.

Did you know? Lapland Longspur breeds on open tundra across Eurasia and North America, including coastal southern Greenland.

Date & Location Seen: _____

lutescens

Immature
orestera

escription: 5". Warblers are small, active insect-gleaning birds of shrubby and wooded areas. Orange-crowned (subspecies *lutescens* described) is **plain olive-yellow throughout** with an indistinct yellow eyebrow, a **yellowish eye ring broken by a thin dark line** through the eye, and **faint olive breast streaking**. Olive-gray tail lacks white markings. MALE: Dull orange crown patch, nearly always hidden; body plumage brighter yellow-olive. FEMALE is duller; JUVENILE shows indistinct buffy wing-bars. Immatures of the Great Basin and Rockies subspecies *orestera* and the eastern subspecies *celata* have gray heads.

Voice: Song is a colorless rapid trill, usually rising then falling slightly in pitch. Call is a sharp, semi-metallic *tik*; also a thin *seet* in flight.

Behavior: Gleans and probes twigs, leaves for insects; often feeds low in shrubs. Nests on or near ground, but territorial males may sing from high perches.

Similar Species: See Yellow (p. 379) and Wilson's (p. 387) warblers. Dullest gray-headed Orange-crowned females (especially of *orestera*) can suggest Nashville (p. 373) and MacGillivray's (p. 375) warblers.

Where, When to Find: Breeds widely in oak woodlands, willow thickets, open forests and tall chaparral nearly throughout (but avoiding Central Valley and arid habitats within the Great Basin). Common early breeder on the west slope of the Sierra Nevada up to 3,000'; juveniles and post-breeding adults disperses upslope to moist meadows and to other nonbreeding areas as early as late May. Common migrant in spring (March to early May) and fall (late July to October) throughout the region. Uncommon but regular in winter, mainly in the Central Valley and on the coast from the Bay Area southward.

Did you know? These warblers and many other small gleaning species probe into eucalyptus blossoms in the winter and often stain their faces black as a result.

Date & Location Seen:

Virginia's Warbler
Male

Adult
ridgwayi

Description: 4 ¾". A small, rather short-tailed warbler with a **complete white eye ring** on a **gray head**, olive upperparts, **yellow underparts including throat**; bright yellow undertail. MALE has clearer gray head; brighter yellow underparts. As with most warblers, young FEMALE in fall is dullest. Like Orange-crowned, bill is especially sharply pointed.

Voice: Call is a soft *plink*, subtly but distinctly different from calls of our other warblers. Song, a few *see-pit* notes, then a quicker series of sweet notes.

Behavior: Frequently bobs tail up and down while foraging. Gleans for insects, spiders in foliage of low trees, shrubs, and even weed stems. Typical of warblers, singing males on territory may sing for many minutes from a high perch. Nests on the ground.

Similar Species: Immature *orestera* Orange-crowneds with grayish heads (p. 371) differ in split (not complete) eye ring, duller and faintly streaked breasts. Female Common Yellowthroat (p. 377) has longer tail, brown/buff tinge to plumage, skulking habits. Closely related **Virginia's Warbler** (*L. virginiae*, 4 ¾"), scarce and local breeder in riparian thickets in the central and southern Great Basin region (mainly White and Glass Mts.), and rare fall visitor to the coast, is grayer throughout, lacks green on wings, has yellow limited to center of breast and undertail.

Where, When to Find: Breeds in montane woodlands where black oaks or maples augment pines and with shrubby understory, from west slope of Sierra Nevada and inner Coast Ranges (north of Bay Area) north to mountains of Siskiyou and western Modoc counties. Fairly common spring migrant (mainly April, early May) through the lowlands and foothills, especially in live oak woodlands. Moves south mainly through mountains; uncommon mid-August to early October through lowlands. A very few winter in coastal areas.

Did you know? The Pacific region subspecies (*ridgwayi*, named for premier American ornithologist Robert Ridgway) may represent a species distinct from eastern *ruficapilla*.

Date & Location Seen:

Male

Fall Immature

Description: 5 ¼". A skulking warbler of dense thickets. **Olive-green above** and **yellow below. Head and chest gray** with **white arcs above and below the eye**. The bill is rather long and bicolored (blackish above, pinkish below); the long legs are pinkish. MALE has black in front of eye, black mottling on the throat; FEMALE and immatures lack black, throat is pale gray to whitish.

Voice: Call is a hard, sharp *tik* or *tsik*. The song is a short chanting series, e.g., *tr-ree, tr-ree, tr-ree, sweet-sweet*.

Behavior: Generally keeps well within low, dense thickets, but migrants on the eastern deserts may be in more open areas. Rarely forages above shrub level, though territorial males typically sing from perches well up in trees.

Similar Species: Nashville Warbler (p. 373) is smaller and shorter-tailed, has a complete eye ring and yellow throat. Some female Orange-crowned Warblers (p. 371) have grayish heads, but they are duller and more uniform in plumage, show indistinct breast streaks, and have grayish legs.

Where, When to Find: Breeds (mainly April to August) in willow thickets, mountain meadows, montane chaparral, dense brush on shaded slopes, and other moist shrubby habitats, mostly in northern and eastern mountains but also on and near the coast; scarcer and more local south of the San Francisco Bay area. Spring migration (April and May) is most noticeable east of the Sierra Nevada; more widespread but still scarce fall migrant (August to early October).

Did you know? "Squeaking" or "pishing" sounds made by the observer will often bring this skulking warbler (as well as various wrens, sparrows and other birds) into view.

Date & Location Seen: _____

_____

Adult Male

Female

scription: 5″. A skulking warbler of wet thickets and marshes. **Bright yellow throat** contrasts with duller underparts (**sides washed with brownish**). Upperparts olive-green; undertail yellow. MALE: **Bold black mask and forehead** bordered behind by white. FEMALE: Lacks mask, has indistinct whitish eye ring; pale yellow throat contrasts with brownish cheeks and sides. Young males have a hint of a black face mask.

ice: Call is a husky *jip* or *tidge*. The distinctive, loud song repeats several two- to four-note phrases, e.g., *wichety, wichety, wichety…* or *wee-wee′chu, wee-wee′chu, wee-wee′chu…*

havior: Skulks in cattails, tules, or moist, shrubby vegetation, feeding on insects. Males may sing from an open perch, and they sometimes give songs in short flights.

nilar Species: The black-masked male is unmistakable. Females can resemble dull females of other plain-winged warblers, such as Yellow (p. 379), Nashville (p. 373), Orange-crowned (p. 371), and MacGillivray's (p. 375), but note Common Yellowthroat's long, rounded tail, contrast between pale yellow throat and dull pale brownish underparts, and indistinct complete eye ring.

here, When to Find: Common summer resident in freshwater and brackish marshes and other wet, dense tangles throughout the lowlands and foothills, though local within arid Great Basin areas; less common in the Central Valley. Populations in the northern counties and east of the Sierra Nevada withdraw southward in winter, when generally uncommon to fairly common west of the Sierra Nevada. Migrants widespread, but less common in the mountains.

d you know? Subspecies *sinuosa*, which breeds in marshes (including salt marshes) and moist riparian and floodplain areas in the San Francisco Bay area, is a state Species of Special Concern.

ate & Location Seen: _____

Male

Immature

Description: 5". A fairly stocky, **short-tailed** warbler that is **mainly yellow throughout**. Plain head lacks markings except for **bold dark eye** and indistinct pale eye ring, MALE: Bright yellow, with **thin red streaks on breast**. FEMALE: Duller, paler, lacking red streaks. Immature females can be very dull, nearly lacking yellow. All birds show yellow patches in tail (so **tail appears all yellow below**), yellow or whitish edges to wing feathers.

Voice: Call is a downslurred *chip*, varying from husky to thin. Sprightly song starts with high *sweet* notes, then a short high twitter and emphatic *see-see-whew!* ending. In flight gives a buzzy *zzeet*.

Behavior: Bobs tail up and down while foraging. Typical warbler gleaning behavior, often quite high in deciduous trees. Nest is a soft cup well up in a tree.

Similar Species: Other mostly yellow warblers (Orange-crowned, Wilson's) have longer, all dark tails. Duller females with more evident eye rings can suggest Nashville Warbler or Common Yellowthroat.

Where, When to Find: Common breeder (mainly late April to late September) in riparian woodlands (e.g., of willow, cottonwood, alder, sycamore) in the lowlands and foothills, and in brushy woodland edges and aspen groves in the higher mountains; now very localized and declining in the Central Valley and much of the San Francisco Bay area. A state Species of Special Concern. Common and widespread migrant in spring (April to early June) and fall (mainly August to September). A very few winter in coastal areas.

Did you know? As with many of our riparian species, Yellow Warbler nests are often parasitized by Brown-headed Cowbirds, though they do show some ability to recognize cowbird eggs and re-nest.

Date & Location Seen: _____

_____

Yellow-rumped Warblers

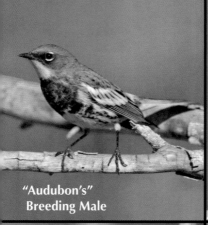

"Audubon's"
Breeding Male

"Audubon's"
Immature
Female

"Audubon's"
Non-breeding

"Myrtle"
Breeding Male

"Myrtle"
Non-breeding

YELLOW-RUMPED WARBLER
Setophaga coronata

Description: 5 ½". Our abundant wintering warbler. Always shows **bright yellow rump patch**, patch of **yellow on sides**, and **white patches near corner of tail**. Gray to gray-brown, with white wing-bars, whitish belly. "Audubon's" subspecies group has **yellow throat patch** (throat may be whitish in immature FEMALES); BREEDING MALE has black chest, large white wing patch. "Myrtle" subspecies group has white throat patch that extends back to a point behind the ear region and thin whitish eyebrow; breeding male has mottled black chest and bold white wing-bars.

Voice: *Chip* call of Audubon's has strong "ch" quality; Myrtle call is flatter *tup*. Song is a loosely-patterned warble.

Behavior: Varied in feeding habits, gleaning foliage, sallying after flying insects, or probing eucalyptus blossoms for nectar. Often forages in the ground in loose flocks (may associate with bluebirds and with juncos and other sparrows).

Similar Species: The yellow rump patch distinguishes even the dullest winter immatures from our other regularly seen warblers.

Where, When to Find: Very common winter visitor (October to April) throughout the lowlands in a variety of habitats. Attracted to groves of winter-flowering eucalyptus, but also in riparian woodlands, chaparral, parks and gardens. "Audubon's" predominates in most areas, but "Myrtle" predominates in many coastal riparian thickets. "Audubon's" breeds (late April to September) in pine-fir forests above 4,000' in all of our high mountain ranges (and more locally above 2,000' in the high Coast Ranges from the San Francisco Bay area south).

Did you know? The "Audubon's" and "Myrtle" subspecies groups have an extensive hybrid zone in British Columbia and w. Alberta, and are usually considered conspecific.

Date & Location Seen:

Immature Female

Male

Description: 5". A warbler that is **gray above** and **white below**, with black markings and with much white in the outer tail feathers. The dark ear patch connects to gray hind-neck; two strong **white wing-bars**. The **tiny yellow spot in front of the eye** is hard to see. MALE: **Black ear patch and throat**, and **bold black streaks on the sides**. Adult FEMALE has dark gray ear patch, some black on lower throat; immature female lacks black on throat.

Voice: Call is a dull *tup*. Song is a series of high, buzzy notes, e.g., *zeea-zeea-zeea-ZEE-zee*.

Behavior: Actively gleans insects from leaves and twigs of oaks and other trees. Often joins other warblers, kinglets and other small insectivorous birds in migration and winter.

Similar Species: Townsend's Warbler (p. 385) is similarly patterned but has extensive olive and yellow coloration. Chickadees (p. 319) lack side streaking, wing-bars, and white tail patches, and have white faces.

Where, When to Find: Breeds in mixed conifer and oak woodlands in the mountains throughout, though local in the southern Coast Ranges and especially scarce/local in northeastern California. Partial to canyon live oaks where they occur, but also in other oaks, in yellow pine, and in Douglas-fir; also in pinyon-juniper associations south through Inyo County. Fairly common migrant from the Cascade/Sierra Nevada crest west, moving earlier in spring (beginning in late March and mainly in April) and later in fall (mid-September through October) than most other warblers. A few winter in woodlands in the coastal regions and Central Valley.

Did you know? You shouldn't fear "confusing fall warblers" because most species, such as the Black-throated Gray and its close relatives, look very similar in spring and fall.

Date & Location Seen: _____

Townsend's Warbler
Adult Male

Townsend's Warbler
Female

Hermit Warbler
Adult Male

Hermit Warbler
Immature Female

TOWNSEND'S WARBLER
Setophaga townsendi

Description: 5". Patterned much like the Black-throated Gray Warbler, including **bold white wing-bars**, but the **upperparts** are **olive-green** and the pale areas of the head and **breast** are **yellow**. ADULT MALE is **black on throat, ear patch**, and much of the crown. IMMATURE males have slightly less black on head and throat. FEMALE duller, with little black on the throat. **Voice:** Call a light *tip*, higher pitched than Black-throated Gray's. Song is also higher. **Behavior:** Actively gleans for insects, particularly moth larvae. Travels about woodlands in mixed-species flocks in winter. **Similar Species:** Distinctive, but beware similar Black-throated Green Warbler (*S. virens*, 5"), a rare vagrant here. **Where, When to Find:** Uncommon migrant through wooded areas in spring (mainly mid-April through May, sometimes into early June); fall migrants (mid-August to mid-October) are common in mountain forests and coastal lowlands. Locally common in winter in coastal slope woodlands.

HERMIT WARBLER *Setophaga occidentalis*

Description: 5". Shares Townsend's white wing-bars and outer tail feathers, but is **gray above, unmarked white below**; MALE **has a bright golden-yellow head** and **black throat**; FEMALE and IMMATURES have little or no black on the throat and a duller yellow head. **Voice:** Song clearer, less wheezy than songs of Townsend's and Black-throated Gray. Call much like Townsend's. **Behavior:** Territorial males sing from high in pines. **Where, When to Find:** Breeds in montane coniferous forests, mainly above 4,000' in the Sierra Nevada and Cascades; southward in the higher inner Coast Ranges to the Santa Cruz Mountains. More widespread in migration, but rare east of the Cascade/Sierra Nevada range; rare in winter in coastal woodlands from the San Francisco Bay area south.

Did you know? A hybrid zone between Townsend's and Hermit Warblers is found in the northern Cascade Mountains. Beware: such hybrids are occasionally noted in our region in migration.

Date & Location Seen: _____

Male

Female

Description: 4 ¾". A small, hyperactive warbler that is **bright yellow-olive above** and **bright golden-yellow below**. The yellow forehead contrasts with a **shiny black cap** (MALES) or mixed black and olive cap (most FEMALES; some females show only olive). The dark eye stands out on the blank yellow face. Wings and tail are unmarked olive-green.

Voice: Call is a distinctive soft *timp*; also gives a slurred *tsilp*. The song is a rapid series of *chip* notes, building in volume and speed, but often trailing off at the end.

Behavior: : Intensely active, gleaning, hovering, and making short sallies for flying insects. The tail is flipped about as the bird forages.

Similar Species: Orange-crowned Warbler (p. 371) is much duller yellow, shows a thin dark line through the eyes, and is shorter-tailed. Yellow Warbler (p. 379) is plumper and shorter-tailed, has yellow tail spots and edges to wing feathers.

Where, When to Find: Common spring (late March through May) and fairly common fall (mainly late August through September) migrant throughout. Often one of the most common and conspicuous migrating songbirds in foothill oak woodlands and in the Great Basin in spring. Breeds fairly commonly in willow thickets along the coast and foothills and in willow thickets and meadows through the higher mountains. Rare in winter in willow thickets of the coastal lowlands.

Did you know? Along with the phalarope, snipe, plover and storm-petrel, this is one of five birds named for famed late 18th and early 19th century American ornithologist Alexander Wilson.

Date & Location Seen: _____

Northern Waterthrush

Black-and-white Warbler
Breeding Male

Tennessee Warbler
Fall

American Redstart
Breeding Adult Male

Backpoll Warbler
Fall

Palm Warbler
Fall
palmarum

Migrants may stray far from their normal route; such "vagrants" may appear here from e. North America, ne. Asia, and Mexico. Forty-six warbler species have been found in our region: here are six "eastern" warblers most frequently encountered in our region – mainly in fall (late August to November), but sometimes in spring (especially mid-May to early June) and winter.

Northern Waterthrush · *Parkesia noveboracensis*

6". Brown terrestrial warbler that walks on ground and bobs tail continuously. Brown above, whitish (tinged yellow) below with long white or pale yellow eye-stripe, extensive dark streaks on breast. Often near ponds or damp understory. Loud *chink* call.

Black-and-white Warbler · *Mniotilta varia*

5 ¼". Boldly striped warbler that creeps along trunks, branches. Note white stripes on back and center of crown, bold white wing-bars.

Tennessee Warbler · *Leiothlypis peregrina*

4 ¾". Small, short-tailed; similar to Orange-crowned, but clearer pale yellow on breast and supercilium, stronger dark eye-line, much white on undertail coverts, brighter olive back. Spring male (rarely seen here) has gray crown, silky white underparts.

American Redstart · *Setophaga ruticilla*

5 ¼". Flashy, active warbler which often spreads tail. Tail with bold black and orange (adult male) or yellow pattern. Adult male black with white belly, orange patches on sides, wings, tail; females and immature male replace black and orange with gray and yellow. Call a thin, downslurred *tsip*.

Blackpoll Warbler · *Setophaga striata*

5 ½". Greenish above, pale yellow on breast with thin streaks, bold white wing-bars, and white tail spots; strong supercilium and dark eye-line; yellowish feet. Spring males (very rare here) have black cap and whisker, white cheek, black-streaked back and breast.

Palm Warbler · *Setophaga palmarum*

5 ½". A largely terrestrial tail-bobber. Dull brownish, faintly streaked on breast, with bright yellow undertail coverts. Whitish supercilium. Spring birds have a rusty crown and a yellow supercilium. Call a weak *tsik*.

Yellow-breasted Chat
Icteria virens

Description: 7 ½". A **large, thick-billed** warbler-like bird with a **deep yellow throat and breast, white spectacle** around the eyes, olive upperparts, whitish belly, and **long olive tail**. The sexes are similar, but FEMALE has less black in front of the eye and a less intensely yellow breast than MALE.

Voice: Distinctive. The loud, rich song is a measured, loose collection of chatters, rattles, caws, and whistles, with notes sometimes repeated rapidly. Call is a nasal *airrh* and a snappy *cheew*.

Behavior: Skulks in dense brush and thickets, where surprisingly hard to see. Territorial males may perch openly for prolonged periods while singing, and often sing exuberantly in flight with deep, snappy wing beats. Feeds on insects and berries.

Similar Species: Unmistakable; Common Yellowthroat (p. 377) is much smaller.

Where, When to Find: Uncommon to fairly common breeder (late April to early September) in extensive riparian thickets in the lowlands and foothills. Most widespread in Sierra Nevada foothills and the northwest; local near the coast and in the northeast and now absent from much of the Central Valley. Its California breeding range has decreased by about one-third, and it is listed as a state Species of Special Concern. Rather rare as a migrant, noted mainly in late April-May and August-September.

Did you know? The relationship of the chat to the wood-warblers has long been studied and debated. Genetic studies led the chat to be placed (2017) in its own monotypic family, Icteriidae.

Date & Location Seen: _____

Male

Juvenile

SPOTTED TOWHEE
Pipilo maculatus

Description: 8 ½". Sparrows (including towhees) are mainly brownish ground-dwelling birds that forage for seeds and insects. Sexes are alike, or nearly so, in most species. This is a large sparrow; MALES with a **black head, white-spotted black wings** and back, and white corners on the black tail. Bright **rufous sides**, flanks and undertail, contrasting with white center breast and belly. **Eyes red**. FEMALES are slightly duller, with slaty heads. JUVENILE is brownish and heavily streaked, but shows distinctive wing spotting and white tail corners.

Voice: Call given by most California birds is a scratchy rising mew, *reee-eeh?* (descending *reeehr* in birds of White and Inyo Mountains). Song is a simple, loud buzzy trill, sometimes with a short whistled introductory note.

Behavior: Towhees are large sparrows that scratch about with their feet in the leaf litter for seeds and insects. Spotteds usually forage well within dense brush, but may often be seen at open edges; readily pop up in response to "pishing". Singing males may perch openly atop shrubs.

Similar Species: Male Black-headed Grosbeak (p. 423) is superficially similar but has a much thicker bill, shorter tail, more extensive orange color, and arboreal habits. Much smaller Dark-eyed Junco (p. 419) lacks white spotting.

Where, When to Find: Common year-round resident in chaparral, other brushlands, and riparian thickets to about 3,000'; above that, fairly common summer resident in similar habitat to about 7,000'. Post-breeding, birds wander upslope, rarely as high as tree line; in fall and winter they withdraw downslope and perhaps southward. Fairly common in residential areas where sufficient cover exists, will emerge to feed on scattered seed.

Did you know? The "double-scratch", a quick forward and backward two-step maneuver, is a unique foraging behavior of towhees and some other sparrows.

Date & Location Seen: _____

Rufous-crowned Sparrow
Aimophila ruficeps

Description: 6". A softly-colored gray-brown sparrow with a **dull rufous crown, black and whitish streaks bordering the sides of the throat,** rufous streaks on the back, and a white eye-ring. Lacks wing-bars. JUVENILE (usually seen with adults) is finely streaked below.

Voice: Call is a plaintive *dear dear dear;* also a soft *tseeet* and a dry chatter. The song is a jumbled series of notes, recalls a House Wren song but thinner and scratchier.

Behavior: Usually found in pairs. Feeds inconspicuously on the ground, where generally secretive; however it is often very responsive to "pishing," approaching the observer closely. Singing males perch openly atop a shrub or rock.

Similar Species: Chipping Sparrow (p. 399) is more cleanly marked, whiter below, with white wing-bars and a black line through the eye; Chippies are gregarious most of the year, and are found in very different habitat.

Where, When to Find: Locally uncommon to fairly common sedentary year-round resident on grass covered arid hillsides with rock outcroppings and sparse low bushes, and in patches of sagebrush, from near sea level to about 3,000'. Avoids dense chaparral and wooded areas. Almost never seen away from areas where it breeds. Range extends from Mendocino and Tehama counties southward through the Coast Ranges, and from near Chico, Butte County southward along the west slope of the Sierra Nevada to the southern edge of our region. Resident also in the Sutter Buttes, and at scattered locations outside the range described above, e.g., near Alderpoint, Humboldt County.

Did you know? Emphasizing that towhees are merely large sparrows, when new genetic data led in 2010 to a rearrangement of towhee genera, this *Aimophila* sparrow was placed in taxonomic order between two of our region's towhees.

Date & Location Seen: _____

Description: 9″. A familiar **large, plain brown** sparrow. **Undertail is rusty orange;** the throat is tinged with orange and bordered below by short, faint streaks. Thin orangish eye-ring. JUVENILE resembles adult but has fine streaking on the breast.

Voice: Call is a sharp metallic *chink*. Song is a series of *chink* notes strung into a loose, accelerating series. Also gives a descending series of rough, squealing notes.

Behavior: Usually found in pairs. Occupies chaparral, coastal scrub, open woodlands, and residential areas. Scratches in the leaf litter and on open ground for seeds, insects. Like many seed-eating species, towhees feed mainly grubs and other invertebrates to their nestlings.

Similar Species: California Thrasher (p. 357) is somewhat similar in plumage, but has a long, thin down-curved bill. Fox Sparrow (p. 409) is whiter below, with heavy spotting.

Where, When to Find: Common to locally uncommon sedentary year-round resident in brushy habitats from central Humboldt, Trinity, and Shasta counties southward, and eastward from the ocean to about 4,000′ in the Sierra Nevada. Largely absent from the Central Valley's floor from about San Joaquin County south; disjunct populations in the Shasta Valley, Siskiyou County and near Tule Lake. A very small isolated population (ca. 700 birds) of subspecies *eremophilus*, considered Endangered (state) or Threatened (federal), resides in willow thickets and adjacent upland shrubs in the Argus and Panamint Mts., southern Inyo County.

Did you know? This and other ground-inhabiting birds suffer heavily from predation by feral cats in urban areas and populations cannot survive around the many sanctioned "feral cat colonies" in the region.

Date & Location Seen: _____

Non-breeding
Adult

Breeding Adult

Juvenile

Description: 5 ½". A small, slim, long-tailed sparrow with gray underparts and rump, streaked brown back, and distinctive face pattern: **black line through the eye, white or buffy eyebrow,** and **rich brown crown** (bright **rusty** in breeding ADULTS). Bill black in breeding adults, otherwise mostly dull pinkish. JUVENILE resembles dull non-breeding adult, but extensively streaked below; this plumage can be held until mid-October.

Voice: Calls include a rich *tseet* and soft *tik*. Song is a colorless dry trill, usually faster and less musical than the trilled song of a junco.

Behavior: Forages primarily on the ground, nests in woodlands and forests with grassy openings. In fall and winter found locally in flocks of 10-50 birds in park-like areas with lawns or weedy fields and scattered trees, in open orchards, and sometimes on residential lawns. Flocks flush up into trees when disturbed. Flocks may mix with other species such as juncos and Yellow-rumped Warblers.

Similar Species: Immature White-crowned Sparrow (p. 415) is much larger with bright pinkish-orange bill. Brewer's Sparrow (p. 477) has finely streaked crown, pale area between bill and eye, and thin white eye-ring.

Where, When to Find: Fairly common to common summer (April to August) resident in open, dry coniferous or pine-oak forests as high as tree line in the northern coastal mountains, the Cascade/Sierra Nevada range, the Warner and White Mts., and locally in the South Coast Ranges and the San Francisco Bay area. Most leave the region in fall and winter; generally rare and local then in open park-like areas, including residential areas and orchards, in the Central Valley and other lowlands. Rare migrant on the coast.

Did you know? Chippies are among the most widespread sparrows in North America, breeding from Alaska to Nicaragua.

Date & Location Seen:

Breeding Adult Male

Female

Description: 5 ¾". A slender, long-tailed sparrow of mountain chaparral with **gray head and underparts. Back streaked rusty brown**, and wing feathers also edged with rusty. **Pink bill** stands out against the gray or (BREEDING MALE) **black face and chin.**

Voice: Call is a high, weak *tik*. The beautiful song is a series of sweet upslurred or downslurred notes, accelerating to a very rapid trill.

Behavior: A bird of moderately dense mixed species chaparral or coastal scrub on dry, sloping and generally south-facing hillsides; best seen when males sing from the top of a low shrub. Feeds on the ground for seeds, insects.

Similar Species: Juncos (p. 419) show extensive white in the tail; no other sparrow is so extensively gray on the head and underparts.

Where, When to Find: Uncommon to rare localized summer resident (late April to August) in foothills around the Central Valley and in the Coast Ranges to about 4,000', north to Lake and Mariposa counties, occasionally to Tehama and Butte counties. Found at higher elevations along the Kern River Highway east of Johnsondale, Tulare County and in mountains bordering the Owens Valley south of Bishop, Inyo County. Breeding locations irregular from year to year; often favors burns and post-fire successional habitat, where the chaparral has been opened up and is not too dense. Migrants found only casually away from breeding habitat.

Did you know? Juveniles of this species and most other plain-breasted sparrows are streaked below for a few weeks after fledging.

Date & Location Seen: _____

Vesper Sparrow

Lark Sparrow

Description: 6 ¼". A large, **streaky** sparrow with **white outer tail feathers**; shows a **white eye ring**, pale crescent behind the **brown ear patch**, and distinctive small chestnut patch (usually concealed) at the bend of the wing. **Voice**: Rich, melodious song: two pairs of slurred whistles, then a series of short, descending trills. Call a soft *seep*. **Behavior**: Forages on bare ground or grassy patches among scattered sagebrush or similar shrubs. **Similar Species**: Smaller Savannah Sparrow (p. 407) has shorter tail, bold eyebrow; more extensively streaked below. **Where, When to Find**: Fairly common summer resident in the Great Basin and brushy mountain meadows east of the Sierra Nevada crest. Uncommon in winter around the fringe of the Central Valley, valleys of the South Coast Ranges, and Owens Valley.

LARK SPARROW *Chondestes grammacus*

Description: 6 ½". A large, handsomely marked and confiding sparrow of open country with scattered trees. **Bold head pattern** includes **chestnut ear patch**, black "whiskers", white markings around the eyes, and chestnut and white crown stripes. **Whitish below** with **black breast spot**. Long **tail has white corners and outer edge. Voice**: Song consists of varied short phrases, often repeated, of sweet notes and rough, burry trills. Call a soft *tsip*. **Behavior**: Feeds in short-grass fields, retreats up into trees when flushed; often gregarious in winter. **Similar Species**: Vesper Sparrow (above). **Where, When to Find**: Fairly common to common through the year in open areas and oak savannas of the lowlands and foothills. Largely absent from northwest coastal counties and the immediate coast; in fall and winter absent north of the Central Valley and from the Great Basin.

Did you know? The "Oregon" Vesper Sparrow (subspecies *affinis*), whose winter range includes central and southern Central Valley grasslands, is a state Species of Special Concern.

Date & Location Seen: _____

Bell's Sparrow

Adult *belli*

Adult *canescens*

Sagebrush Sparrow
Adult

BELL'S SPARROW
Artemisiospiza belli

Description: 5 ½". **Plain dark gray head and back**; back **unstreaked**. White eye ring, spot in front of eye; **broad black whisker mark**, black spot in center of whitish breast. JUVENILE duller, streaked brown. **Voice:** Song a rich, flowing jumble of rising and falling phrases. Call soft, tinkling junco-like notes. **Behavior:** Terrestrial; forages for seeds and insects in moderately dense, continuous hillside chaparral. Males sing atop low shrubs; best brought into view by "pishing". **Similar Species:** Compare Sagebrush Sparrow (below). Juvenile Black-throated Sparrow (p. 477) differs from juvenile in having bold, long eyebrow and more limited streaking below. **Where, When to Find:** Uncommon local year-round resident in inner Coast Ranges south from Trinity County, extending to coast south of Marin County; also locally on the west slope of the central Sierra Nevada. Pale subspecies *canescens*, intermediate in appearance to Sagebrush Sparrow, nests locally in Inyo County and into the Mojave Desert, also in arid hills on the San Joaquin Valley's west side north to Fresno County.

SAGEBRUSH SPARROW *Artemisiospiza nevadensis*

Description: 6". Like Bell's, but with **pale gray face, buffy brown back with blackish streaks, narrow whisker mark**. JUVENILE duller, browner, more streaked overall. **Voice:** Song a strongly defined pulsating pattern of rising and falling phrases in a minor key. Call like Bell's. **Behavior:** Terrestrial; runs with tail in air, like a tiny thrasher. Defends a territory of several acres. **Similar Species:** See Bell's (above). **Where, When to Find:** Uncommon to locally common summer resident in sage scrub and chaparral in the Great Basin south through Mono County. Uncommon in winter in Owens Valley; casual west of the Sierra Nevada in fall, winter.

Did you know? Based on genetic and other evidence, these two species were split (from the former Sage Sparrow) in 2013.

Date & Location Seen: _____

Savannah Sparrow
nevadensis

Grasshopper Sparrow

Description: 5 ½". A small sparrow of open areas with **streaked back, breast and flanks**; often shows a yellow tinge in front of the eye. Note **small bill, short, notched tail**, and **bright pink legs. Voice**: Calls include a sharp *tip* and a high *tsee*. Song is high and buzzy. **Behavior**: Feeds in loose flocks on the ground in open grassy areas; usually perches on weed stems, fences or wires (less often in trees). **Similar Species**: Song Sparrow (p. 411) has a longer rounded tail and grayer face, and inhabits wet brushy areas. See Vesper Sparrow (p. 403). **Where, When to Find**: Common resident in coastal grasslands, wet meadows, and margins of tidal marshes south to Elkhorn Slough, Monterey County (subspecies *alaudinus*); also in the Great Basin region south to Owens Lake (*nevadensis*). Fall and winter visitors (chiefly *nevadensis*) blanket the region's warmer grassland areas (late August to April).

GRASSHOPPER SPARROW *Ammodramus savannarum*

Description: 5". A small, chunky grassland sparrow with short tail, **flat head, large bill**, and **unstreaked breast**. Crown dark with **pale central stripe, yellow-orange between eye and bill, white eye ring. Voice**: Most frequent song one or two high chip notes followed by a short, grasshopper-like *buzz*. **Behavior**: Skulking. Forages on the ground, climbs tall stem to sing; also sings from fence wires. **Similar Species**: Compare Savannah Sparrow (above). **Where, When to Find**: Uncommon and local summer resident (May through September); nests semi-colonially in foothills, low mountain valleys, and grasslands west of the Cascade/Sierra Nevada range; variable in occurrence from year to year. Rare (perhaps more numerous, but undetected because of its secretive nature) in the Central Valley and coastal areas in winter.

Did you know? Grasshopper Sparrow and coastal fog belt resident *alaudinus* subspecies of Savannah Sparrow are state Species of Special Concern, both mainly because of habitat loss or alteration.

Date & Location Seen:

_____

_____

"Thick-billed"

"Sooty"

"Slate-colored"

"Red"

Description: 7". A **large** sparrow, variable in bill size, shape, and plumage color. Our breeding "Thick-billed" birds have **thick, swollen bills, gray heads** and upperparts, **rusty on wings and tail,** and white underparts with breast spots like inverted "V"s. In winter and migration we have mainly "Sooty" birds, which are more uniformly **dark brown above** (including wings, tail; some are grayer on the head), **densely marked with brown spots below,** with smaller bills. Much less common in winter are "Slate-colored" birds, which resemble Thick-billeds but have smaller bills; "Red" birds, **streaked bright rufous below, rufous and gray above,** are rare.

Voice: Variable song combines clear slurred whistles and short trills; often includes mimicry of other birds' calls. Resembles Green-tailed Towhee's song. Calls vary: Thick-billed a metallic *chink*, Sooty and Red a smacking *thick*, and Slate-colored a more slurred *tewk*.

Behavior: Scratches on the ground, towhee-like, for seeds and insects. Singing birds tee up on the tops of shrubs or low conifers.

Similar Species: Song Sparrow (p. 411) is much smaller, with bold face pattern and streaked back. Compare with thinner-billed Hermit Thrush (p. 351).

Where, When to Find: Thick-billed is a common breeder (April to September) in montane chaparral throughout the foothills and mountains (as low as 3,500', as high as 9,000'); winters locally at lower foothill elevations and in coastal mountains in small numbers. Sooty is a common, widespread winter visitor (October to March) to foothills and lowland areas west of the Cascade/Sierra Nevada crest, including chaparral and scrub of the inner Coast Ranges. Winter ranges of Slate-colored and Red much as Sooty, except Slate-colored is scarce in lowland areas.

Did you know? Each of the four groups of Fox Sparrows noted above comprises multiple subspecies; as many as four species may be involved.

Date & Location Seen: _____

Description: 6 ¼". A common and familiar long-tailed sparrow of wet brushy or marshy areas. **Boldly streaked below**, often with a blackish **central breast spot**. Strongly patterned face with **broad gray eyebrow** and **black whisker stripe**. The **wings and tail are tinged rusty**. JUVENILE more lightly streaked, with buffy wash below.

Voice: Sprightly but variable song starts with a Beethoven-like motif of piping notes, followed by lower husky notes and short trills. Call is a distinctive *chemp*.

Behavior: Singing males may perch openly for many minutes, but otherwise these sparrows forage low, often on wet ground. Readily responds to "pishing". Flight is relatively weak, with the tail pumped up and down.

Similar Species: Lincoln's Sparrow (p. 413) is smaller, more finely streaked, and strongly buffy across the breast. Savannah Sparrow (p. 407) has shorter, notched tail, bright pink legs, and (often) yellow eyebrow.

Where, When to Find: Common year-round resident in or very near marshes, riparian woodlands, and other wet, densely-vegetated habitats throughout the region. Also in oak woodland understory and coastal sage scrub along the immediate coast, where fog and rain supply its moisture requirements; not found in drier chaparral. Limited to marshes and riparian areas in the Great Basin. Migrants and winter visitors from more northerly breeding subspecies are sometimes found in other habitats.

Did you know? Of some 25 subspecies of Song Sparrows occurring in North America, three are endemic to our region's tidal marshes, in San Francisco, San Pablo, and Suisun bays. All three (*maxillaris, samuelis,* and *pusillula*) are classified as state Species of Special Concern, as is the "Modesto" Song Sparrow, subspecies *mailliardi,* resident in the north-central portion of the Central Valley.

Date & Location Seen:

_____

_____

Description: 5 ¾". A rather retiring **finely streaked** sparrow of damp brushy and weedy areas. The **breast is washed with buff** and has fine streaks (and usually a small central spot). Also note the broad gray eyebrow, narrow buff eye ring, and **buffy stripe at side of throat**. The wings are tinged rusty. Slender and long-tailed shape, often with **peaked crown.**

Voice: Song is a hurried warble, usually rising then falling in pitch; sometimes delivered from surprisingly high in a tree. Calls include a sharp *thik* and buzzy *zzeeet*.

Behavior: Moves furtively through low, dense weedy growth and damp brushy areas, though "pishing" will often bring birds into view.

Similar Species: Song Sparrow (p. 411) is more boldly streaked and lacks buffy breast, but beware close similarity of Lincoln's to juvenile Song. If it's in the lowlands from late May through August, it's almost certainly a juvenile Song. Swamp Sparrow (*M. georgiana*, 5 ¾") has blackish and gray streaked upperparts and rufous wings, faint, blurry streaks on sides of grayish breast. Locally uncommon winter visitor to north coast marshes; rare elsewhere.

Where, When to Find: Fairly common, highly localized summer resident (May to September) in the Cascade/Sierra Nevada range in boggy, well-grown mountain meadows that are fringed or intermixed with willow thickets. Locally uncommon to rare in the Warner Mts., Klamath Mts., and North Coast Ranges; absent as a breeder from South Coast Ranges. Fairly common winter visitor (September to April) in damp, weedy fields, riparian understory, freshwater marshes, and woodland edges throughout the lowlands. Migrants are noted widely (mainly September-October and late March to late April).

Did you know? Named by Audubon in 1834 for Thomas Lincoln, his companion when they discovered the species, in present-day Quebec.

Date & Location Seen:

Adult *gambelii*

Immature *gambelii*

Adult *pugetensis*

Adult *oriantha*

WHITE-CROWNED SPARROW
Zonotrichia leucophrys

Description: 7". A familiar species, large and long-tailed with **bold black and white crown stripes, plain gray underparts**, streaked back, and **orangish bill**. Crown stripes are dark brown and creamy on IMMATURE. Coastal fog zone breeders "Puget Sound" (*pugetensis*) and "Nuttall's" (*nuttalli*) White-crowns have yellower bills, duller head stripes, streaked black and tan backs, and a brown tinge below. "Mountain" breeders (*oriantha*) differ from taiga-breeding "Gambel's" (*gambelii*) in having black between the eye and a darker pink bill.

Voice: Song consists of wheezy whistles and trills in a distinctive pattern, such as *dzew, zeedle zhee-jee dzu*; songs of *pugetensis* and *oriantha* include sweet repeated trills. All populations readily sing through winter. Common calls include a sharp *pink* and high *seet*.

Behavior: In winter, feeds in flocks on the ground near or within brushy areas. They readily visit backyard feeders.

Similar Species: Golden-crowned Sparrow (p. 417) has duller grayish bill, duller and browner underparts, and different crown pattern. Compare immatures with much smaller Chipping Sparrow (p. 399).

Where, When to Find: Common breeder *pugetensis* occupies the humid coast belt of Del Norte and Humboldt counties; widespread and common (especially in coast regions) in winter. Similar, sedentary *nuttalli* is locally common in a narrow coastal strip from Cape Mendocino south through the region. Fairly common *oriantha* breeds in willow thickets in high mountain meadows in the Warner Mountains and the Sierra Nevada; very rare outside breeding area, migrant in southern Great Basin, winters in western Mexico. Most of the region's wintering birds (late September to April) away from coastal areas are *gambelii*: common nearly everywhere (except in the higher mountains), in brushy areas, weedy fields, chaparral, and gardens.

Did you know? This species has been the subject of many pioneering studies of song learning and dialects, physiology, and migration.

Date & Location Seen: _____

Golden-crowned Sparrow
Breeding Adult

Golden-crowned Sparrow
Immature

White-throated Sparrow
Non-breeding White-striped Morph

Description: 7". A large sparrow, **dull gray below** and striped on the back, with a dull pinkish-gray bill and **yellow suffusion on the forecrown.** ADULT'S **crown bordered with black; forehead bright yellow** (pattern is stronger and bolder in BREEDING plumage, with black extending down to the eyes). IMMATURE'S head plainer, with dull yellow tinge to forecrown.

Voice: Calls include a sharp *chewp* and a drawn-out *tseeet*. Sweet song, a series of 2-5 long, plaintive whistles, usually going down the scale, *"Oh dear me"*, is often heard upon their arrival in fall, and near departure in spring.

Behavior: Feeds in small flocks in dense brushy areas, usually avoiding open areas; will flock with White-crowned Sparrows, but often in pure groups.

Similar Species: Immature White-crowned Sparrow (p. 415) has creamy white eyebrow and central crown stripe, pinkish bill, "cleaner" gray underparts. **White-throated Sparrow** (*Z. albicollis*; 6 ¾") is a rare but regular fall and winter visitor mainly to coastal and Central Valley woodlands. Usually seen singly, foraging with White-crowned or Golden-crowned Sparrows. Shows strongly outlined white throat; broad eyebrow is yellow in front of eye, either white or tan behind; dark crown stripes and eye-line. Call a sharp, metallic *pink*. May hear pure, whistled song *"pure sweet Canada Canada Canada"* in late winter.

Where, When to Find: Common fall and winter visitor (late September through April) in well-vegetated suburban areas, tall dense brush, woodland understory, and woodland edges as high as lower mountain slopes; scarcer in the Great Basin, especially in Mono and Inyo counties.

Did you know? Although scarce, apparent hybrids of White-crowned x Golden-crowned sparrow are known; apparent White-throated x Golden-crowned hybrids are even more rare.

Date & Location Seen: _____

Description: 6 ¼". A **dark-hooded** sparrow with a **light pink bill** and **flashing white outer tail feathers.** In our common **"Oregon"** birds, MALE has **black head,** contrasting with **pinkish-brown back,** white chest, and **pinkish sides.** FEMALE'S head dark slaty-gray to duller grayish brown. JUVENILE is streaked on the back and breast. **Male "Slate-colored"** birds have a **dark gray hood with a concave bottom edge** bordering white underparts; upperparts slightly paler gray or with varying brown at the center of the back; female brownish-gray overall.

Voice: Song is a simple, slightly musical trill, usually quite rapid, but sometimes with distinctly spaced notes. Calls include a sharp *tik* and high twittering.

Behavior: Forages mainly on the ground, hopping about grassy open areas for seeds and insects; requires nearby trees and brush for cover. Forms flocks in winter, often with other sparrows, bluebirds, Yellow-rumped Warblers and goldfinches.

Similar Species: Streaky juvenile may suggest Vesper Sparrow (p. 403). Slate-colored's resemblance to Black Phoebe (p. 283) is merely superficial.

Where, When to Find: "Oregon" is a common breeder in oak woodlands, coastal forests, mixed coniferous forests, and montane forests to tree line; also in eucalyptus forests, and well-wooded lowland residential areas. In winter (mid-October to March) they are common and widespread, mostly below levels of heavy snow, and common at feeders. Slate-coloreds are rare but regular in winter, the majority found in Oregon flocks east of the Cascade/Sierra Nevada crest.

Did you know? Juncos are among our hardiest songbirds, some overwintering even in the high mountains.

Date & Location Seen: _____

Summer Tanager Male

Summer Tanager Female

Western Tanager Breeding Male

Western Tanager Female

SUMMER TANAGER
Piranga rubra

Description: 7 ¾". ADULT MALE **entirely rosy red** year-round; first-spring male's head usually red, otherwise **mostly mustard-yellow**, like FEMALE. Lacks wing-bars. **Voice:** Call, a sharp *chi-tuk!* Song similar to Western Tanager (below), but sweeter, less burry. **Behavior:** Gleans within canopy, sallies for flying bees, wasps. **Similar Species:** Compare Western Tanager (below). **Where, When to Find:** Western subspecies *cooperi* an uncommon localized summer resident (May to mid-September) in riparian desert woodlands (especially cottonwoods). In region, breeds regularly only at China Ranch, Inyo County. Also a rare but regular visitor (probably mainly eastern subspecies *rubra*), mostly in fall migration and winter along the coast. A state Species of Special Concern.

WESTERN TANAGER *Piranga ludoviciana*

Description: 7". BREEDING ADULT MALE has red to **orange-red head** (first-spring male duller); otherwise **bright yellow** with **black back, wings and tail**; two **wing-bars** (front yellow, rear white). FEMALE olive-green above, pale yellow below, with **two white wing-bars**. WINTER adult males show almost no orange on face. **Voice:** Call a rising *pr-d-dik*. Song a series of hoarse, burry robin-like phrases: *pr-rit, pree-ur-rit, pree-u,* etc.; call often interspersed. **Behavior:** Sluggishly gleans insects through foliage, often high in trees; also sallies after flying insects. Feeds largely on berries and nectar in winter. **Similar Species:** Adult male unmistakable. Female's and immature male's heavy bill differentiate from slender-billed orioles. **Where, When to Find:** Common spring migrant (late April – May), fairly common fall migrant (late July to early October) throughout. Common breeder (May to August) in lowland mixed and riparian woodlands and montane forests to 8,000'. Rare but regular in coastal lowlands in winter.

Did you know? Genetic studies show that the "tanagers" of this genus are more closely related to our grosbeaks and buntings than to the diverse tanagers of the New World tropics.

Date & Location Seen:

_____

_____

Breeding Adult Male

Fall Immature Male

Female

Description: 8 ¼". The **very thick bill, white wing patterning** and **yellow underwing linings** are distinctive in all plumages. BREEDING ADULT MALE **head mostly black**; back streaked; **collar, breast, sides and rump rich burnt orange**; black wings and tail have bold white markings. Fall IMMATURE MALE like female, but with more richly colored breast. FEMALE has **brown crown stripes** and eye-line; **fine, tawny streaking mainly on sides of breast.**

Voice: Song is a rollicking and varied series of rich whistled notes. Calls include a sharp *pik* and (usually in flight) a wheezy *wheet?* Begging juveniles give an incessant *wheee-u.*

Behavior: Arboreal foragers, they take fruits, berries and seeds as well as insects; often visit sunflower seed feeders. The energetic song is sometimes given in flight in spring.

Similar Species: American Robin (p. 353) is very different in shape and behavior, and lacks white in the wings. Compare with Spotted Towhee (p. 393).

Where, When to Find: Common breeding visitor (mid-April to early September) in woodlands (oak, conifer, and riparian) and mixed coniferous forests of the mountains and foothills, including some well-planted suburban residential areas. Spring migrants (mid-April through mid-May) are common and widespread throughout; smaller numbers of migrants pass through from early July to late September, but this species remains only very rarely in winter.

Did you know? The Rose-breasted Grosbeak (*P. ludovicianus*, 8") is the Black-headed's eastern North American relative, yet grosbeaks in our region after late September and through the winter are just about as likely to be Rose-breasted as Black-headed.

Date & Location Seen: _____

Breeding Adult Male

Female

Description: 6 ¾". ADULT MALE is **bright, deep blue** on the head, underparts and rump; the black face sets off the **thick, silvery beak**. Two **thick, cinnamon wing-bars**. FEMALE is **tawny-cinnamon on the head, underparts and rump**; cinnamon wing-bars. The thick bill is distinctive. First spring males resemble females but have some blue coloring, especially on head.

Voice: The song is a continuous rich warble. Calls include a sharp *penk* and a buzzy *zzzzt*.

Behavior: Forages on weed stems, on the ground, and in low shrubs, taking both seeds and insects. Shares, with the other *Passerina* buntings (p. 427), the distinctive habit of switching its tail from side to side.

Similar Species: Female Lazuli Bunting (p. 427) is smaller with a shorter tail and much smaller bill. Male Blue Grosbeaks in poor light may look all black, resembling a cowbird.

Where, When to Find: Uncommon and local breeding visitor (end of April to August) in the Central Valley and adjacent foothills, in the Owens Valley north to Fish Slough, Mono County, and in the valleys between the Inner and Outer Coast Ranges north to Santa Clara County. Breeds in brushy riparian edges, willow bottomlands, and wet weedy fields. Refuges are good places to look for this colorful bird, among them Yolo Bypass and White Slough Wildlife Areas; Sacramento, Colusa, and San Joaquin National Wildlife Refuges, and the Cosumnes River Preserve. Very rare along the coast, mostly in fall migration.

Did you know? Though called a grosbeak, this species is, in fact, an outsized bunting closely related to the Lazuli.

Date & Location Seen: _____

_____

Breeding Adult Male

Female

escription: 5 ½". On BREEDING ADULT MALE, the **head and upperparts** are **bright blue, breast tawny-orange**, belly white. **Thick upper wing-bar bold white,** lower wing-bar narrower. IMMATURE to first spring MALES have more limited blue. FEMALE has **plain gray-brown head** and upperparts, **tawny breast, narrow white to buffy wing-bars**. JUVENILE resembles female, but breast is finely streaked.

oice: Song is a rapid, jumbled warble, with many notes given in pairs, delivered from a conspicuous perch. Call is a sharp *pit*; in flight gives a distinctive buzzy *zzzitt*.

ehavior: Forages for seeds on weed stems; also feeds in shrubs and on the ground. Agitated birds "switch" their tails from side to side.

milar Species: Blue Grosbeak (p. 425) is larger and heavier billed. Indigo Bunting (*Passerina cyanea*; 5 ½"), a rare migrant and summer visitor, is similar to Lazuli in size and shape; male Indigo is entirely deep blue, female is rich cinnamon-brown with blurred breast streaks and no wing-bars. Compare female to juvenile Scaly-breasted Munia (p. 457).

/here, When to Find: Common summer resident (May through August) in shrubby riparian growth, broken montane chaparral, and meadows with high, dense herbaceous vegetation throughout the region, from near sea level to about 6,000' on the west slope of the Sierra Nevada; higher on the east side. Common spring (mid-April to May) and fall (August to mid-September) migrant throughout, accidental in winter.

id you know? Lazuli and Indigo Buntings can be "fire followers" in that they are often common in the years following a burn in chaparral or forest. A singing male of either species atop a fire-blackened snag is a fine treat for the eye and ear.

ate & Location Seen: _____

"Bicolored Blackbird"
Adult Male

Adult Male

Female

Red-winged Blackbird
Agelaius phoeniceus

Description: 8 ¾". A familiar dark-eyed blackbird of marshy areas and open fields. ADULT MALE is **black** throughout, with a **bright red wing patch** that is usually bordered behind by creamy yellow. At rest, this patch is usually partly concealed. In fresh fall plumage the male's black back feathers are edged with rusty. FEMALE is **striped above and below**, with a buffy eyebrow and throat, and usually a reddish-brown tint to the wings and back. The IMMATURE male is like a dark female with a limited red wing patch. "Bicolored Blackbird" (subspecies *californicus* resident in the Central Valley, *mailliardorum* resident on the central coastal strip) differs in that the male nearly or totally lacks yellow border on its red wing patch, female is blacker below, more like Tricolored Blackbird (p. 431).

Voice: Song is a loud, semi-musical *cong-ka-REEE*. Calls include a harsh *check*, a harsh, slow rattle, and a high whistled *teeew*.

Behavior: Males sing from atop reeds or other emergent vegetation in marshes, wet meadows, and fields; displaying males flare out their red wing patches, but the red appears more limited on the folded wing of a resting bird. The nest is woven around stems of herbaceous plants. Large flocks (often mixed with starlings and other blackbirds) occur in winter.

Similar Species: See Tricolored Blackbird (p. 431), which is very similar but more localized. Female might be confused with a large sparrow or finch, but note longer, sharper bill, walking behavior.

Where, When to Find: Common breeder around freshwater and brackish marshes; lake margins; wet, weedy pastures and meadows; and dry fields with tall weeds (such as mustard). Widespread in winter in open fields, agricultural areas and marshes, and some open urban parks.

Did you know? Some consider this to be the most abundant bird in North America.

Date & Location Seen:

Adult Male

Female

TRICOLORED BLACKBIRD
Agelaius tricolor

Description: 8 ¾". Closely related to the Red-winged Blackbird. ADULT MALE is shiny black with a silvery sheen throughout, with a **deep red wing patch bordered by a broad white stripe** (more buffy in fresh fall plumage). At rest usually only the white stripe is visible. FEMALE is **sooty gray** (often appearing almost blackish) **on the belly**, with **whitish streaking on the breast** and a pale eyebrow, whisker mark and chin. In fresh fall plumage, the **back feathers are edged gray**.

Voice: Song is a harsh, nasal version of Red-winged's; a colony of singing males provides quite an acoustic experience. Calls lower and more nasal than those of Red-winged.

Behavior: Breeds very locally in dense colonies of dozens to thousands of birds in cattail and bulrush marshes, also Himalayan blackberry patches, nettles, and fields of triticale or other annual grain crops near water. Breeding birds may travel miles to forage for insects in fields, grasslands. Often cocks its tail, like cowbirds, when feeding on the ground.

Similar Species: Red-winged Blackbird (p. 429) very similar. Tricoloreds have more pointed wings and longer, more slender bills; males differ in their glossier plumage and darker, more limited red wing patch with a broad white border. Female Tricolored is sootier (lacking rufous) than female Red-winged, and the belly is more uniformly dark, lacking streaking.

Where, When to Find: In most years, more than 90% of breeding adults are found in Central Valley colonies. Smaller colonies occur throughout most of the remainder of the region, though this species is absent or a very local breeder in northwestern counties. Populations move extensively in winter; large concentrations gather in the Delta region and coastal areas, including Monterey and Marin counties, often associated with dairies.

Did you know? Tricoloreds, largely limited to California, numbered in the millions in the 1930s. With the population estimated at about 177,000 birds in 2017, California listed the species as Threatened in April 2018.

Date & Location Seen: _____

Adult

Fall Immature

Description: 9 ½". Not a lark, but a relative of the Red-winged Blackbird. Stocky and short-tailed, with a long, pointed bill. **Cryptically streaked brown above;** head with bold stripes. **Bright yellow below with black "V" on chest** and streaked white sides. **Tail bordered with white.** Winter birds and especially immatures are less boldly marked.

Voice: Loud, bubbly song is a burst of fluty whistles; calls include a harsh *chuck*, a low rattle, and in flight a high *wheet?*

Behavior: Found in pairs or small groups on open ground, foraging for insects and seeds. Males sing from atop shrubs or on fence lines or utility wires. Walks on ground, flicking open white-edged tail.

Similar Species: Stocky, triangular shape may suggest a starling in poor light. Pipits and larks are slimmer, lack extensive yellow below.

Where, When to Find: Fairly common year-round resident in agricultural lands, grasslands and desert scrub throughout the region, mostly at lower elevations but regularly up to 5,000' in the northeast. Migrants are sometimes found at higher elevations in fall. A large influx of wintering birds occurs from late September to March in open areas at lower elevations throughout. Very common in winter.

Did you know? Meriwether Lewis recognized that meadowlarks he heard and saw in Idaho in 1805 differed from those in the east. But it wasn't until 1844 that Audubon formally described the Western Meadowlark, naming it *neglecta* to chide naturalists who'd overlooked during the intervening 39 years the differences compared to the Eastern Meadowlark that Lewis noted.

Date & Location Seen: _____

_____

Breeding Adult Male

Adult Female

Description: 9 ½" (male); 8 ½" (female). Unmistakable; ADULT MALE'S **bright yellow head and breast** contrast sharply with its black body; also shows a **white patch partway out the wing**. FEMALE is smaller and duller, with yellow limited to the face and breast; IMMATURE MALE is intermediate.

Voice: Raucous song heard at breeding colonies begins with a harsh, rasping note and ends with a long, descending buzz. Call a low, rich *k-ruk*.

Behavior: Colonial nester, often with other blackbirds, in freshwater marshes with tules, cattails, or other plants that provide nest substrates above fairly deep standing water.

Similar Species: Yellow on head and chest distinguish it from all other blackbirds.

Where, When to Find: Fairly common summer resident (late April through August) in marshes of the Klamath Basin, Modoc Plateau and east of the Cascades/Sierra Nevada range southward to Owens Valley; also locally in marshy high mountain lakes and reservoirs. Uncommon in the Central Valley, sparse localized breeder coastward. It is a state Species of Special Concern. Migrants (April to mid-May, August to early October) are uncommon to rare but are seen widely, even to the coast, usually with other blackbirds. A few winter in the Central Valley; most leave the state in winter.

Did you know? Those who believe the Yellow-headed Blackbird's song is the least musical of all those produced by our region's songbirds seldom get contradicted.

Date & Location Seen: _____

_____

Brewer's Blackbird Adult Male

Brewer's Blackbird Female

Great-tailed Grackle Male

Great-tailed Grackle Female

Description: : 9". A familiar blackbird. ADULT MALE **shiny black** throughout, with iridescent purple highlights on head; glaring **pale yellow eyes**. IMMATURE MALE often with buffy feather edges on head and back. FEMALE **solidly dull gray-brown**, with **dark eyes. Voice**: Song an unmusical, forced *k-squeeesh*. Call a hard *check*. **Behavior**: Often tame around outdoor eateries, parking lots, parks; walks on the ground, picking up seeds, insects, food scraps. Gathers in large flocks in winter, often with other blackbirds and starlings. Nests in dense foliage of trees, hedges. **Similar Species**: Compare Great-tailed Grackle (below). Smaller Brown-headed Cowbird (p. 439) has smaller, thicker bill and shorter tail. Other female blackbirds (pp. 429, 431) have streaks. **Where, When to Find**: Common year-round resident in open lowland areas; numbers increase in winter. Also breeds around clearings, lakes and meadows in the mountains, withdrawing in winter.

GREAT-TAILED GRACKLE *Quiscalus mexicanus*

Description: 18" (male), 15" (female). MALE **glossy black** with very l**ong, keel-shaped tail**; eyes whitish. FEMALE **warm sooty-brown above**, paler **tan-brown below; eyes whitish** (light brown in juveniles). **Voice**: Male's song loud, mechanical; includes whistles, harsh grating sounds. Calls include harsh *chuck* and wooden *cut-a-cut-a-cut*. **Behavior**: Nests in loose colonies, especially in marshes. Walks, probing for grubs, seeds; also bird eggs, small fish. **Similar Species**: Compare Brewer's Blackbird (above). American Crow (p. 305) is smaller, with much shorter tail. **Where, When to Find:** Locally uncommon to fairly common year-round resident in marshy areas of the Central Valley, coastal counties from Sonoma County southward, and the central and southern Great Basin. Also found locally at higher elevations and northward, where some winter.

Did you know? This grackle spread from Arizona and Mexico to California by 1964. Recorded now in all 58 counties; numbers gradually increasing.

Date & Location Seen: _____

_____

Male

Female

Juvenile

Description: 7 ½". A small, short-tailed blackbird with dark eyes and a **stubby, finch-like bill**. MALE'S **dark brown head** contrasts with its **black body**. FEMALE is plain gray-brown. JUVENILE resembles female, but paler, faintly streaked below, and with pale scalloped edges to wing and back feathers. Molting young male in first fall has patches of black and tan, and can present a very confusing appearance.

Voice: Male's song a gurgling *glug-glug-gleeee*, delivered with bowed head and partly spread wings and tail. Calls include a sharp rattle and (in flight) high whistles.

Behavior: Cowbirds feed mainly on the ground, tail cocked up, for seeds and insects. Gather in large flocks in winter, often with other blackbirds, starlings. In the breeding season males display and chase females; females sneak through woodlands looking for open cup nests of other songbird species in which to deposit their eggs. "Brood parasites," cowbirds leave it to foster parents to care for their eggs and young.

Similar Species: Larger Brewer's Blackbird (p. 437) has a thinner bill, longer tail; male has pale eyes and shiny black head. Streaked juveniles suggest sparrows or a female Red-winged Blackbird.

Where, When to Find: Year-round locally common resident in the region in lowland areas that experience mild winters. Locally common to uncommon spring and summer resident in foothills and middle elevations of mountains, in meadows and open areas. Winter flocks gather in lowland open areas, dairies, and agricultural fields.

Did you know? A huge increase in cowbirds with grazing, agriculture, and urbanization has had severe impacts on many species (e.g., flycatchers, vireos and warblers) that they parasitize; intensive cowbird trapping efforts have aided these host species in many areas.

Date & Location Seen: _____

_____

Hooded Oriole
Adult Male

Hooded Oriole
Female

Bullock's Oriole
Adult Male

Immature
Male

Bullock's Oriole
Female

HOODED ORIOLE
Icterus cucullatus

Description: 8". Slender, long tailed, with **thin, slightly curved bill**. ADULT MALE **deep yellow** with **black face and throat**, back and tail. FEMALE olive-gray above, entirely yellow below. JUVENILE similar, but bill shorter; first-spring male like female, but throat black. **Voice:** Calls, a distinctive rising whistle, *wheet?* (loudest in males); also staccato chatters. Infrequently delivered song a jumble of short whistles and chatters. **Behavior:** Probes in foliage and flowers for insects and nectar; visits hummingbird feeders. Woven nest hung from underside of a palm frond (rarely in other trees). **Similar Species:** Compare Bullock's Oriole (below). Female Western Tanager (p. 421) stockier, with thicker bill. **Where, When to Find:** Uncommon and local breeding visitor (late March to August) in lowland parks, residential areas in Central Valley and surrounding foothills, and Inner Coast Ranges/valleys north to Mendocino County; rare elsewhere; very partial to fan palms. Rare in winter.

BULLOCK'S ORIOLE *Icterus bullockii*

Description: 8 ¼". Stocky, short tailed, with **straight bill**. ADULT MALE **bright orange**, with **black crown**, back, eye-line, and stripe on chin. **Large white patch on wing** coverts. **Tail yellow-orange with black center and tip**. FEMALE has gray back, white belly. First spring male similar, but chin and eye-line black. **Voice:** Song a rollicking *chick-chicky, tew, tew*. Calls include dry chatter, soft *hyew*. **Behavior:** Forages for insects in broad-leafed trees, nectar from flowers of trees, shrubs. Woven nest hung in a deciduous tree. **Similar Species:** Compare Hooded Oriole. **Where, When to Find:** Fairly common breeding visitor (April to mid-August) in oak and riparian woodlands, well-treed residential areas in coastal lowlands and up into the foothills; uncommon in mixed coniferous forests. A few winter in coastal lowlands, especially around flowering eucalyptus groves.

Did you know? Many woven oriole nests incorporate green plastic Easter basket "grass" or monofilament fishing line.

Date & Location Seen: _____

Male

Female

HOUSE FINCH
Haemorhous mexicanus

Description: 6". One of our most common and familiar native birds. The **stubby bill** is slightly curved along the top; long tail is only slightly notched. MALE is variably **red to orange-red** (or even orange or yellow, depending upon the bird's diet) on the forehead, eyebrow, chin, throat, breast and rump (brightest males have more extensive red wash). **Sides and belly with long, distinct streaks.** FEMALE has **long gray-brown streaks below; head relatively unpatterned**, with only slight thin eyebrow.

Voice: Song is a cheery, musical warble, descending slightly before usually ending with a nasal *wheer* note. "Happy" sounding calls include a variety of bright, inflected chirp notes.

Behavior: Abundant and confiding, often nesting in planters, porches and under eaves; Feeds on seeds, buds; commonly visits seed feeders. Often found in flocks in fall and winter.

Similar Species: See Purple (p. 445) and Cassin's (p. 467) finches. In flight House shows smaller head, shorter wings, longer tail than those species. Females are told from various streaky sparrows by curved bill, blurred streaking, plain head, and sweet chirping calls.

Where, When to Find: Common and ubiquitous year-round resident in grasslands, woodlands, lowland areas, treeless scrub, foothills, and even heavily urbanized areas; absent only from dense mountain forests and extensive tracts of chaparral. Year-round resident to about 6,000' on the east side of the Sierra Nevada; largely restricted to the foothills on the west side.

Did you know? This species occupies one of the widest ecological niches of any bird, ranging from hot deserts to ocean coasts to dense metropolitan areas.

Date & Location Seen:

Adult Male
californicus

Female
californicus

PURPLE FINCH
Haemorhous purpureus

Description: 6". A red finch of coastal, foothill and mountain woodlands with a stout bill and **notched tail**. ADULT MALE is washed with **raspberry red through the head, breast and rump**. The brown back and wings are also washed pinkish; a few blurry streaks on the sides. On FEMALE (IMMATURE MALE similar through first year), **patterned head** shows dark ear patch and crown, indistinct whitish eyebrow and whisker stripe; **blurry brown stripes below**; olive-brown back with indistinct blurry streaks. Our West Coast subspecies *californicus* is distinctive in plumage and vocalization from the East's nominate *purpureus*.

Voice: Song is a rich rapid warble with a few inflections and short trills. Calls are a sharp *pik* (given in flight) and *cheer-i-lee*.

Behavior: Feeds on buds, flower parts, berries, seeds, and insects; also visits feeders. Found singly or in small, loose flocks in winter.

Similar Species: House Finch (p. 443), much more abundant in lowlands, has smaller bill (slightly curved on top), smaller head, longer tail, and sharper and more extensive streaking on underparts; male's more restricted color is more orange-red, female has unpatterned head. See Cassin's Finch (p. 467).

Where, When to Find: Common breeding (May to August) resident down to near sea level in riparian and oak woodlands and mixed oak-coniferous forests west of the Central Valley and on the west slope of the Cascade/Sierra Nevada range into the red fir belt. Favors moist, shaded areas. Rare and localized breeder east of the Cascade/Sierra Nevada crest. Populations move downslope in fall; in winter, common in wooded habitats in foothills and lowlands west of the crest.

Did you know? Unlike House Finches, male Purple (and Cassin's) Finches do not attain their red color until a year old; they often sing and may even breed while in this "female-like" plumage.

Date & Location Seen:

Male

Female

Description: 5 ½ - 7 ¾". Flocking finch that specializes on conifer seeds, extracted (often audibly) with **unique crossed mandibles**. Most ADULT MALES **orange-red to brick red overall**, brightest on crown and rump; may instead be pale rose or scarlet (rarely yellow) overall. ADULT FEMALES **yellowish olive**; JUVENILES boldly streaked. Appears large-headed and short-tailed in flight. **Bill sizes and shapes and body sizes vary considerably** throughout the species' range.

Voice: Distinctive *jeep-jeep* calls delivered in flight. Ten different call types have been identified, about half of which have occurred in California; the types may indicate discrete, reproductively isolated populations that travel together.

Behavior: Nomadic in search of plentiful, ripening cone crops. Targeted conifers range in elevation from near sea level, e.g., Sitka spruce and Douglas-fir, to near tree line, e.g., whitebark and limber pines. Twists the mandibles to pry the cone's scales apart, enabling the tongue to extract the nut. Breeds where and when pine nuts, other conifer seeds are abundant. Feeds from ground level, on fallen cones, to tree tops.

Similar Species: Larger Pine Grosbeak (p. 467) has two white wing bars; bill is stubbier and mandibles do not cross.

Where, When to Find: Movements irregular; range includes North Coast Ranges from Mendocino County northward, Santa Cruz Mts., Modoc Plateau, Warner Mts., Cascade/Sierra Nevada range up to tree line, and bristlecone pine forest of the White Mts. Birds may be fairly common in one year, often absent in others. Irregularly will wander to planted pines within lowland urban areas.

Did you know? In 2017 Cassia Crossbill (*L. sinesciurus*), which is endemic (or nearly so) to Cassia County ID, was recognized as a separate species. The taxonomy of Red Crossbills remains problematic. There may be multiple cryptic crossbill species (meaning crossbill species that differ genetically and vocally but closely resemble one another) involved.

Date & Location Seen: _____

Description: 5". A streaky goldfinch relative with short notched tail, long wings, and slender pointed bill. **Streaked above and below**, with **yellow fringes to flight feathers**. Brightest birds, usually ADULT MALES, have **broad yellow wing-bar**, a yellow stripe on the spread wing, and yellow wash on breast. Dull birds have whitish wing-bars but still show traces of yellow wing stripe. All show dark rear portion of ear patch with pale neck sides curving behind.

Voice: Calls include scratchy *sheee-u,* rough *pit-pit* notes, and a buzzy, rising *zzhreeee?* Song is a rambling mix of call notes, trills.

Behavior: Siskins feed on seeds, catkins, buds and insects; when winter flocks "invade" lowlands they often frequent thistle feeders. Nests high in conifers.

Similar Species: Goldfinches (pp. 451, 453) lack streaking. House, Purple and Cassin's Finches (pp. 443, 435, 467) are much larger and heavier-billed, lack yellow in wings.

Where, When to Find: Fairly common to common summer resident and breeder (April through July) in the Cascade/Sierra Nevada range and the White Mts., the humid coast belt and Coast Ranges south to southern Monterey County; in the north, eastwardly across the state to Warner Mts. Nests mainly in pine trees, from near sea level to tree line. Erratic in its occurrence in fall and winter. Generally scarce in winter in lowlands, but in some years very large winter influxes occur there, with birds feeding at seeding trees, weedy fields, and thistle feeders.

Did you know? The Pine Siskin's seasonal movements in search of food are not well understood overall. But they are dramatic: recaptures of banded siskins show that some appear on approximately the same date in different years at places separated by half a continent or more.

Date & Location Seen: _____

Lesser Goldfinch
Adult Male

Lesser Goldfinch
Female

Lawrence's Goldfinch
Male

Lawrence's Goldfinch
Female

LESSER GOLDFINCH
Spinus psaltria

Description: 4 ½". ADULT MALE **olive-green above**, bright **yellow below**; forehead and cap black. FEMALE **dull olive above, pale yellow below**; IMMATURE male intermediate. All have dark gray bill, whitish wing-bars, and a **white patch at the base of the primaries** (largest in adult males). **Voice**: Calls include plaintive whistled *teeey-yee?* Song a rambling collection of call notes, sweet inflected notes, imitations of other species' call notes. **Behavior**: Feeds low on buds, catkins, weed seeds; visits thistle feeders. **Similar Species**: Slightly larger American Goldfinch (p. 453) lacks green tones to upperparts, lacks white patch on wing; strongly brown-tinged in winter. **Where, When to Find**: Common resident in chaparral, riparian woodlands, and well-planted residential areas of the lowlands and foothills throughout most of the region, never far from water. Generally absent from the high mountains.

LAWRENCE'S GOLDFINCH *Spinus lawrencei*

Description: 4 ¾". MALE **pale gray** throughout, with **black cap, face and chin, yellow patch on breast**, and **extensive yellow wing markings**. Bill pale pinkish gray. FEMALE like male, but lacks black on head, yellow slightly less extensive. **Voice**: Distinctive call a very high, tinkling *tink-u*, often delivered in flight. Song a tinkly jumble of call notes, with imitations of other species' call notes. **Behavior**: Feeds on seeds of annuals; especially fond of fiddlenecks in spring. Usually in small, loose groups. **Similar Species**: Yellow wing edges help distinguish dullest females from dull female Lesser Goldfinch. **Where, When to Find**: Fairly common breeder in arid interior valleys and foothills, dry woodlands and brushy areas with some water and riparian vegetation nearby. More scarce in winter, but abundance anywhere, in any season, varies greatly year-to-year. Rare on the coast, very rare in northern counties and east of the Sierra Nevada.

Did you know? Outside of California, Lawrence's Goldfinch breeds regularly only in northwest Baja California.

Date & Location Seen:

Breeding Adult Male
salicamans

Non-breeding
Adult Male

Non-breeding
Female

Description: 5″. Our largest goldfinch, but still a small bird. BREEDING MALES of our subspecies *salicamans* are not bright pale yellow as in other subspecies but are a more **muted and dull yellow,** with **black forehead,** black wings with one white wing-bar and **yellow "shoulder" patch**, white rump and undertail, and **pink bill.** BREEDING FEMALE is **duller overall, lacks black forehead** and yellow shoulder patch. WINTER adult male is tan above, pale gray below with partially yellow face, throat; yellow shoulder patch. Winter adult female like winter male but less extensively yellow; bill is gray.

Voice: Song is a rapid jumble, faster and shorter than songs of our other goldfinches and lacking mimicry. Calls include *yip-yip* (or *potato chip!*), given in flight, light twitters and squeaky whistles.

Behavior: Forages in trees at catkins and seed pods; in low, weedy growth on thistle-heads, dandelions, other flowers in the sunflower family; and at thistle feeders. Nests in streamside groves of willows, alders, and cottonwoods; also in early successional shrub growth with nearby seed sources. Winter flocks may occur with juncos, other goldfinches, and Yellow-rumped Warblers.

Similar Species: See Lesser Goldfinch (p. 451).

Where, When to Find: Common local breeder (April to July) in lowlands (especially the near-coastal strip), valleys and foothills west of the Cascade/Sierra Nevada range; more local in the northeast; rare to absent in west slope foothills south of Mariposa County. Widespread and fairly common in winter; found in parks and residential areas with seed-producing trees such as sycamores, birches, and alders.

Did you know? Cowbirds parasitize American Goldfinch nests, but not very successfully. No cowbird nestling is known to have survived longer than 15 days, apparently because a goldfinch's seed diet provides insufficient nutrition.

Date & Location Seen: _____

Breeding Male

Female

Description: 6 ¼". This dumpy, stout-billed Old World sparrow was introduced to North America from Europe about 1851, and was widespread in the region by the 1880s. MALE has a **black bib** (partly obscured by gray feather tips in fall, winter), **gray crown**, pale gray cheeks, **rufous neck sides** and rufous areas on striped back and wings, and one thick white wing-bar. Bill black in breeding season, otherwise yellowish. FEMALE is dingy gray-brown with tan and brown back stripes, broad creamy eyebrow; dull yellowish bill.

Voice: Incessant chirping calls, *chillip, churp, shrillip, shur...* These also repeated monotonously as male's song. Also, various twangy chatters.

Behavior: Gregarious. Bold and tame, picking seeds, scraps from the ground; also takes insects. Nest is a messy ball of grasses or straw jammed into a cavity, roof tile, or even street sign or old Cliff Swallow nest; nest is sometimes a free-standing structure in a tree. Roosting flocks make a din at dusk.

Similar Species: Our native sparrows (classified in a different family) are slimmer, have shorter and more sharply pointed bills, and differ in face pattern.

Where, When to Find: Common to abundant year-round resident in all urban areas, and around ranch yards, dairies and almost any other area with plenty of people or livestock. Generally forsakes natural habitats and is absent from the mountains except around settlements and towns.

Did you know? Within the roughly century and half since the species' introduction, U. S. populations have evolved measurably different body shapes and proportions that better equip birds to survive in their local environments.

Date & Location Seen:

RECENTLY INTRODUCED EXOTIC SPECIES

Red-masked Parakeet

Scaly-breasted Munia
Adult
punctulata

Juvenile

Description: 13 ½". The most numerous of several introduced parrot species in the region; native to western South America. **Green with bright red head**, large **red patch on leading edge of underwing**; tail long, pointed. Heavy ivory colored bill. JUVENILE lacks red markings. **Voice**: Harsh, loud, nasal *eeeh, eeeh* cries. **Behavior**: Travels, forages in flocks (mated birds often paired within flock); roosts in tall, dense trees, feeds on berries, seeds, small fruits, blossoms. **Similar Species**: Occasionally encountered are related (and established in Los Angeles area) Mitred Parakeet (*P. mitratus*, 15"), , with heavier bill, more restricted red on face, green wing linings, and Blue-crowned Parakeet (*Thectocercus acuticaudatus*, 14 ½"), with reddish underside of tail, bluish on head (in adults). **Where, When to Find**: Widespread in San Francisco's parks and neighborhoods, especially where trees are fruiting. The north waterfront from the Ferry Building to the Presidio is dependable, as are larger open areas. Also present locally further south on the San Francisco peninsula.

SCALY-BREASTED MUNIA *Lonchura punctulata*

Description: 4". Small introduced finch, formerly known as Nutmeg Mannikin. **Deep chestnut head and chest, white underparts with black scaling,** dull yellowish uppertail coverts; conical black bill (Indian subcontinent subspecies *punctulata*). JUVENILE rich tan-buff throughout. **Voice**: Distinctive *kib-bee, kib-bee* calls often betray presence. **Behavior**: Found in tight flocks, feeding on grass, weed seeds; globular nest placed in trees. **Similar Species**: Adults distinctive; compare juveniles with female buntings, which have much smaller bills. **Where, When to Find**: Small numbers have nested near Almaden Lake, Santa Clara County since 1997. Populations are spreading rapidly in southern California; populations in our area should be monitored.

Did you know? Red-masked Parakeets are "The Wild Parrots of Telegraph Hill" in San Francisco, made famous by Mark Bittner's book.

Date & Location Seen:

Northern Goshawk
Adult

Juvenile

Northern Goshawk
Juvenile

Flammulated Owl

Great Gray Owl

Jorthern Goshawk *Accipiter gentilis*

1", wingspan 41". Red-tailed Hawk-sized, with longer tail; wavy tail bands re diagnostic. Conspicuous white eyebrow separates adult's dark gray rown from blue-gray upperparts. Underparts appear gray at a distance; has uffy white undertail coverts. Juvenile brown above, underparts extensively treaked dark brown. Smaller, shorter-winged Cooper's Hawk (p. 117) usually acks bold eyebrow; adult is rusty-barred below, juvenile lacks undertail treaking. Call near nest a strident *kak-kak-kak-kak*. Rare resident of mature orests in northern half of the region, and south through the Sierra Nevada, nostly 5,000-9,000'. Casual elsewhere. A state Species of Special Concern. reys on squirrel-sized mammals, birds up to grouse size. Aggressively defends est, attacking humans who get too close.

Jammulated Owl *Psiloscops flammeolus*

¾". A small, secretive migratory owl that preys on nocturnal insects. Short ar tufts (seldom seen), mottled gray and reddish plumage; our only small wl with dark eyes. Call a series of soft ventriloquial *oop* notes, sometimes receded by grace notes. Heard often, seen rarely; well-camouflaged against runk of oak or ponderosa pine. Fairly common summer resident (May to eptember) in suitable mixed or coniferous forests to about 10,000'. Breeds rom Greenhorn Mts. north through the Cascade/Sierra Nevada range, in the Varner Mts., on Lassen Bench, in Trinity and Siskiyou Mts., in Coast Ranges o Mendocino County, locally in Monterey County.

Great Gray Owl *Strix nebulosa*

.7". Our largest owl, mottled brown and gray, with a very large head, gray acial disk, yellow eyes, and a white "bow tie." Call a series of short, deep, mphatic *whoo* notes. Very local resident 2,500-8,000' on the west slope of he Sierra Nevada from Fresno County north to El Dorado and Placer counties; nas also nested in northern Modoc County. Chooses large trees within closed canopy mixed and coniferous forests with adjacent moist meadows, where it nunts small rodents from low perches, dusk to early morning. Endangered in California; estimated population about 300 birds.

**Calliope Hummingbird
Adult Male**

**Calliope Hummingbird
Female**

**Williamson's Sapsucker
Male**

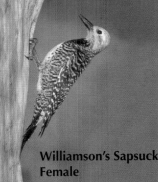

**Williamson's Sapsucker
Female**

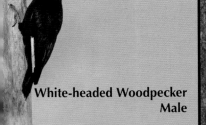

**White-headed Woodpecker
Male**

**Black-backed Woodpecker
Male**

Calliope Hummingbird
Selasphorus calliope

3 ¼". Our smallest hummingbird; short-billed and short-tailed. Male has purplish red rays on throat; female has buff-tinted sides and sides of neck, tail tip shorter than wing-tip. Calls very high-pitched. Breeds (late April to July) in the higher mountains east of the humid coast belt, east to Warner Mts. and south to Tulare County. A few found irregularly in spring migration (April to mid-May) in foothills and lowlands, mainly at feeders and around flowering plants.

Williamson's Sapsucker
Sphyrapicus thyroideus

9". Male is a striking black woodpecker with yellow belly, red chin, white head stripes, and large white wing patch; female has brown head, barred brown and black back, yellow belly and black breast. Call a clear *QUEEah*. Uncommon summer resident in high pine and fir forests above about 7,000' throughout the Cascade/Sierra Nevada range, and in Warner and White Mts. Winter whereabouts less well known: some winter in the yellow pine belt throughout. Casual in fall and winter in foothills and lowlands.

White-headed Woodpecker
Dryobates albolarvatus

9 ¼". Unmistakable black woodpecker with white head; large white wing patches show in flight. Male has red crescent on hindneck. Call a sharp doubled note, *pee-dink* or *peek-it*. Fairly common year-round resident east of the humid coastal belt in mountains from Mendocino County northward, east through the Warner Mts., and down the Cascade/Sierra Nevada range in pine forests about 4,000' to 8,000', especially Jeffrey, ponderosa and sugar pines. Casual to planted pines in lowlands in winter.

Black-backed Woodpecker
Picoides arcticus

9 ½". A three-toed woodpecker with a long, heavy bill, black face and back, white underparts barred black; male's crown yellow. Call a single sharp, low-pitched *pik*. Drumming is loud, far-carrying. Flakes off loose bark to expose larvae; wanders in search of recent burns, to forage on trunks of dead or dying pines. Rare to uncommon resident in coniferous forests mainly 6,000-9,000' in the Cascade Range, Warner Mts., and on west slope of Sierra Nevada south to Tulare County; scarcer on east slope, south to Mono County.

Canada Jay
griseus

Pinyon Jay

Clark's Nutcracker

Canada Jay   *Perisoreus canadensis*

11 ½". Dark gray cap, nape, upperparts, and flight feathers; pale gray underparts, face, and collar. Juvenile dark sooty gray overall. Calls include whistled *wheeoo*, low *chuck*. Inquisitive; a 'camp robber.' Uncommon resident (subspecies *griseus*) in broken or solid forests east of the humid coast belt, 4,000-7,000' from Shasta County northward, including Warner Mts. Also (*obscurus*) in humid coastal forests south to Cape Mendocino, and in the vicinity of Fort Bragg, Mendocino County.

Pinyon Jay   *Gymnorhinus cyanocephalus*

10 ½". An entirely dull blue, crestless jay, shaped like a small, long-billed crow. Walks on ground; nasal, laughing *ha-a-a* calls distinctive. Found locally in flocks in pinyon-juniper and yellow pine forests; locally common resident to 8,000' in the Great Basin region. Found locally on the east side of the Sierra Nevada from Alpine County southward. Rarely and erratically, flocks wander more widely in fall, winter; have reached the coast.

Clark's Nutcracker   *Nucifraga columbiana*

12". A raucous crow-like bird, gray overall with a white patch on black wings, broad white borders to black tail, and white undertail. Wing beats deep and slow, like crow. Call is a harsh grating note. Uses its long, pointed black bill to extract seeds from pine cones, which it caches in large numbers; also walks on ground for seeds, insects. Locally common in summer in coniferous forests above about 8,000'. Nests as early as mid-February. More widespread within the mountains in fall. Numbers erratic; in very rare invasion years a few may be found in the lowlands in fall and winter.

Townsend's Solitaire
Adult

Townsend's
Solitaire
Juvenile

Green-tailed Towhee

"Hepburn's" *littoralis*

Gray-crowned Rosy-Finch
Winter *dawsoni*

ownsend's Solitaire   *Myadestes townsendi*

½". A slender, long-tailed thrush with a buffy wing patch that's prominent
1 flight; perches upright, often on high, conspicuous perch. Adults gray with
/hite eye-ring, white tail sides; juveniles scaly brown, with buffy spots. Call
loud, whistled *heep*; long, rambling fluty song is sometimes given in flight.
'lycatches" in summer; eats mistletoe and juniper berries in winter. Fairly
ommon breeder above about 5,000' in forested areas of the Inner Coast
anges from Lake County northward, and in more easterly mountains south
rough the Sierra Nevada. Fall, winter movements are complex; many
emain in juniper forests when berries are plentiful, some are found at lower
levations. Rare winter visitor to coastal lowlands.

reen-tailed Towhee   *Pipilo chlorurus*

¼". Large sparrow with olive upperparts, reddish cap, white throat, gray
nderparts, and green-tinged wings and tail. Call a kitten-like *mew*? Lively
ong of buzzy trills and short whistles suggests Fox Sparrow. Fairly common
reeder (May to early September) in mountain brush fields and chaparral
/ith scattered trees below 8,500' in the Warner Mts., Cascade/Sierra Nevada
ange, and White Mts. Less common in the Inner Coast Ranges from Lake
ounty northward. Uncommon migrant in lowlands east of the Sierra Nevada,
re elsewhere.

ray-crowned Rosy-Finch   *Leucosticte tephrocotis*

¼". Dark brown, with gray on head, black forehead; pink on wings and
nderparts; underwing silvery. Female shows less pink. Call, a high chirping
heew. Resident subspecies *dawsoni* nests above tree line on only the highest
eaks, in the Sierra Nevada from Sierra County to Tulare County, in the White
1ts., and – perhaps only sporadically – on Mt. Lassen. Accessible sites include
quaw Valley High Camp (Placer County), and near Ellery Lake (Mono County)
1st east of Tioga Pass. More extensively gray-faced "Hepburn's" (*littoralis*)
ests on Mt. Shasta. Winter flocks found irregularly at lower elevations in
he Great Basin and at feeders in the mountains may include both breeding
ubspecies (but mainly *dawsoni*), or other subspecies that resemble *dawsoni*
ut breed out of state.

Pine Grosbeak
Adult Male

Pine Grosbeak
Female

Cassin's Finch
Adult Male

Cassin's Finch
Female

Evening Grosbeak
Male

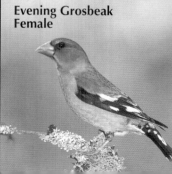

Evening Grosbeak
Female

ine Grosbeak   *Pinicola enucleator*

". A large, rather plump boreal finch with two bold white wing-bars and a long il. Stubby black bill is strongly curved. Adult male's gray plumage is tipped sy, females and immatures are grayer overall, with yellow-olive (or russet) ead and back. Song a short rich warble; alarm call of our endemic subspecies *alifornica* is a sharp, musical *chee-vli*. Uncommon and unobtrusive (especially winter) year-round resident in coniferous forests of the Sierra Nevada from umas County to Tulare County, usually near meadows or water, from 6,000' tree line. Yuba Pass, Yosemite National Park's Bridalveil Campground, and inaret Vista above Mammoth Lakes are good spots.

assin's Finch   *Haemorhous cassinii*

". Bill longer and more sharply pointed than on the closely related Purple inch (p. 445). Adult male has red cap, deep pink wash to breast and rump, ne streaks on flanks, and pale back streaks. Female and immature male like orresponding Purple Finch plumages, but with finer, sharper streaking. Song nger, more varied, flutier than Purple's; call a dry *tr-dlip*. A common summer esident (some winter; numbers vary) in open coniferous forests above about ,000' throughout the region, favoring drier areas than Purple where ranges verlap. Migration and winter movements poorly understood. Often common Great Basin in spring.

vening Grosbeak   *Coccothraustes vespertinus*

". A stocky, noisy finch with a large, conical bill. Males with dark olive and ellow body, bright yellow forehead and eyebrow, and large white patch on econdaries. Females more grayish tan, with a second white wing patch. Call a loud, strident *clee-ip*, or *peer*. Sparse to fairly common breeder in mature oniferous forests above 3,500' in the Cascade/Sierra Nevada range south Tulare County, in the Warner, Siskiyou, and Trinity Mts., and – at least poradically – in Humboldt County's coastal forests. Usually found in flocks. Nomadic in search of food; irregular in winter to coastal lowlands, possibly cluding birds (judging by flight call) from distant populations.

Greater Sage-Grouse
Displaying Male

Greater Sage-Grouse
Female

Chukar

Gambel's Quail
Male

Gambel's Quail
Female

Greater Sage-Grouse *Centrocercus urophasianus*

Male 28", female 22". A very large pheasant-like bird with a long pointed tail and black belly. Larger males have black throat and white chest. In display with other males at a lek site, cocks and spreads tail in fan shape, raises plumes, puffs out white chest, and displays yellow air sacs. A local species restricted to sagebrush regions in northeastern California; isolated populations in Mono and northern Inyo counties: in the Bodie Hills, Long Valley, and above tree line in the White Mts. A state Species of Special Concern, formerly more numerous and widespread. Remaining populations should be carefully monitored.

Gambel's Quail *Callipepla gambelii*

10". Found in desert scrublands in southeastern Inyo County from eastern Death Valley National Park and south locally to the San Bernardino County line. Some of these populations (e.g., Argus Mts.) may be introduced. Although resident, there may be at least some movement (e.g., periodically present at Furnace Creek Ranch, then disappear for years, then reappear). Plumages closely resemble related California Quail (p. 69), including teardrop-shaped crest in both sexes. Male Gambel's has rufous (not brown) crown and black (not scaled) belly surrounded by white; female plainer than male and duller, with white belly. Calls similar to California's but higher-pitched.

Chukar *Alectoris chukar*

14". An Old World species introduced in the early 1930s. Large and quail-like with buffy throat and face outlined in black, bold black bars on sides and flanks. Juvenile duller. Stout bright red legs. Extensive rufous in tail feathers best noted in flight. Gives loud clacking calls in a series, also *whitoo* alarm calls. Forms large coveys especially in late summer when augmented by young. Walks long distances in search of food and water; most dependably found around springs on steep rocky slopes in arid mountains. Most common and widespread in the "dry mountains" of eastern Inyo and southern Mono counties. Local north to northeastern California; very local elsewhere, such as in the San Joaquin Valley's arid western foothills.

First-fall

**Franklin's Gull
Breeding**

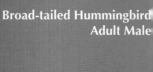

**Broad-tailed Hummingbird
Adult Male**

**Ladder-backed
Woodpecker
Male**

Female

**Brown-crested Flycatcher
*magister***

ranklin's Gull   *Leucophaeus pipixcan*

4 ½". A small dark-mantled gull. Hooded in all plumages, entire head of adults black in breeding season. Adults have extensive white in black wingtips. n winter, forehead and throat white, thick broken white eye-ring. Immature's ead pattern like winter adult but wing coverts are fringed buff; black tail and, not extending to outer tail feathers. Rare but regular spring (mid-March o June) and rare to casual fall (mid-August – early November) migrant in ortheastern California and east of the Sierra Nevada. Very rare but fairly videspread migrant elsewhere. Recorded all months.

road-tailed Hummingbird   *Selasphorus platycercus*

". Uncommon summer (late April to July) resident to canyons in the White nd Inyo Mts., Mono and Inyo counties. Adult males have bright rose-red orget and green crown with white eye-ring. Females and immatures like emale type Rufous and Allen's (p. 251), and identification extremely difficult, out larger and longer billed, and color below more blended, less rufous, more uffy; color extends to sides of neck. Adult males give loud cricket-like trill hat is diagnostic. Chip notes are more metallic sounding than Rufous and \llen's. Casual on east side of Sierra Nevada; most reports elsewhere may be rroneous, owing to identification difficulties.

adder-backed Woodpecker   *Dryobates scalaris*

¼". Like Nuttall's Woodpecker (p. 259), but buffier and more spotted below vith buffy nasal tufts. White cross bars extend through nape; face whiter; ail more barred. Red crown of male more extensive than Nuttall's. Calls imilar to those of Downy Woodpecker (p. 261), quite unlike Nuttall's. Rare o uncommon local Inyo County resident, generally east of the Owens Valley vhere Nuttall's is found and occasional hybrids are noted.

rown-crested Flycatcher   *Myiarchus tyrannulus*

¾". Larger than Ash-throated Flycatcher (p. 287) with yellower belly and nuch bigger bill; reddish in tail feathers extends to tips. Calls differ from Ash-hroated; most frequent note is a loud, sharp liquid *whit*. Known only as a ummer resident (May to mid-August) from the China Ranch oasis, extreme astern Inyo County; casual elsewhere in the county. Accidental on the arallones (Sept. 1983).

Gray Vireo

Lucy's Warbler
Male

Verdin
Adult

Black-tailed Gnatcatcher
Breeding Male

Verdin
Juvenile

Gray Vireo
Vireo vicinior

½". Like Plumbeous Vireo (p. 293) but shorter wings with longer tail that is flipped about like a gnatcatcher. Faint wing-bars, white eye-ring. Song like Plumbeous, but sweeter, with notes delivered more rapidly; also a sharp descending musical trill. Uncommon summer resident in open pinyon pine woodland in the Grapevine Mts., eastern Inyo County; reports from elsewhere in our region are unsubstantiated. A state Species of Special Concern.

Lucy's Warbler
Leiothlypis luciae

¼". Tiny warbler, pale gray above, creamy-white below; rump chestnut (adults) or pale rusty (juveniles); dark eye stands out on pale face. Adult male has chestnut crown patch. Call a sharp metallic *plink*; song a lively short trill followed by whistled notes. Summer resident (late March to mid-July) in mesquite woodland of eastern Inyo County along the Amargosa R., at Furnace Creek Ranch, and in the Saline Valley. Singing territorial males recorded north to Oasis, Mono County. Very rare but annual fall and winter visitor elsewhere in region, mostly along the coast. A state Species of Special Concern.

Verdin
Auriparus flaviceps

½". A small active light gray bird with yellow head, dark lores; small chestnut patch at bend of wing; sharply pointed bill. Juvenile lacks yellow and chestnut, has pale base to bill. Calls include a sharp *tseep*, a whistled *tee-tew*, and chipping notes. Resident locally in southern Inyo County from Pearsonville and nearby side canyons of the eastern Sierra Nevada; recorded north to Haiwee Reservoir. Also resident along the Amargosa R. in southeastern Inyo County and very locally in Death Valley (e.g., Furnace Creek).

Black-tailed Gnatcatcher
Polioptila melanura

½". Bluish-gray above, whitish below; graduated tail with prominent white tips on outer tail feathers. Males in breeding plumage show shiny black cap; reduced in winter to a line above eye. Calls rather harsh, suggestive of House Wren. Song a harsh *jee-jee-jee-jee-jee*. Uncommon and local resident in dense mesquite along the Amargosa R. east of Tecopa; also at a few locations on the eastern side of the Panamint Valley. No credible records from Death Valley or elsewhere in the region.

Cactus Wren

Sage Thrasher

LeConte's Thrasher

Crissal Thrasher

Cactus Wren   *Campylorhynchus brunneicapillus*

8 ½". An outsized, long-billed wren; heavily spotted below with chestnut crown and white eyebrow. Upperparts and tail heavily barred; white tail corners. Distinctive call a repetitious low *kur-kur-kur*; other harsh grating calls. Local Inyo County resident in canyons on east side of Sierra Nevada to west of Pearsonville; also very locally elsewhere at Lee Flat in Nelson Range and Joshua Flats, Inyo Mts. Regular occurrence strongly tied to extensive Joshua tree woodland. Casual elsewhere; recorded north to southern Mono County.

Sage Thrasher   *Oreoscoptes montanus*

8 ½". Small, boldly streaked thrasher with short bill, yellow eyes, and white cornered tail. Song a series of warbled phrases; calls include a *chuck* and low *churr*. Summer resident (late March – September) in sage throughout the Great Basin. Rare migrant and winter visitor elsewhere in region. The Bendire's Thrasher (*Toxostoma bendirei*, 9 ¾"), a state Species of Special Concern, breeds in the region only in Joshua tree woodland at Lee Flat in the Nelson Range (west of the Panamint Mts.). Brownish-gray overall, stippled below with arrow-shaped spots; gold eye. Accidental elsewhere in the region; several records from the Farallones, has wintered near Sacramento.

LeConte's Thrasher   *Toxostoma lecontei*

11". A sandy colored thrasher with a dark eye, blackish tail, pale tawny undertail coverts and long slim decurved bill. Call a loud whistled *hooweep*. Song is loud and melodious. Rather shy; runs on ground with tail cocked up. Uncommon, local and declining resident in open arid areas with saltbush and/or creosote of Inyo and extreme southern (Fish Slough) Mono counties; formerly found north to Benton. Population on the San Joaquin Valley's western fringe (north to Coalinga, Fresno County) is a state Species of Special Concern; the portion of this population in our region is apparently extirpated.

Crissal Thrasher   *Toxostoma crissale*

11 ½". Brownish-gray throughout with chestnut undertail coverts, thin black and white lines bordering throat, long, thin decurved bill, and slightly pale eye. Distinctive call *chor-lee* or *toit toit toit*. Musical and varied song. Uncommon resident in dense mesquite thickets of eastern Inyo County along Amargosa R. north to Death Valley Junction. A state Species of Special Concern.

Brewer's Sparrow

Black-throated Sparrow Adult

Juvenile

Bobolink Breeding Male

Bobolink Non-breeding Female

Scott's Oriole Adult Male

Scott's Oriole First-Spring Female

Brewer's Sparrow — *Spizella breweri*

5 ½". A small, slender, pallid gray-brown sparrow with finely streaked crown, thin whitish eye-ring and slightly outlined ear patch bordered below by whitish stripe; brown rump. Song a remarkably long series of varied bubbling notes and buzzy trills. Common call a thin *sip*. Common summer resident (late April – September) in sagebrush throughout Great Basin, including locally up eastern side of the Sierra Nevada. Rare but widespread migrant (mostly September) and casual winter visitor elsewhere in region.

Black-throated Sparrow — *Amphispiza bilineata*

5 ½". Distinct diamond-shaped black throat bordered by white stripe; broad white eyebrow; streaked juvenile plumage (seen into early October) lacks black throat. Song is two clear notes followed by trill; calls are faint tinkling notes. Fairly common summer resident (April – early September) on arid slopes in southern Mono County; rare to uncommon and local farther north in Great Basin to Modoc County. Has bred at burn sites in the Sierra Nevada. Casual migrant (mostly September) and winter visitor elsewhere in region.

Bobolink — *Dolichonyx oryzivorus*

7". Breeding male is black below; hindneck buff; scapulars and rump white. Female and all fall plumages are a rich buffy color; striped head; tail feathers sharply pointed. Rare and local summer resident (late May – August) in the Surprise Valley, Modoc County; not present every summer. Otherwise a casual spring (late May – June) and very rare fall (mid-September – October) migrant; nearly all fall migrants on coast.

Scott's Oriole — *Icterus parisorum*

9". Adult male is black with lemon yellow underparts, rump, tail base and shoulder patch. Female is dull olive above with dusky back streaks, yellow-green below. Older adult females and immature males intermediate. Bill long and straight. Fluty whistled song suggests Western Meadowlark; calls include a *chuck*. Local summer resident (April – July) in Joshua tree and pinyon pine woodland on east side of Sierra Nevada west of Pearsonville and in the desert ranges of Inyo County north to Benton Range, Mono County. Casual elsewhere in region.

Black-footed Albatross

Laysan Albatross

Northern Fulmar Dark Morph *rodgersii*

Light Morph *rodgersii*

Pink-footed Shearwater

Flesh-footed Shearwater

Black-footed Albatross — *Phoebastria nigripes*

1". Large, very long-winged seabird; common far offshore (sometimes seen from shore), especially May to mid-August. Like a huge dark shearwater, but wing beats slow, with long glides. Entirely blackish-brown; adults show white on face, uppertail coverts. Heavy black bill, black legs. Our visitors breed mainly in Leeward Hawaiian Islands. **Laysan Albatross** (*P. immutabilis*, 0") a rare to uncommon offshore visitor mainly in winter. White body with ragged dark and white pattern on underwings. Breeds mainly on Northwestern Hawaiian Islands, including Midway and Laysan.

Northern Fulmar — *Fulmarus glacialis*

8". A bull-necked gull-like "tubenose" with a flap-and-glide flight on stiff wings. Evenly gray to gray-brown throughout; tail darker. Stout yellowish bill with obvious nostril tubes. Less common light morph is mostly white with light gray back, some gray markings on wings and tail. Our birds breed mainly on islands off Alaska coast; very common in our waters some winters (mainly October to March), scarce during others. Rare (nonbreeders) in summer. During major flights may be found inshore around piers. Albatrosses, fulmars, shearwaters and storm-petrels secrete a concentrated salt solution from their nostril tubes; these are quite prominent on fulmars.

Pink-footed Shearwater — *Ardenna creatopus*

8". Shearwaters are highly marine birds with stiff flap-and-glide flight low over water, arcing higher in strong winds. This is a large species with relatively languid flight (wing beats easily counted). Gray-brown head and upperparts, mostly white belly and underwings; pinkish bill, legs, and feet. Visits (mainly April-November, with peak July-October) from breeding areas on islands off Chile. Common well offshore, but can be seen from coastal seawatch points in warmer months.

Flesh-footed Shearwater — *Ardenna carneipes*

8". Much like Sooty Shearwater (p. 481), but broader winged; plumage entirely dark, including underwing; pinkish bill base, legs, and feet. Size and leisurely flight like Pink-footed. Rare but regular offshore, mainly August-November but with records throughout the year. Breeds on islands around Australia, New Zealand.

Sooty Shearwater

Short-tailed Shearwater

Manx Shearwater

Buller's Shearwater

Black-vented Shearwater

Sooty Shearwater
Ardenna grisea

17 ½". Dark brown shearwater with rapid wing beats, flap-and-glide flight; underwings flash silvery white. Dark bill is long, thin. Usually the most numerous shearwater off California. Abundant well offshore (but huge flocks also often seen from coastal seawatch points), especially April through September. Our birds visit from breeding islands off s. Chile and New Zealand/se. Australia.

Short-tailed Shearwater
Ardenna tenuirostris

16 ½". Nearly identical to Sooty, but bill shorter and thinner, forehead steeper (dark cap usually contrasts with pale throat); wing linings average slightly darker and more uniform than on Sooty. Migrants returning to s. Australian breeding colonies from Bering Sea are seen here mainly November-March.

Buller's Shearwater
Ardenna bulleri

17". A striking shearwater with black crown and clean white underparts, including underwings. Dark wing coverts and outer wing contrast with pale gray back and inner flight feathers. Tail relatively long, wedge-shaped. Fall visitor; can be common (mainly August to mid-November) in Monterey Bay and elsewhere offshore. Breeds on islets off New Zealand.

Black-vented Shearwater
Puffinus opisthomelas

14 ½". Like a small version of Pink-footed, but with slender dark bill, stronger contrast between dark upperparts and mostly white underparts. Rapid wing beats alternate with short glides. Irregular visitor (mainly September to March) from breeding areas on islands off Baja. An inshore species, often visible from shore. **Manx Shearwater** (*P. puffinus*, 13 ½"), rare visitor (mainly August-October), is darker above, whiter below (white includes undertail coverts), and shows pale crescent behind dark "ears."

Fork-tailed Storm-Petrel

Leach's Storm-Petrel

Ashy Storm-Petrel

Black Storm-Petrel

Fork-tailed Storm-Petrel   *Hydrobates furcatus*

3 ¾". Storm-petrels are small seabirds that fly low over the ocean surface employing deep, staccato wing strokes interspersed with short glides. Fork-tailed is gray, with strongly forked tail, blackish underwing, dark eye patch. Compare with darker gray Ashy Storm-Petrel (below), and beware possible confusion of distant birds with phalaropes. Found far offshore year-round (mainly in far north), but late fall and winter gales may bring numbers inshore. A few breed on islets off Humboldt and Del Norte counties; most breed further north, to Alaska. Fork-tailed, Ashy, and Black Storm-Petrels are state Species of Special Concern. Physical degradation of nesting habitat and the introduction of non-native mammalian predators are the species' main threats.

Leach's Storm-Petrel   *Hydrobates leucorhous*

8". Dark, medium-large storm-petrel, usually only seen far offshore (rare inside Monterey Bay); mainly April to November. Most have white rumps, divided by a variably dusky line down the middle; dark-rumped birds that breed off Baja are only rarely seen in our waters. Flight is bounding, erratic, occasionally well above water surface.

Ashy Storm-Petrel   *Hydrobates homochroa*

7 ½". A nearly endemic California breeder, with declining colonies on offshore islets and on the Farallon Islands (and Channel Islands of southern California). All ashy brown; smaller, paler-bodied than Black, with some pale gray mottling on the underwings; more fluttering flight. Found in our waters year-round, but large concentrations often present in fall (e.g., in Monterey Bay). Rare north of Mendocino County.

Black Storm-Petrel   *Hydrobates melania*

8 ¾". Our largest all-dark storm-petrel. Long wings, flies with deep wing beats and many course changes. Entirely blackish-brown with pale brown bar across upperwing. Visits mainly August to October; can occur in large rafts (often with Ashy) in Monterey Bay; casual north of Sonoma County. Breeds off Baja (and a few on Channel Islands). Tiny, short-tailed Least Storm-Petrel (*O. microsoma*, 5 ¾"), also all dark, visits irregularly (Monterey Bay) in fall from Mexico, mainly in "El Niño" warm water years.

Pomarine Jaeger
Adult

South Polar Skua

Parasitic Jaeger
Adult

Long-tailed Jaeger
Adult

Pomarine Jaeger
Stercorarius pomarinus

21". The jaeger most commonly seen on one-day boat trips. Gull-like seabird with powerful falcon-like flight; steals food from gulls, terns, shearwaters. Long "spoon-tipped" central tail feathers of adult distinctive when present, as is blackish face, heavy chest band (some birds are all dark). Note double white flash on underside of wingtips in flight. Younger birds have heavy barring, lack "spoons." Jaegers breed on Arctic tundra; winter offshore; a few (nonbreeders) summer. Common August-November, uncommon April-May; casual inland.

South Polar Skua
Stercorarius maccormickii

21". "A jaeger on steroids" – heavy-bodied and thick-necked, with powerful flight. All brown (juveniles dark dusky, adults paler; light morph birds even "blonde" on head, underparts). Dark adults show golden hindneck. All show bold white patch at base of primaries. Antarctic breeder, moving in small numbers to our offshore waters mainly August to October.

Parasitic Jaeger
Stercorarius parasiticus

19". The jaeger most often seen from land. Lighter in build than Pomarine; adult has pointed central tail feathers, less extensive black on face. Parasitic chases small gulls and terns, and is often seen from shore around flocks of Elegant Terns. Fairly common near shore, mainly August-October. Rare inland migrant, mainly September.

Long-tailed Jaeger
Stercorarius longicaudus

22". Our most slender jaeger. Adult has longer pointed central tail feathers than Parasitic, limited white in primaries; juvenile much like Parasitic but grayer overall, usually whiter on belly. Migrant far offshore late July-September, with a few in late spring; rare inland migrant, mainly late August to September.

Marbled Murrelet
Non-breeding

Marbled Murrelet
Breeding

Ancient Murrelet
Immature

Guadalupe
Murrelet

Scripps's Murrelet

Craveri's Murrelet

Marbled Murrelet
Brachyramphus marmoratus

10″. Murrelets, murres, auklets and guillemots are small to medium-sized diving birds collectively known as "alcids" (from the family name Alcidae); they propel themselves underwater with their wings (very narrow in murrelets). Breeding birds dark brown above, mottled brown and white below; winter birds slaty above, white below, with white collar and patches along sides of back. This enigmatic species nests high in old-growth conifers and is considered Endangered (state) or Threatened (federal); at sea found mainly within a few miles of shore (often visible from shore). Uncommon along forested coastlines, with the largest numbers from Del Norte to Mendocino County. In spring, adults are sometimes seen and heard near dawn as they fly between their nest sites and the ocean.

Ancient Murrelet
Synthliboramphus antiquus

10″. A murrelet with a short pale bill. Gray back contrasts with black crown, hindneck and flight feathers, Adults have black throats (more prominent in breeding birds). Uncommon and irregular visitor offshore (though often visible from shore), mainly mid-October through March. Casual inland in late fall.

Scripps's Murrelet
Synthliboramphus scrippsi

9 ¾″. A small black and white alcid, found usually in pairs offshore (very rarely seen from shore), August through October. Clean separation along neck between slaty upperparts and white underparts; small, thin bill. In flight shows narrow wings that are white underneath. A scarce breeder on s. California and nw. Baja islands. A few birds, usually seen far offshore, show white over the eye; these are **Guadalupe Murrelets** (*S. hypoleucus*, 9 ¾″), which breed mainly on Guadalupe Island off Baja. Scripps's and Guadalupe Murrelet were, until very recently, considered a single species, the Xantus's Murrelet; both are Threatened (state). **Craveri's Murrelet** (*S. craveri*, 8 ½″) rare, irregular visitor offshore August through September (primarily in warmer water years), is much like Scripps's but with longer bill, blacker upperparts, dusky underwings, more black at bill base.

Tufted Puffin
Breeding Adult

Cassin's Auklet

Cassin's Auklet

Rhinoceros Auklet
Breeding Adult

Rhinoceros Auklet
Immature

Tufted Puffin
Fratercula cirrhata

16″. A large dark alcid. Breeding adult unmistakable with swollen red and yellow bill, white face, long yellow tufts projecting behind eyes, orange feet. Winter adult has dark face, smaller bill; juvenile even smaller-billed (but bill still outsized, orangish), can be whitish on belly, with hint of pale on sides of face. Uncommon and irregular offshore, mainly August to mid-October. Small numbers breed on Farallon Islands and islets of far north (Castle Rock, Trinidad, etc., where can sometimes be seen from mainland). A state Species of Special Concern; the population has not recovered from mid-20th century declines.

Cassin's Auklet
Ptychoramphus aleuticus

9″. A small chunky dark gray alcid, whitish on belly; at close range note light spot at bill base and white crescents above and below eye. Flight more twisting than murrelets', wings broader-based, more triangular. Found year-round offshore in small to large groups; thousands often present in productive waters around upwelling zones, as in Monterey Bay and over Cordell Bank; small numbers regularly seen from shore. Huge numbers breed on the Farallon Islands; smaller colonies elsewhere. A state Species of Special Concern; population declines over recent decades are generally attributed to reductions in prey abundance.

Rhinoceros Auklet
Cerorhinca monocerata

15″. A chunky gray-brown alcid with a stout, yellowish bill; breeding birds have white face stripes, "horn" on bill. Much larger and longer-billed than similarly-plumaged Cassin's. In flight suggests dark football with whirring wings, whitish belly. Common winter visitor offshore September through March (fewer in summer), sometimes seen in large numbers from coastal points such as Pt. Pinos. Casual inside San Francisco Bay. Nests on Castle Rock, South Farallon, and Año Nuevo islands; also in smaller numbers on other offshore islets.

Black-legged Kittiwake Juvenile

Juvenile

Arctic Tern Breeding Adult

Sabine's Gull Breeding Adult

Sabine's Gull Juvenile

Black-legged Kittiwake · *Rissa tridactyla*

17". A northern gull that is irregularly found – sometimes in numbers – in offshore waters (sometimes also at coastal piers and promontories) mainly from November through mid-April. Some summer after flight years. Adult has plain yellow bill, black legs, solid black tips to pale gray wings; dark gray nape smudge in winter. Juvenile has black bill and legs, bold black wing covert bar, black tip to slightly notched tail, broad black collar. Casual inland.

Arctic Tern · *Sterna paradisaea*

15 ½". Dainty offshore tern, much like Common Tern (p. 209) but with shorter bill, shorter legs, shorter neck, more rounded head. Adult underwings translucent white, with narrow black outer trailing edge. Juvenile much like Common, but secondaries entirely whitish. Fairly common far offshore, mainly fall (mid-August to early October), but a few from early May to early June. Casual inland, mainly June.

Sabine's Gull · *Xema sabini*

13 ½". An especially beautiful small gull with a buoyant, tern-like flight that migrates (mainly May, August to mid-October) well offshore; infrequently seen from shore. Readily identified at any age by its striking plumage pattern seen from above: dark back and wing coverts, white flight feathers with black triangle forming outer wing. Breeding adults (as seen in May and again in August) have slate-gray heads. Bill black with yellow tip. Tail slightly forked. Juvenile has brown back and hindneck, black tail tip. Rare inland, mainly in fall (late August to early October).

Acknowledgments, Photographer Credits

By far the most difficult part of writing this book was to learn and to concisely describe where, when, and in what numbers one might find the region's bird species. Our efforts to describe their status and distribution owe much to publications by those who came before, beginning with Joseph Grinnell and Alden Miller in 1944 (the Helpful Resources section cites most of the publications mentioned here), and continuing with the 1998 annotated field list from Guy McCaskie, Paul De Benedictis, Richard Erickson, and Joseph Morlan. Other authors dealt with sizeable parts of our region. David Gaines lyrically detailed the distribution and abundance of the birds of Yosemite and the East Slope in 1988. Stanley Harris described the birds of northwestern California; Don Roberson did the same for Monterey County; and Ted Beedy, Ed Pandolfino, and Keith Hansen covered the Sierra Nevada's bird life.

Countywide breeding bird atlases provide localized insight into bird status and distribution. Because of their atlases' extensive accounts and historical insights, special thanks go to Dave Shuford (Marin County), Don Roberson and Chris Tenney (Monterey County), Bill Bousman (Santa Clara County), and John Hunter, David Fix, Gregory Schmidt, and Jude Claire Power (Humboldt County). To date, other authors have produced highly useful atlases for seven other counties, as well.

Bird status and distribution are not static, so we are particularly grateful to authors who've published relevant articles in *Western Birds*, and to those who regularly contribute to *North American Birds (NAB)*. NAB's Regional and

Subregional Editors faithfully produce seasonal summaries that identify trends and notable occurrences, portraying the changing panorama of Northern California's bird life. Birders who regularly contribute observations to eBird (and eBird reviewers who vet these observations) have our thanks as well. We also thank those – too numerous to name – who have birded with us over the years and have enhanced our understanding of the region's bird life by word and by example.

Steve Rottenborn, a former member of the California Bird Records Committee and currently a Regional Editor of *NAB*, has earned our deep gratitude for reviewing this book's species accounts. Of course, any errors there or elsewhere in the book are our sole responsibility.

The writing of *Birds of Northern California* started in 2013 following the release of *Birds of Southern California* in 2012. Bob and Christina Morse have collaborated with local authors and photographers to produce regional, photographic field guides for the western US over the last 14 years. We were fortunate to have Dave Quady serve as the lead author for *Birds of Northern California*. He has coordinated the writing of the text with all the authors (as well as writing a large portion of the text himself), coordinated the selection of the photographs and, as noted above, has rightfully acknowledged the people who have made significant contributions to our existing knowledge of the California birds. Kimball Garrett and Jon Dunn (authors of *Birds of Southern California*) used their extensive, detailed knowledge of the birds of California for this book. Brian Small, primary photographer of *Birds of Southern California* provided many of the book's photographs and serves as our fourth author of *Birds of Northern California*.

Others, such as Rusty Scalf, prepared the maps that

grace this book's pages. Nick Hausman was the initial graphic designer and his early work is much appreciated. Our current graphic designer, Christina Merwin, hired in 2014 to complete the book's design, spent hundreds of hours integrating the text and photographs for the book. She was able to implement creative photo layouts, e.g. the flycatcher photos p. 272 – 280. Christina Morse, in her first efforts at publishing, has taken the leadership role for this book and worked with the entire team to produce what you now see in this regional guide.

Brian E. Small provided 468 images from his collection of high quality wildlife photographs; all of the book's photographs that are not specifically credited to another photographer on the next page are his. All of us owe a great debt to all the photographers, amateurs, professionals and friends whose works appear in this book. They consistently met the challenge of capturing a bird's key field marks in photographs of high technical and artistic merit. Photographer names are listed below.

Lastly, we want to thank the many photographers that have shared their images, whether selected or not. Their time and effort is deeply appreciated by all of us.

We hope you enjoy the end result of all these professionals who now bring you *Birds of Northern California*.

The letters following the page numbers refer to the position of the photograph on that page (T = top, MT = middle, top, B = bottom, MB = middle, bottom, L = left, R = right, C = center, M = middle, N = inset).

Lee Barnes: TL70, TR70; B106, TL184, T206. **Brian Bell:** BLN184. **Tom Blackman:** TL198, BR478, TRN478, TR480,

BL480, BLN480, TR486, T488, MR488. **Keith Brady**: TL318, BL466, BR466, TN470. **Jim Burns**: TN118, TRN126, BR490. **Mike Danzenbaker**: B140, TN178, BN214, TN366, BTR480, BL486, BR486, TN490. **Mike Donahue**: BTN124. **Jon Dunn**: TN72. **Tony Godfrey**: BRN130. **Tom Grey**: B164. **Ed Harper**: B26, TR464. **Ralph Hocken**: TL58. **Dave Kutilek**: BN462, BL488. **Peter LaTourrette**: TR68, TL74, BN74, T, MB164, N216, T302, BN312, B392, TL466, TL486, TN486. **Greg Lavaty**: BR290, TN304, ML488. **Robert Lewis**: TR466. **Kevin Li**: T308. **Jerry Liguori**: TR114, TN222, BR270, B432. **Stuart MacKay**: BL58. **Curtis Marantz**: B72. **Todd McGrath**: BL482; BR482. **Bob McKay**: TL114. **Dick McNeely**: TL58, BL290. **Dennis Paulson**: BLN88. **Jeff Poklen**: TR198. **Jim Pruske**: TN26, BL62, 134, 216, B364. **Dave Quady**: BR166, BL184. **Bob Royse**: TR8, TR130, B192, B206, T278, TR388, B408, BR416, TL470. **Bart Rulon**: 34, BL414. **Tom Ryan**: TTN124. **Larry Sansone**: BL32, BR32, N34, BR40, TR58, BN104, B110, B114, BN116, B118, BN120, T122, BBN124, BR150, BL166, TTR176, TBR176, BTR176, BR180, BR182, TR186, B186, T190, TR192, TL194, BL194, BR194, BN198, B200, BR208, TL214, 228, T232, B232, TN236, 242, TN268, TL270, B276, TN308, BN308, TTN310, TBN310, BN310, TN312, TR316, B338, B360, 368, B374, T376, BR380, BL388, BR408, T452, BN452, T456, TN456, TRN458, TR466, TR478, BL478, TL480, BBR480, TL482, TL484, BL484, BR484, BN486, BR488. **Robert Shantz**: T124, BL126. **Arnold Small**: BL198. **Bryan Smith**: 148. **Bob Steele**: N200. **Rick Taylor**: N136. **Glen Tepke**: B244, 314, TL316. **Jerry Ting**: BN28, BR88, TR194, BL288, TN422, TN428. **Khanh Tran**: T72. **Hank Tseng**: T238. **George Vlahakis**: B124, B312. **Brian Wheeler**: B126, T268, B268, TL458, TR458. **Jim Zipp**: TR98, BL98, TN266, ML476.

Index/Checklist

Use this checklist to keep a record of the birds you have seen. Bold numbers ar
for the main Species Account page and any bird that is pictured. Common local bir
denoted by 'clb'.

☐ Albatross, Black-footed, **479**
☐   Laysan, 479
☐ Auklet, Cassin's, **489**
☐   Rhinoceros, **489**
☐ Avocet, American, **139**
☐ Bittern, American, **93**, 103
☐   Least, **93**, 101
☐ Blackbird, Brewer's, clb, 361, **437**, 439
☐   Red-winged, clb, 361, **429**, 431, 439
☐   Tricolored, 361, 429, **431**
☐   Yellow-headed, 361, **435**
☐ Bluebird, Mountain, **347**
☐   Western, **347**
☐ Bobolink, **477**
☐ Brant, **31**
☐ Bufflehead, **61**, 67
☐ Bunting, Lazuli, 425, **427**
☐   Indigo, 427
☐ Bushtit, clb, 321, **323**
☐ Canvasback, **51**
☐ Chat, Yellow-breasted, **391**
☐ Chickade, Black-capped, **319**
☐   Chestnut-backed, **319**, 321, 323, 383
☐   Mountain, **319**, 321, 323, 383
☐ Chukar, **469**
☐ Condor, California, **107**
☐ Coot, American, clb, 133, **135**
☐ Cormorant, Brandt's, 87, **89**
☐   Double-crested, clb, **87**, 89, 97
☐   Pelagic, **89**
☐ Cowbird, Brown-headed, 379, 425, 437, **439**, 453
☐ Crane, Sandhill, 95, **137**
☐ Creeper, Brown, **329**
☐ Crossbill, Red, **447**
☐ Crow, American, 437, **305**

☐ Cuckoo, Yellow-billed, **221**
☐ Curlew, Long-billed, 105, **159**, 161
☐ Dipper, American, **341**
☐ Dove, Eurasian Collared-, clb, **215**, 219
☐   Mourning, clb, 215, **219**
☐ Dowitcher, Long-billed, 175, **177**, 179
☐   Short-billed, **177**, 179
☐ Duck, Harlequin, **59**
☐   Long-tailed, **61**
☐   Mandarin, 37
☐   Ring-necked, 51, **53**
☐   Ruddy, **67**
☐   Tuffed, 53
☐   Wood, **37**
☐ Dunlin, **165**, 167
☐ Eagle, Bald, 107, **127**
☐   Golden, 107, 125, **127**
☐ Egret, Cattle, 97, **99**, 103
☐   Great, **97**, 99, 103
☐   Snowy, 97, **99**
☐ Falcon, Peregrine, 269, **271**
☐   Prairie, **271**
☐ Finch, Cassin's, 443, 445, 449, **467**
☐   Gray-crowned Rosy-, **465**
☐   House, clb, **443**, 445, 449
☐   Purple, 443, **445**, 449, 467
☐ Flicker, Northern, clb, **263**
☐ Flycatcher, Ash-throated, 285, **287**, 471
☐   Brown-crested, 287, **471**
☐   Cordilleran, 275, 281
☐   Dusky, 275, 277, **279**
☐   Dusky-capped, 287
☐   Gray, 275, **279**
☐   Great Crested, 287
☐   Hammond's, 275, **277**, 279, 281
☐   Least, 277

Olive-sided, **273**
Pacific-slope, 275, 277, **281**
Willow, 181, 273, **275**
Fulmar, Northern, **479**
Gadwall, **39**
Gallinule, Common, **133**, 139
Gnatcatcher, Black-tailed, **473**
Blue-gray, **339**
Godwit, Marbled, 159, **161**
Goldeneye, Barrow's, 61, **63**
Common, 61, **63**
Goldfinch, American, 449, 451, **453**
Lawrence's, 449, **451**
Lesser, clb, 449, **451**, 453
Goose, Cackling, 31, **33**
Canada, 31, **33**
Greater White-fronted, **27**, 33
Ross's, **29**
Snow, **29**
Goshawk, Northern, 117, **459**
Grackle, Great-tailed, **437**
Grebe, Clark's, 83, **85**
Eared, 79, **81**
Horned, **81**, 83
Pied-billed, **79**
Red-necked, 81, **83**
Western, 83, **85**
Grosbeak, Black-headed, 353, 393, **423**
Blue, **425**, 427
Evening, **467**
Pine, 447, **467**
Rose-breasted, 423
Grouse, Greater Sage, **469**
Ruffed, 71, **73**
Sooty, 71, **73**
Guillemot, Pigeon, **185**
Gull, Bonaparte's, **187**
California, clb, 189, 191, 193, **197**, 199
Franklin, 187, **471**
Glaucous, **201**
Glaucous-winged, 195, 199, **201**
Heermann's, **189**

Herring, 195, 197, **199**, 201
Iceland, **199**
Mew, **191**, 193
Ring-billed, clb, 191, **193**, 197
Sabine's, 187, **491**
Western, clb, 189, **195**, 199, 201
Harrier, Northern, **113**, 125
Hawk, Broad-winged, 119
Cooper's, 113, 115, **117**, 119, 459
Ferruginous, 123, **125**
Red-shouldered, 117, **119**, 123
Red-tailed, clb, 113, 119, 121, **123**, 125, 459
Rough-legged, **125**
Sharp-shinned, **115**, 117, 267
Swainson's, **121**, 123
Heron, Great Blue, clb, **95**, 97, 137
Green, 93, **101**
Hummingbird, Allen's, **251**
Anna's, clb, 247, **249**
Black-chinned, **247**
Broad-tailed, 251, **471**
Calliope, 251, **461**
Costa's, 247, **249**
Rufous, **251**
Ibis, Glossy, 105
White-faced, **105**
Jaeger, Long-tailed, **485**
Parasitic, **485**
Pomarine, **485**
Jay, Blue, 299
California Scrub-, clb, **301**
Canada, **463**
Pinyon, 301, **463**
Steller's, **299**, 301
Woodhouse's Scrub-, **301**
Junco, Dark-eyed, 393, 401, **419**
Kestrel, American, **267**
Eurasian, 267
Killdeer, clb, **147**
Kingbird, Cassin's, **289**
Eastern, **289**
Tropical, **289**

☐   Western, 285, 287, **289**
☐ Kingfisher, Belted, 265, **253**
☐ Kinglet, Golden-crowned, 329, **343**
☐   Ruby-crowned, 295, **343**
☐ Kite, White-tailed, **111**
☐ Kittiwake, Black-legged, **491**
☐ Knot, Red, **165**, 177
☐ Lark, Horned, **307**, 369
☐ Longspur, Chestnut-collared, 369
☐   Lapland, **369**
☐ Loon, Common, 75, **77**
☐   Pacific, **75**, 77
☐   Red-throated, **75**, 77
☐   Yellow-billed, 77
☐ Magpie, Black-billed, **303**
☐   Yellow-billed, **303**
☐ Mallard, clb, **39**
☐ Martin, Purple, **309**, 361
☐ Meadowlark, Western, **433**, 477
☐ Merganser, Common, **65**
☐   Hooded, **67**
☐   Red-breasted, **65**
☐ Merlin, 267, **269**, 271
☐ Mockingbird, Northern, 291, **359**, 367
☐ Munia, Scaly-breasted, 427, **457**
☐ Murre, Common, **185**
☐ Murrelet, Ancient, 185, **487**
☐   Craveri's, 185, **487**
☐   Guadalupe, **487**
☐   Marbled, 185, **487**
☐   Scripps's, 185, **487**
☐ Nighthawk, Common, **239**, 241
☐   Lesser, **239**, 241
☐ Night-Heron, Black-crowned, 93, **103**
☐ Nutcracker, Clark's, **463**
☐ Nuthatch, Pygmy, 325, **327**
☐   Red-breasted, **325**
☐   White-breasted, **325**
☐ Oriole, Bullock's, clb, **441**
☐   Hooded, clb, **441**
☐   Scott's, **477**
☐ Osprey, **109**
☐ Owl, Barn, 227, **223**

☐   Barred, 227, **233**
☐   Burrowing, **231**
☐   Flammulated, 225, 237, **459**
☐   Great Gray, 209, **459**
☐   Great Horned, clb, **227**, 235
☐   Long-eared, 225, 227, **235**
☐   Northern Pygmy-, **229**
☐   Northern Saw-whet, 225, 229, **237**
☐   Short-eared, 223, 231, **235**
☐   Snowy, 223
☐   Spotted, 227, **233**
☐   Western Screech-, **225**, 229, 237
☐ Oystercatcher, Black, **141**
☐ Parakeet, Blue-crowned, 457
☐   Mitred, 457
☐   Red-masked, **457**
☐ Pelican, American White, **91**
☐   Brown, **91**
☐ Phainopepla, 359, **367**
☐ Phalarope, Red, 181, **183**
☐   Red-necked, 181, **183**
☐   Wilson's, **181**, 387
☐ Pheasant, Ring-necked, **71**, 221
☐ Phoebe, Black, clb, **283**, 285, 341, 419
☐   Eastern, 283
☐   Say's, 279, **285**
☐ Pigeon, Band-tailed, 215, **217**
☐   Rock, clb, **215**, 217
☐ Pintail, Northern, **47**
☐ Pipit, American, 307, **363**, 369, 433
☐   Red-throated, 363
☐ Plover, American Golden-, **143**
☐   Black-bellied, **143**
☐   Mountain, **149**
☐   Pacific Golden-, **143**
☐   Semipalmated, **145**
☐   Snowy, **145**
☐ Poorwill, Common, 239, **241**
☐ Ptarmigan, White-tailed, 73
☐ Puffin, Tufted, **489**
☐ Quail, California, clb, 469, **69**
☐   Gambel's, **469**
☐   Mountain, **69**, 73

Rail, Black, **131**
    Ridgway's, **129**
    Virginia, **129**
    Yellow, **131**
Raven, Common, clb, **305**
Redhead, 47, **51**, 53
Redstart, American **389**
Roadrunner, Greater, **221**
Robin, American, clb, **353**, 355, 365, 423
Sanderling, clb, **169**
Sandpiper, Baird's, **171**, 173, 175
    Least, 169, 171, **173**, 175
    Pectoral, **171**, 175
    Rock, 165, **167**
    Semipalmated, 175
    Sharp-tailed, 171
    Solitary, **151**, 155
    Spotted, **151**, 153
    Western, 165, 169, **175**
Sapsucker, Red-breasted, **257**
    Red-naped, **257**
    Williamson's, 263, **461**
Scaup, Greater, 53, **55**
    Lesser, 53, **55**
Scoter, Black, **59**
    Surf, **57**, 59
    White-winged, **57**, 59
Shearwater, Black-vented, **481**
    Buller's, **481**
    Flesh-footed, **479**
    Manx, **481**
    Pink-footed, **479**
    Short-tailed, **481**
    Sooty, **481**
Shoveler, Northern, **45**
Shrike, Loggerhead, **291**, 359
    Northern, **291**
Siskin, Pine, **449**
Skimmer, Black, **213**
Skua, South-Polar, **485**
Snipe, Wilson's, 177, **179**, 387
Solitaire, Townsend's, 359, **465**
Sora, **131**

Sparrow, Bell's, **405**
    Black-chinned, **401**
    Black-throated, 405, **477**
    Brewer's, 399, **477**
    Chipping, 395, **399**, 415
    Fox, clb, **409**
    Golden-crowned, **417**
    Grasshopper, **407**
    House, clb, **455**
    Lark, **403**
    Lincoln's, 411, **413**
    Rufous-crowned, **395**
    Sagebrush, **405**
    Savannah, 403, **407**, 409
    Song, 407, 409, **411**
    Swamp, 413
    Vesper, **403**, 419
    White-crowned, clb, 209, 399, **415**, 417
    White-throated, **417**
Starling, European, clb, 309, 341, **361**, 365
Stint, Red-necked, 169
Stilt, Black-necked, **139**
Stork, Wood, 18
Storm-Petrel, Ashy, **483**
    Black, **483**
    Fork-tailed, **483**
    Leach's, **483**
Surfbird, 163, **167**
Swallow, Barn, clb, 315, **317**
    Bank, 311, **313**
    Cliff, **315**, 317, 455
    Northern Rough-winged, **313**
    Tree, 309, **311**, 315
    Violet-green, **311**
Swan, Mute, 35
    Trumpeter, 35
    Tundra, **35**
Swift, Black, **245**
    Vaux's, **243**
    White-throated, 243, **245**
Tanager, Summer, **421**

☐   Western, **421**, 441
☐ Tattler, Wandering, 151, **153**
☐ Teal, Blue-winged, **43**, 49
☐   Cinnamon, **43**, 49
☐   Green-winged, **49**
☐ Tern, Arctic, **491**
☐   Black, **207**, 211
☐   Caspian, **205**
☐   Common, **209**, 491
☐   Elegant, 205, **211**
☐   Forster's, 187, 203, **209**
☐   Least, **203**
☐   Royal, 211
☐ Thrasher, Bendire's, 475
☐   California, **357**, 397
☐   Crissal, 359, **475**
☐   LeConte's, 357, **475**
☐   Sage, **475**
☐ Thrush, Gray-cheeked, 175
☐   Hermit, 349, **351**, 409
☐   Swainson's, **349**, 351
☐   Varied, 353, **355**
☐ Titmouse, Juniper, **321**
☐   Oak, **321**, 323
☐ Towhee, California, clb, 357, **379**
☐   Green-tailed, 409, **465**
☐   Spotted, 353, **393**, 423
☐ Turkey, Wild, **71**
☐ Turnstone, Black, **163**, 167
☐   Ruddy, **163**
☐ Verdin, **473**
☐ Vireo, Bell's, **293**, 297
☐   Cassin's, **293**, 295
☐   Gray, **473**
☐   Hutton's, 293, **295**, 343
☐   Plumbeous, **293**
☐   Warbling, **297**
☐ Vulture, Turkey, clb, **107**
☐ Warbler, Black-and-white, **389**
☐   Black-throated Gray, **383**, 385
☐   Black-throated Green, 385
☐   Blackpoll, **389**
☐   Hermit, **385**

☐   Lucy's, **473**
☐   MacGillivray's, 371, **375**, 377
☐   Nashville, 371, **373**, 375, 377, 379
☐   Orange-crowned, **371**, 373, 375, 377, 379, 387, 389
☐   Palm, **389**
☐   Tennessee, **389**
☐   Townsend's, 383, **385**
☐   Virginia's, **373**
☐   Wilson's, 333, 371, 379, **387**
☐   Yellow, 371, 377, **379**, 387
☐   Yellow-rumped, clb, 347, **381**, 419
☐ Waterthrush, Northern, **389**
☐ Waxwing, Bohemian, 365
☐   Cedar, **365**
☐ Whimbrel, **159**, 161
☐ Wigeon, American, **41**
☐   Eurasian, **41**
☐ Willet, clb, 153, **157**
☐ Woodpecker, Acorn, **255**
☐   Black-backed, **461**
☐   Downy, 259, **261**, 471
☐   Hairy, **261**
☐   Ladder-backed, 259, **471**
☐   Lewis's, **255**, 361
☐   Nuttall's, **259**, 261, 471
☐   Pileated, **265**
☐   White-headed, **461**
☐ Wood-Pewee, Western, **273**, 275
☐ Wren, Bewick's, clb, 333, 335, **337**, 345
☐   Cactus, **475**
☐   Canyon, **331**, 345
☐   House, **333**, 335, 337, 339, 345
☐   Marsh, **335**, 337, 345
☐   Pacific, **333**
☐   Rock, **331**
☐ Wrentit, **345**
☐ Yellowlegs, Greater, **155**, 157
☐   Lesser, 151, **155**, 181
☐ Yellowthroat, Common, 373, **377**, 379, 391

About The Authors

David E. Quady   Dave Quady has birded extensively throughout northern California since the late 1970s. He wrote the owls section of National Geographic Society's *Complete Birds of North America*, and he teaches owl classes and leads field trips for Golden Gate Audubon Society. Dave and his family reside in Berkeley. He is now past-President of Western Field Ornithologists.

Jon L. Dunn   Jon Dunn has been a leader for WINGS, leading bird watching tours worldwide since 1977. He has extensive knowledge of the identification and distribution of North American and Asian birds and has written and co-authored books and numerous papers on these subjects. He is co-author of the National Geographic Society's *Field Guide to the Birds of North America*. He was co-author with Kimball Garrett of *Birds of Southern California: Status and Distribution, Peterson Field Guide to Warblers, Birds of the Los Angeles Region,* and *Birds of Southern California.* Jon is a member of the American Ornithological Society's Committee on Classification and Nomenclature—North and Middle America, has served for 27 years on the California Bird Records Committee, and served for many years on the American Birding Association Checklist Committee.

Kimball L. Garrett   Kimball Garrett has, since 1982, been the Ornithology Collections Manager at the Natural History Museum of Los Angeles County. He is past-President of Western Field Ornithologists, a longtime member of the California Bird Records Committee, and co-editor of the Southern California regional reports for *North American Birds*. He was co-author with Jon Dunn of *Birds of Southern California: Status and Distribution, Peterson Field Guide to Warblers, Birds of the Los Angeles Region,* and *Birds of Southern California.*

Brian E. Small   Brian is a professional wildlife photographer and co-author of three photographic field guides *Birds of Eastern North America, Birds of Western North America,* and *Birds of Southern California.* He is co-author of a bird identification column in *BirdWatching.* Thousands of his images are featured in books, magazines, calendars, websites and smartphone apps.

Short Index to Species

Use this index to find the main account for every species illustrated in the guide. A complete index is on pages 496 – 500.

Albatross 479
Auklet 489
Avocet 139

Bittern 93
Blackbird 429-431, 435-437
Bluebird 347
Bobolink 477
Brant 31
Bufflehead 61
Bunting 427
Bushtit 323

Canvasback 51
Chat 391
Chickadee 319
Chukar 469
Condor 107
Coot 135
Cormorant 87-89
Cowbird 439
Crane 137
Creeper 329
Crossbill 447
Crow 305
Cuckoo 221
Curlew 159

Dipper 341
Dove 215, 219
Dowitcher 177
Duck 37, 53, 59-61, 67
Dunlin 165

Eagle 127
Egret 97-99

Falcon 271
Finch 443-445, 465-467
Flicker 263
Flycatcher 273-281, 287, 471
Fulmar 479

Gadwall 39
Gallinule 133
Gnatcatcher 339, 473
Godwit 161
Goldeneye 63
Goldfinch 451-453
Goose 27-29, 33
Goshawk 459
Grackle 437
Grebe 79-85
Grosbeak 423-425, 467
Grouse 73, 469
Guillemot 185
Gull 187-201

Harrier 113
Hawk 117-125
Heron 95, 101
Hummingbird ... 247-251, 461, 471

Ibis 105

Jaeger 485
Jay 299-301, 463
Junco 419